RETHINKING DEMOCRACY

RETHINKING DEMOCRACY

Edited by
Andrew Gamble and Tony Wright

Wiley
In association with *The Political Quarterly*

This edition first published 2019
© 2019 The Political Quarterly Publishing Co. Ltd.

John Wiley & Sons

Registered Office
John Wiley & Sons Ltd, The Atrium, Southern Gate, Chichester, West Sussex, PO19 8SQ, UK

Editorial Offices
101 Station Landing, Medford, MA 02155, USA
9600 Garsington Road, Oxford, OX4 2DQ, UK
The Atrium, Southern Gate, Chichester, West Sussex, PO19 8SQ, UK

For details of our global editorial offices, for customer services, and for information about how to apply for permission to reuse the copyright material in this book please see our website at www.wiley.com/wiley-blackwell.

The right of Andrew Gamble and Tony Wright to be identified as the editors of the editorial material in this work has been asserted in accordance with the UK Copyright, Designs and Patents Act 1988.

Wiley also publishes its books in a variety of electronic formats. Some content that appears in print may not be available in electronic books.

Designations used by companies to distinguish their products are often claimed as trademarks. All brand names and product names used in this book are trade names, service marks, trademarks or registered trademarks of their respective owners. The publisher is not associated with any product or vendor mentioned in this book.

Limit of Liability/Disclaimer of Warranty: While the publisher and authors have used their best efforts in preparing this book, they make no representations or warranties with respect to the accuracy or completeness of the contents of this book and specifically disclaim any implied warranties of merchantability or fitness for a particular purpose. It is sold on the understanding that the publisher is not engaged in rendering professional services and neither the publisher nor the author shall be liable for damages arising herefrom. If professional advice or other expert assistance is required, the services of a competent professional should be sought.

Library of Congress Cataloging-in-Publication Data
Library of Congress Cataloging-in-Publication data is available for this book
ISBN 9781119554226
A catalogue record for this book is available from the British Library.

Cover design by Rob Bowker

Printed in the UK by Hobbs the Printer

1   2019

For

our grandchildren,

citizens of the future.

Contents

Notes on Contributors

Vernon Bogdanor is Professor of Government, King's College, London.

Colin Crouch is Professor Emeritus, University of Warwick; external scientific member, Max Planck Institute for the Study of Societies, Cologne.

Alan Finlayson is Professor of Political and Social Theory in the School of Politics, Philosophy, Language and Communication Studies at the University of East Anglia.

Andrew Gamble is Professor of Politics at the University of Sheffield and Emeritus Professor of Politics at the University of Cambridge. He is a former editor of *The Political Quarterly*.

Joni Lovenduski is Professor Emerita at Birkbeck and Chair of the Board of *The Political Quarterly*.

Helen Margetts is Professor of Society and the Internet at the University of Oxford, a Turing Fellow and Director of the Public Policy Programme at the Alan Turing Institute for Data Science and Artificial Intelligence.

Martin Moore is Director of the Centre for the Study of Media, Communication and Power, and Senior Research Fellow at King's College London.

David Runciman is Professor of Politics at the Department of Politics and International Studies (POLIS), University of Cambridge.

Gerry Stoker is Chair of Governance, University of Southampton and Centenary Research Professor, University of Canberra.

Albert Weale is Emeritus Professor of Political Theory and Public Policy in the School of Public Policy, University College London.

Tony Wright is a former Labour MP and former editor of *The Political Quarterly*, now Professor of Government and Public Policy at University College London.

1. Introduction

ANDREW GAMBLE AND TONY WRIGHT

2018 IS THE centenary of the 1918 Act which introduced universal suffrage for all male citizens over twenty-one and all female citizens over thirty. Women had to wait another ten years until 1928 for that anomaly to be corrected, but the fundamental principle of universal suffrage for all citizens had been conceded. This reform marked a decisive stage in the emergence of a full democracy in Britain and seems a good moment for some stocktaking and rethinking. Has democracy delivered what those who fought so hard to establish it hoped for? How far is it an unfinished revolution? The present time is a difficult one for democracies everywhere. The populist surge, from Brexit to Trump, and now Italy, has raised questions about the condition and conduct of representative politics; and democratic politics is under attack on several fronts and in a range of places. There is much to discuss and to rethink about democracy.

This collection of essays is a response to these issues and concerns. We asked our contributors to write pieces which would reflect on one or more aspects of democracy. We did not assign them a particular theme or set of questions but asked them to explore the issues in the way they thought most appropriate. In the tradition of *Political Quarterly*, we also asked that the essays should not be narrowly academic but written for an informed and non-specialised readership.

They did not disappoint us. The essays collected here explore the problems of democracy from many different perspectives, and although some of the contributors address similar themes, they do so from different angles. Each contributor develops an argument which sheds new insight on the current state of democracy. Some suggest ways it might be improved, some dissect myths that have grown up about how democracy operates, while others analyse the developments which are undermining democracy and could conceivably threaten its survival in the next hundred years. We think our democracies are now so well established that they have become permanent and irreversible, but in politics nothing is guaranteed to last for ever, and what seems solid and impregnable in one era can seem fragile and vulnerable in the next. Democracy is not a finished state. It is a living process and if there is no longer the will or the belief in its value then it may not endure. If we lose the art of active citizenship, we will lose the freedoms and the rights which democracy has bestowed.

This is one of the key themes of Tony Wright's opening essay, pointing out that democracies can die and when they do, it is norms not institutions which are the key factor. If important aspects of a democratic culture weaken, if the civilised management of disagreement is lost, then the will to

Published by John Wiley & Sons Ltd, 9600 Garsington Road, Oxford OX4 2DQ, UK and 350 Main Street, Malden, MA 02148, USA

sustain the institutions of democracy can decline also. He notes that there has been an explosion of accountability in recent times but governments are accountable for less and less, which means that elected governments are often perceived as no longer delivering for their citizens. But the essay ends on an optimistic note. Representative democracy can be renewed and enriched in ways that were not possible before, including through the new digital media, but it also needs a culture of democratic citizenship, one that is pluralist and encourages civility. Without it, the greatest risk is not that democracies will collapse but that they will steadily deteriorate.

Joni Lovenduski is more pessimistic about the possibilities of renewing representative democracy. All democratic governments notionally support equality for women, but none have achieved it. She argues that the political institutions of representative democracy pre-dated the mobilisation of women, and as a result, women were trapped in the private sphere. The operating institutions of representative democracy have always been unable to accommodate both ascribed and real differences between women and men. Democracy raises expectations of inclusion and equality, but in reality, women have been ignored and have often been absent in both the theory and practice of democracy. One hundred years after the breakthrough in securing votes for women, they are not yet citizens on the same terms as men.

David Runciman asks why democracies are so surprising. In many recent results of elections and referendums, the winners have often been as taken aback as the losers. Part of this is because representative democracies are no longer very representative. The political class has become increasingly divorced from those it represents. The tremors that were an early warning of the later earthquake were ignored. Voting behaviour is driven by tribal loyalties and voting against someone is often more important than voting for someone, which makes differential turnout a very important factor in elections. Some element of surprise is good for democracy and forces the political class to listen, but too many surprises make good government much harder to achieve.

Vernon Bogdanor looks at the history of constitutional reform over the last hundred years and why, after the lively debate before 1914 on Ireland and the suffrage, the constitution was little discussed for fifty years until it became once more a major issue with the return of the old question of Ireland, the new question of Europe, and the eruption of Scottish nationalism. He explores the introduction of the referendum into British constitutional practice, arguing that the 1975 referendum established the precedent that for fundamental decisions, a vote in Parliament is no longer enough. The people also have to be consulted. In the Brexit vote the sovereign people have triumphed over the sovereign Parliament. Brexit is coming about against the wishes of both government and Parliament. The crisis of British representative democracy, he argues, is that the constitutional reforms of the Blair government shared power amongst the elite but did little to transfer power

2

from the elites to the people. What is now needed is a major reform of local government to energise citizens once again. The age of pure representative democracy is coming to an end.

Albert Weale picks up on another aspect of the practice of representative democracy in the UK, the greater difficulty parties currently have in forming majority governments. The electoral system no longer delivers the parliamentary majorities of the past: two of the last three elections have produced a hung Parliament. Weale argues that there are good reasons why this is not likely to change and that this makes it urgent to find fair and open ways to make possible political negotiations among different groups in order to achieve strong and effective governments. He supports the principle of double majorities, seeing it as desirable that governments should command a majority both in Parliament and in the electorate. The coalition government of 2010–15 satisfied that principle, while the May government does not.

Alan Finlayson reflects on the nature of political communications in contemporary democracies and the impact of digital media, a theme which is also the focus of several other essays in this collection. Finlayson considers digital media and the digital public sphere, noting the anxieties which have arisen around fake news, irrationality, and hate speech. He argues that rather than just bemoaning these things, we need to develop new strategies to combat them. He discusses the effectiveness of some of the right-wing bloggers, noting that nothing similar exists on the left. What is required are new forms of egalitarian self-education, and new ways of communicating political messages, using the new styles of the digital media.

Martin Moore also analyses the impact of digital media, looking in particular at election campaigns as communication campaigns. He notes that there have always been exaggerated fears and hopes around the political effects of every major change in communication, but he accepts that some of the changes introduced by digital media do pose real challenges to established democratic principles and protections, such as safeguarding the secrecy of the vote and shielding voters from undue influence. He uses the recent revelations about Cambridge Analytica to pinpoint the dangers and what might be done about it.

Helen Margetts looks at a different angle of digital media and democracy. She examines the evidence of the impact of digital media on political behaviour, noting that up to now this has been hard to research because researchers cannot access the data which the big platforms hold. This means we actually know very little about the relationship between social media and democracy, but that has not prevented many people speculating as to what that relationship is, and reaching sometimes apocalyptic conclusions. Margetts focuses on what we do know, such as the way the new digital platforms have transformed the costs and benefits of every kind of political participation, which has both good and bad effects. She seeks to dispel some of the myths which have gathered around social media and argues that these new media platforms need to be accepted as part of the democratic

3

system, and that although many political institutions have not yet adjusted, eventually they will. To speed up the process, we need to separate fact from myth and analyse in much greater depth the scale and scope of the democratic pathologies such as fake news with which digital media have become associated.

Almost every piece in this collection touches on populism and the final two chapters make it their main focus. Colin Crouch contrasts two concepts of democracy, liberal and populist, and relates them to his thesis of post-democracy which he first advanced more than ten years ago in 2005. Post-democracy was the process by which democracies were being hollowed out and the political class divided from the mass of citizens, leading to feelings of anger and resentment. Crouch identified xenophobic populism as one possible response to the increasing detachment of the political class, but he did not think back then that it would become the dominant one. He analyses the consequences of xenophobic populism in the vote for Brexit and the vote for Trump.

Gerry Stoker takes up the theme of the politics of resentment and shows how rooted it is in the geographical, educational and generational divides of modern Britain. Reinforcing some of the arguments of Wright and Bogdanor, he argues that the right democratic response to the politics of resentment is not to condemn it but to understand it, and to mobilise a new politics of place and identity to counter it. One of the implications is that liberal democracies, if they are to survive and contain and even roll back the populist insurgencies which are currently besieging them, need to pay much more attention to democratic accountability exercised locally. Citizens need to regain a stake in their local communities and influence over the decisions that most immediately affect them.

Andrew Gamble's concluding chapter surveys the progress and the setbacks to democracy in Britain over the last hundred years and identifies some of the things which need to change if democracy and the public domain which supports it is to be preserved and extended in the future.

The editors would like to thank the contributors and also the *Political Quarterly* Editorial Board for their assistance in the writing of this book. Special thanks also go to Emma Anderson for production, Clara Dekker for the copyediting and Anya Pearson for organising events around the book.

2. Democracy and Its Discontents

TONY WRIGHT

'THAT'S DEMOCRACY.' This is the claim routinely heard as political opponents exchange verbal blows, with each side asserting their occupancy of the democratic high ground. In Britain, it is the contested claim between those who see the EU referendum as the definitive expression of popular democracy and those who regard it as a threat to its representative version. In the battle for control inside the Labour party, an assertion of the democratic primacy of an activist membership collides with a more pluralist conception of democracy. In Catalonia, the assertion of democratic rights by the separatists is met by the assertion of democratic rights by other Spaniards. In the United States, the democratic authority of a rogue president rubs up against the kind of checks-and-balances democracy of the Founding Fathers. In Russia, Putin wins an election and claims democratic legitimacy. Such examples could be endlessly multiplied. All kinds of regimes, including many oppressive ones, have wanted to call themselves democracies. If everybody can make the claim of 'that's democracy' to support their position, it suggests that democracy is both potent and promiscuous.

It also means that any discussion of it can easily become muddled. Consider, for example, the latest version of the Economist Intelligence Unit's annual Democracy Index, an audit of the state of democracy in every country in the world. In its most recent report, the United Kingdom's democratic score has improved from the previous year, largely on the basis of the high turnout in the 2016 referendum on the EU. In one sense this makes sense, as electoral participation is an important measure of democracy. Yet does it mean that the quality of democracy in Britain has improved? This seems unlikely. It would be difficult to claim that the referendum campaign produced a more informed electorate. For example, an Ipsos Mori survey shortly before the referendum found that Leave voters overestimated the number of EU immigrants by a factor of four (and Remain voters by a factor of two). As for the turnout boost produced by non-voters voting, the political science evidence on non-voters is that 'however ignorant voters tend to be, non-voters—adult citizens who are eligible to vote but choose to abstain —tend to be worse'.[1]

None of this diminishes the significance (or validity) of the result, but it does illustrate some of the difficulties about the discussion of democracy. These difficulties were already there in the origins of the democratic idea in the city states of ancient Greece. Democracy combined 'demos' (the people) with 'kratos' (control), but who were the people and what were they controlling? The different answers to this question meant that 'there was no such thing as ancient Greek democracy—no one *single* thing, that is'.[2] Citizenship

© The Author 2019. The Political Quarterly © The Political Quarterly Publishing Co. Ltd. 2019
Published by John Wiley & Sons Ltd, 9600 Garsington Road, Oxford OX4 2DQ, UK and 350 Main Street, Malden, MA 02148, USA

excluded women and slaves, but even beyond this exclusion the 'demos' might mean people in a broad sense or the rule of the many poor. It was this latter sense, with its association of mob rule and the prospect of the propertyless expropriating the propertied, that was to identify democracy as a bad word for much of its history. How a bad word became not merely a good word but the defining source of political authority in the modern world is a remarkable story.

The reinvention of democracy took the idea of the people ruling themselves and put it into the idea of people ruling through their representatives. Not only did this overcome the problem of scale (the face-to-face direct democracy of Athens was only possible because of a citizen body numbered in the thousands), but also mitigated the problem of majoritarian tyranny that so exercised the minds of such nineteenth-century figures as Tocqueville and Mill as they contemplated the advance of democracy. Government through representatives was the best insurance against democratic excess and the best guarantee of good government. The equal right to vote for representatives became the key democratic demand, a right slowly gained by all citizens (with Britain in the slow lane, not getting there until 1918, and even then, not quite).

However, it soon became apparent that a democracy required something more than voting. The rise of fascism in the interwar years showed that people were quite capable of voting for tyranny (hence Clement Attlee's oft-quoted verdict that he could never consent to 'a device so alien to our traditions as the referendum, which has only too often been the instrument of Nazism and Fascism'). This did not happen in Britain, but there was much discussion on the left about whether the conflict between a capitalism in crisis and the demands of a democracy could be reconciled by constitutional means. When the post-1945 world talked about democracy, therefore, it was not just representative democracy but 'liberal' democracy. In other words, democracy was shorthand for a whole bundle of attributes that constituted decent government. Elections certainly, free and fair, but also much more, including freedom of expression, the right of opposition, the protection of minorities, a free media, basic human rights, the rule of law and an independent judiciary, along with all the other constitutional checks and instruments of accountability. A democratic government is one that can be kicked out, but also one that can be kicked while it is in. Elections are a necessary but not sufficient condition for democratic government.

It was the failure to understand that democracy is not a single event but a dense and continuous process that allowed the claim to be made ('that's democracy') by the Brexit camp after the EU referendum that 'the people' had spoken and therefore any further discussion of the issue was somehow illegitimate. In fact, there is not a single 'people' (as the referendum clearly showed) and it is dangerous to claim that there is. And democracy goes on. As the political theorist John Dunn has observed, political legitimacy is strengthened by the fact that in a democracy, losers can believe they may be winners next time and so stay in the game.[3] The referendum was an expression of democracy; but so is the campaign to revisit it. It is also dangerous for democracy when a newspaper denounces independent judges as 'enemies of the people' for deciding that a government must operate through parliament, not least because that phrase has been the chilling language of tyrants everywhere.

But these are, nevertheless, local issues, while the contemporary challenges facing democracy are more general ones. The consolidation of democracy after 1945 was reinforced after the 1989 collapse of communism, bringing new countries into the democratic European fold and enabling it to be reliably announced that the final triumph of liberal democracy had arrived. It was only a matter of time before other countries in the world developed in a democratic direction as their economies and societies progressed. How different it all looks now. Western democracies are in trouble, as mainstream politics is confronted by the populist surge, while non-democracies (notably China) confidently reject the democratic model of development. Even in Europe, there is democratic decline, with countries like Hungary and Poland embracing an 'illiberal democracy' of conservative nationalism that restricts freedoms and interferes with the courts. Democratic advance has gone into reverse. The number of 'full democracies' in the Democracy Index has fallen sharply (with the United States dropping into the 'flawed democracy' category).

Something serious is happening. The most recent Pew Centre Survey, covering thirty-eight countries, revealed that while support for democracy remained strong 'large numbers in many nations would entertain political systems that are inconsistent with liberal democracy'.[4] About a quarter of people in a cluster of established democracies—including Britain and the United States—would support the idea of a strong leader able to make decisions without interference from a parliament or a court. Against this kind of background, it is not surprising if the current condition of liberal democracy is the subject of much anguished investigation and rethinking. What has gone wrong? And how might it be put right?

Just as democracy came to grief in the conditions of the interwar years, it is not accidental that its current troubles have coincided with a period of rapid economic and social dislocation, culminating in the financial crash and its austere consequences. Democracies have to be able to deliver for their citizens. Joseph Chamberlain had famously described the 'ransom' that would have to be paid by the propertied classes to a democratic electorate; and the assumption was that a democracy would be required to produce both a better and a more equal life for its citizens. 'The logic of universal suffrage', wrote Harold Laski, 'is either an equal society or such a continuous expansion of material welfare as softens the contrast between rich and poor.'[5] The post-1945 generation of social democratic politics, with its rising living standards and diminished inequality, seemed to exemplify this logic. The fact that today's world is so sharply different is fundamental to democracy's current condition. As the financial journalist, Philip Coggan, sums up the evidence: 'Some modern democracies today look more like tyrannies of the rich than tyrannies of the poor, with income and wealth inequality increasing, and the beneficiaries using their wealth to buy access to politicians.'[6]

At some point, this would bring its political consequences. Democracy had proved to be quite compatible with an acceleration of inequality, but there were consequences nevertheless. Those individuals and communities left behind by globalisation, their real incomes declining and their services eroded, increasingly divorced from a class of the super-rich, would eventually produce a response. Initially, it was evident in the developing disengagement from the institutions and practices of democratic politics, a process described by Peter Mair as 'the hollowing of Western democracy'.[7] The populist revolt may be more recent, but its roots were already there. When the revolt came, exemplified by Brexit and Trump but going much wider, it took the form of a general attack on the elites who had been running the system. Although this kind of anti-elitism is the stock-in-trade of all populist rhetoric, along with simplistic solutions, the fact is that the elites had a lot to answer for. In this sense, democracy was doing its job, by enabling people to send a signal that all was not well with their lives and that they wanted something done about it.

Simply to denounce the populist threat to democracy without responding to its causes is therefore an abdication. Populism is democracy's fire alarm. Nor is it adequate simply to claim that populists exploit fears about culture and identity, especially in relation to immigrants, when this is not the 'real' issue. Of course, they seek to exploit such fears, often in crude and dangerous ways, but this does not mean that issues of culture, identity and place do not matter. They matter hugely, and always have done. If an elite of 'anywheres' (in David Goodhart's nice phrase)[8] seems not to understand this, then people will look elsewhere. For example, it is not irrational for people, especially those at society's sharp end, to be concerned about the impact of immigration, or to think that a country should be able to decide for itself who can live and work in it. (If the EU had been more sensible about this, then events may have been different, with Britain leading those countries wanting a less integrationist European Union.) The proper response of democratic politics to a crude populism is to attend to the circumstances in which it can flourish.

In a similar way, only those who are politically tone deaf could fail to understand the potency of the appeal of democratic self-government in the EU referendum campaign. Many people clearly felt, despite all the warnings about the damaging economic consequences, that they would like to govern themselves. They regarded the nation state as the maximum arena of accountability. Of course, all this may be illusory, since supranational power clearly requires a supranational response, but it is potent nevertheless. It requires a better answer than it received during the referendum campaign, when the argument about democracy was never really engaged with by those wanting Britain to stay in the EU club.

Its importance was recognised by Theresa May (or whoever wrote her speech) when she stood in Downing Street after the referendum, having just become Prime Minister, and declared that her intention was to 'do everything we can to give you more control over your lives'. The fact that she did not seem to have any idea what this meant in practice, as has become clear since, did not detract from its significance. The 'demos' was being promised its 'kratos'. This played to a pervasive sense that control had been lost. People might feel empowered as consumers, bombarded with invitations to buy the latest gadgetry, but disempowered as citizens. Their jobs might be lost because of a decision taken on the other side of the world and their services might be provided by companies over whom they had neither knowledge nor control. Regulators and quangos had taken over functions from the politicians and public officials. Markets had implanted themselves into the public realm. The effect of all this was a sense of control lost and responsibility dissolved.

Yet there is something of a paradox here, since in many respects the accountability of governments has dramatically increased in recent times. The traditional vertical structure of formal political accountability—in which representatives are accountable to electors, ministers accountable to parliament, officials accountable to ministers—has been supplemented by a vast network of horizontal accountability actors and mechanisms. Some of these are formal, established within the political system, but many are informal and exist outside it. The new communication technologies have had a major impact on this process. The effect is that the operation of government is scrutinised more closely and intensively than ever before. The political theorist, John Keane, has coined the term 'monitory democracy' to describe this development, arguing that 'the constant public scrutiny of power by hosts of differently sized monitory bodies with footprints large and small makes it the most energetic, most dynamic form of democracy ever'.[9]

Indeed, some have even begun to question whether this process has gone too far, with results that are inimical to good government. The suggestion is that it can merely provide ammunition for an increasingly aggressive partisan battle, or that it inhibits the capacity to govern effectively. The fact that accountability is good does not mean that ever more accountability is even better. What matters is having the right kind of scrutiny and accountability, a matter of quality and not just of quantity. Accountability should keep government on its toes, not knock it off balance. This argument aside though, the key point is that the explosion of accountability that has taken place has not been accompanied by a strengthened attachment to, or trust in, the institutions of democratic government, as might have been expected. In fact, the reverse has happened. No doubt there are many reasons for this—some cultural, some about a changed environment, some about expectations and performance—but it is significant nevertheless. Government itself is far more accountable than it used to be, but at the same time, accountable for less and less.

However, this evolution in how democracy operates also provides a reminder that the character of representative government is not static. It not only takes different institutional forms in different places, but also evolves over time in response to new demands and pressures. This is not always recognised by those who are so exercised by the infirmities of representative democracy that they enthusiastically write its obituary, sometimes accompanied by a proposal that it should be replaced with something else. Thus recently, the author of *Against Democracy* recommends a return to Plato and 'the rule of the knowers' because the electorate is too ignorant; while the author of *Against Elections* wants to 'democratise democracy' by also returning to the world of Athens and replacing elections with the lottery of random selection.[10] The problem with all such proposals is not that they are without interest, but that they end in a kind of fantasy universe of their own making.

Stripping away some of the fantasies about democracy is the purpose of another recent work by two American political scientists. In *Democracy for Realists* they argue that 'conventional thinking about democracy has collapsed in the face of modern social-scientific research'.[11] They assemble a vast body of this research on electoral behaviour to demonstrate that voters do not perform the role that classical democratic theory attributes to them. Voters are as they are; and it is merely romantic to construct democratic theories on a false view of what they are like and how they behave. In their view, Schumpeter was on to something when he observed that, compared with the rest of life, 'the typical citizen drops down to a lower level of mental performance as soon as he enters the political field. He argues and analyses in a way which he would readily recognise as infantile within the sphere of his real interests'.[12] Those proposals which suggest that the remedy for democracy's ills is more democracy are therefore misguided. It is not more democracy that is needed, but better democracy, at least if the purpose is good government.

This is a sober analysis. It presents a particular challenge to those who pin their hopes on a more participatory kind of democracy. It means an acceptance that most people do not want to pay a great deal of attention to politics because they have far too much else in their lives to attend to. Once elected, they just want politicians to go away and not bother them again for a few years, when they will then decide—on the basis of how they feel at the time—whether they should be kept on or booted out. That is why political ignorance is so widespread. It would be good if citizens were better informed, or at least kept a watching eye on what was going on, but there should be no unrealistic expectations about this. In many respects, representative democracy is deliberately founded upon this sort of division of labour between voters and politicians.

This is not quite as dispiriting as it sounds, unless democracy is thought to consist entirely of elections. Even then, it certainly beats some of the populist politics that is now in evidence, and which seems to be the contemporary challenger of representative democracy. It also leaves plenty of scope for making representative democracy work better. As A.C. Grayling writes in his recent anti-Brexit philosophical polemic:

[T]he political history of what we can call the 'Western liberal democracies' is the history of the development and application of a compromise aimed at resolving the dilemma of democracy—the dilemma of finding a way to locate the ultimate source of political authority in democratic assent, without democracy collapsing into mob rule or being hijacked by an oligarchy.[13]

Representative democracy was the form of that compromise. It is now under attack and needs defending—but also developing.

It is not necessary to embrace the current death literature about democracy to feel anxious about its contemporary condition. A generation ago, Francis Fukuyama famously announced the final victory of liberal democracy; but now his message is that all political systems are prone to decay and therefore: 'No one living in an established liberal democracy should ... be complacent about the inevitability of its survival.'[14] Reformers who have taken liberal democracy for granted and saw only its democratic limitations, wanting to go 'beyond' it to something better, are now obliged to become its defenders and protectors. As Al Gore has put it: 'People who took liberal democracy more or less for granted are now awakening to a sense that it can only be defended by the people themselves.'[15] In established democracies like Britain, those political reformers who casually describe the political system as 'broken' (or worse) might usefully reflect on what a broken liberal democracy is actually like.

This is emphatically not an argument for the status quo. Democracy must always be work in progress. The task of making representative democracy thicker and richer is a permanent one. In a country like Britain, where political power is traditionally concentrated and centralised, there is ample scope for institutional reform of various kinds. Democratic experiment should also be encouraged and nourished. Direct democracy can never substitute for the complexities of policy making that only a representative system can negotiate, but this does not mean that there are not issues where (with a clear framework of rules) direct democracy might play a role. In Ireland, for example, it has unlocked social issues, and could do the same in Britain on an issue like assisted dying. The same applies to selection by lot, as a supplement to election. There is particular scope for democratic experiment at a local level, where people have a more direct knowledge of the issues (and people) involved. The new means of communication have opened up new participatory possibilities, especially if sustained by a real commitment to civic education and the hard work by citizens that a more engaged democracy requires.

It is not enough, though it is necessary, to defend liberal representative democracy without also exploring how it can be strengthened and improved. This has received too little attention. 'The fact is that during the past two hundred years we have thought little about the institutional design of democracy', write leading political scientists, adding: 'Since the great explosion of institutional thinking, when the present democratic institutions were invented—and they were invented—there has been almost no institutional creativity.'[16] The only real exception is in relation to proportional electoral systems, and that was in the nineteenth century. There is no reason to think that the present form of representative government is democracy's last word; and every reason to apply some institutional imagination in exploring how it might be developed. This is particularly necessary in Britain, where the institutional landscape has remained remarkably the same and where muddling through has been preferred to principled reform.

Yet in many ways this institutional focus is misleading. It is always tempting to think that a problem with democracy can be remedied by an institutional reform or a new piece of political machinery. Institutions certainly matter; and they have important consequences. A striking example is offered by the 1918 legislation that brought near-universal suffrage to Britain. The Speaker's Conference on which this legislation was based had included a recommendation for an electoral system of proportional representation. However, this was opposed by the Conservatives and not introduced, which as a result 'produced a Conservative hegemony in British government until 1945'.[17] Institutional forms are important. However, it is too easy to respond to democracy's current difficulties simply by reciting a list of desired institutional and constitutional reforms.

For example, it is often suggested that Britain is democratically deficient because it lacks a written constitution (though actually it is uncodified rather than unwritten). This cannot be true, since Britain is conspicuously more democratic than many countries with written constitutions. It is the quality of democracy that matters, not the possession of a paper constitution. Indeed, constitutional entrenchment has been found to make it more difficult to bind national minorities to democracy. The written Spanish constitution ensured confrontation with the separatism of Catalonia by making independence referendums illegal, while the unwritten British constitution enabled a politically agreed referendum in Scotland. In the United States, a written constitution has protected the dominance of politics by money and prevented reform. There is much to be said for deciding political issues politically, not judicially, and having the flexibility to respond to changing circumstances. This is not an argument against writing constitutions down; but it is an argument for not thinking that writing a constitution down is a guarantee of an effective democracy.

Similar considerations apply to the never-ending discussion in Britain about the House of Lords. Everybody seems to agree that some kind of reform of this preposterous house of patronage is needed, but there is no agreement on what this should be. To some reformers, it is self-evident that it should become an elected body, because that is what democracy demands. How, in a democracy, can you have a chamber of parliament that is not elected and accountable? This is a strong argument, but it is not conclusive. For example, it might be decided, democratically, that it is conducive to good government to have a second chamber of appointees, informed and independent, whose job is to scrutinise legislation and advise on improvements. Such a body, a chamber of scrutiny, could only advise, deferring always to the elected chamber, but nevertheless performing a useful function. Other variants could be explored. This would not be 'undemocratic'; indeed, its purpose would be to improve the quality of democracy.

Nor is it always the case that 'more democracy' is the remedy for democracy's difficulties, at least if the objective is good government (which presumably is what most people want). For example, there are good democratic reasons for electing judges, or for having them appointed by those who have been elected. Both practices are features of American democracy. Yet in Britain, we are right to think that good government would be ill-served by the democratic politicisation of the judiciary. On a different front, the leaders of all the political parties in Britain are now elected by the votes of their membership instead of by the votes of an electoral college of parliamentary colleagues, as was the previous practice. This is 'more democratic', but it may not produce better leaders, especially when party memberships are tiny and unrepresentative. This is a reminder that democracy is both a virtue and a mechanism, something to be valued for itself but also designed to produce good government.

Democracy is not just (or primarily) a set of institutions. It has a character and a spirit. It is a way of doing politics that involves the civilised management of disagreement. The ability to settle differences without violence, and for opponents not also to be regarded as enemies, is a considerable historical achievement. Democracy is a culture, requiring nurture and protection. A recent study of *How Democracies Die* identifies norms, not institutions, as the key factor: 'Without robust norms, constitutional checks and balances do not serve as the bulwarks of democracy we imagine them to be.'[18] In the United States, democracy is in trouble not because of constitutional deficiencies, but because a political culture of aggressive partisanship has undermined the conventions which made the system work.

In Britain, politics has been rooted in conventions. These were seen as much more reliable in terms of good government than words in constitutions. They carried with them expectations about behaviour, with consequences if these expectations were not met. It is no longer possible to be so sanguine. The EU referendum has exposed the frailties of a system which did not know what its constitution was, or what rights its parliament had (with judges called upon to try to find out). A culture of divisiveness has descended, shredding conventions. Now judges are denounced, the civil service impugned, the BBC attacked and experts dismissed. This is what happens when the norms and conventions that sustain democracy are eroded.

It is because democracy is fundamentally about culture, a way of doing politics (there are other ways), that this is where attention should be directed. We recognise this when we talk about the need for a culture of citizenship, but it applies more widely. Institutions and culture should be mutually reinforcing. Surveys regularly report that people say they like democracy, but not politics or politicians. Of course, it is much easier to dismiss politics and politicians ('they are all the same') than to engage with them, but this nevertheless suggests that there may be something about the activity of politics that produces democratic discontent.

Politics should inspire, but it also disappoints. There is always a gap between rhetoric and reality. Policy making is complex and difficult, because that is what many problems are, and it is often the least bad option that has to be taken. It might help if this was openly acknowledged by politicians, instead of the pretence that they are in command of every issue and can magic up solutions. Once out of office, and in memoir mode, they frequently tell a more truthful story. Thus Nick Clegg, former Deputy Prime Minister, declares that politicians are 'trapped in a fatal pretence: that they are in complete control, when everyone knows they are not'.[19] This kind of pretence was much in evidence in the EU referendum, only shattered by the negotiations that followed. If the business of politics is conducted on the basis of a pretence, then it is hardly surprising if people come to feel pretty disillusioned about it.

This is not the only problem about the way politics is conducted. It seems almost designed to put people off. The endless repetition of banalities is bad enough, but when accompanied by the compulsory party point-scoring, it is even worse. Arguments should be real, not routinised. The frenetic pace of contemporary politics contributes to the problem; a slower democracy would be a better one. Critics have long lamented the sterile adversarialism of the British way of doing politics, but it is a culture that is embedded and resistant to change. It is supported by an electoral system that institutionalises adversarialism (although there is no evidence that democratic discontent is less in countries with other electoral systems). Reformers usually identify the unfairness of this system, but a more serious charge against it at present is that it consolidates division and prevents compromise and agreement. As David Runciman has expressed: 'It produces a reckless, cavalier politics that panders to popular discontent rather than trying to channel and ameliorate it.'[20] A different kind of politics needs a different electoral system; but a different electoral system also requires a different kind of politics.

It is not enough to criticise politicians though. It often seems that the only popular politicians are dead ones, but it is the living ones we should be interested in. It is remarkable how much energy goes in to the politician-bashing business, but how little goes in to the task of encouraging good people to enter political life. Good governments require good politicians (in the several senses of 'good'), yet these are in permanently short supply—and perhaps especially so at present. There will never be a shortage of bad (or self-important) people who want to get themselves elected to public office, some of whom manage to do so through the opaque party selection processes. But in a system where governments are formed out of the tiny gene pool that is the majority parliamentary party, it is essential for good government that there are enough good people to go around (and Prime Ministers routinely lament that there are not). We should therefore be far more interested in the whole business of political recruitment than we currently are.

The same applies to political leadership. The fact is that the quality of political leadership in a democracy matters hugely. A leader who has the capacity to tell a convincing story about the direction of travel, and can articulate a positive vision, can inspire confidence and trust. In the absence of this, democratic discontent will grow and with it the appeal of varieties of populism. In troubled times, the quality of democratic leadership becomes even more important, as the current experience of different democracies shows. Democracy and leadership are not antithetical, as some (particularly on the left) are inclined to believe. People look to leaders who can steer a course they can believe in, and in whom they can invest trust. This has never been more necessary than at present.

Representative democracy requires both representatives and representative institutions. We should pay more attention to the nature of both. If we are electing representatives to devote themselves to the issues of the day on our behalf, and to apply their judgement to them, we need to know if this is what they are actually doing. Similarly, if our representative institutions are supposed to enable this function to be performed, then we need to know if this is what is happening in practice. Party loyalty is important, but it should not substitute for judgement. Britain's part in the Iraq war happened because Parliament and parliamentarians failed to stop it. The courts asserted Parliament's rights in relation to Brexit only because Parliament had failed to assert them for itself. If we believe in the importance of representative democracy, then we need to ensure that both representatives and representative institutions are doing their job. Representation has to be practised as well as proclaimed.

The context within which representation now operates has changed significantly. The explosion of voice in all its forms has altered the relationship between the represented and their representatives. The political class has lost its old insulation and is exposed to public scrutiny and pressure as never before. The new communication technologies have overcome some of the problems of scale that prevented Athenian-type direct democracy finding a place in the government of mass societies. What this means is that representative democracy can now be supplemented (and enriched) in ways that were not possible before. This will not weaken representative democracy but will strengthen it. The task for representatives, and for representative institutions, is to find imaginative ways to connect with this new environment.

However, none of this will happen if we fail to nourish a culture of democratic citizenship. This is more important than particular policies or specific institutional reforms (though both matter). The real problem with a populist kind of politics is not that it attacks an establishment elite, or that it trades in simplicities, but that it is fundamentally anti-pluralist. In the name of the 'people', it denounces all opponents and wages war on those institutions which stand in its way. It is not possible to conduct liberal democracy on this basis. It dissolves the norms of democratic politics and fosters a toxic divisiveness. This is Trump's America; but it is also (in milder form) Brexit Britain. Robust argument is the meat and drink of democracy, but partisan bile turns into its poison. That is why it must be flushed out of the system.

This is made harder by the coarsening of political exchange that has taken place. The digital revolution promised an unprecedented expansion and enrichment of democratic possibilities, with opportunities to communicate, inform and mobilise on a scale never seen before. The prospect was of a citizenry armed with information and the means to use it, in a way that could transform democratic participation. Some of this has happened, but so has much else. Instead of a richer democratic conversation, we have warring tribes inhabiting their own digital bunkers and shouting abuse at each other while feeding off junk news often manufactured by powerful interests. Opinion substitutes for knowledge. Targeting substitutes for debate. A culture of civility that democracy requires, along with trusted sources of information and a shared public space, is in danger of being lost. There is awareness of the problem, but uncertainty about what can be done about it (or about the giant tech companies that provide the platform for this kind of misinformation, manipulation and abusive bigotry). Doing nothing should not be an option if we care about liberal democracy.

Something profound is happening. Within the space of a generation the Western world has passed from democratic triumphalism to gloomy anticipations of democratic decline and possible death. At the very least 'Western democracy is going through a mid-life crisis'.[21] It faces challenges it seems unable to meet, while authoritarian nationalists and assorted populists trade on its difficulties. The coupling of liberalism and democracy starts to be uncoupled, increasingly antagonists rather than partners. Democratic collapse may be unlikely, but democratic deterioration is not. We are in uncharted territory. In the words of a leading democratic scholar: 'We still have only limited understanding of the processes by which democracies collapse and even less of the processes by which they deteriorate.'[22] If democracy is to continue to be the way in which Western societies negotiate their differences and meet their challenges, it will have to be re-energised and renewed. Business as usual is not an option. Democracy is worth defending; but that means deciding what kind of democracy we want to go into battle for.

Notes

1 J. Brennan, *Against Democracy*, Princeton, Princeton University Press, 2017, p. 26.
2 P. Cartledge, *Democracy: A Life*, Oxford, Oxford University Press, 2016, p. 219.
3 J. Dunn, 'Situating political accountability', in A. Przeworski, S. Stokes and B. Manin, *Democracy, Accountability and Representation*, Cambridge, Cambridge University Press, 1999, p. 332.
4 Pew Research Centre Survey, Democracy Report, October 2017.
5 H. Laski, *Democracy in Crisis*, London, Allen and Unwin, 1933, p. 233.
6 P. Coggan, *The Last Vote: The Threats to Western Democracy*, London, Penguin, 2014, p. 26.
7 P. Mair, *Ruling the Void: The Hollowing of Western Democracy*, London, Verso, 2013.
8 D. Goodhart, *The Road to Somewhere: The Populist Revolt and the Future of Politics*, London, Hurst, 2017.
9 J. Keane, *The Life and Death of Democracy*, London, Simon and Schuster, 2009, p. 743.
10 Brennan, *Against Democracy*; D. Van Reybrouck, *Against Elections: The Case for Democracy*, London, The Bodley Head, 2016.
11 C. Achen and L. Bartels, *Democracy for Realists*, Princeton, Princeton University Press, 2016, p. 12.
12 J. Schumpeter, *Capitalism, Socialism and Democracy*, 1942, quoted in Achen and Bartels, p. 10.
13 A. C. Grayling, *Democracy and Its Crisis*, London, Oneworld, 2017, p. 181.
14 F. Fukuyama, *Political Order and Political Decay*, London, Profile Books, 2014, p. 548.
15 Interview with Al Gore, *Observer Magazine*, 30 July 2017.
16 B. Manin, A. Przeworski and S. Stokes, 'Elections and representation', in Przeworski, Stokes and Manin, *Democracy, Accountability and Representation*, p. 51.
17 M. Pugh, *Electoral Reform in War and Peace*, London, Routledge & Kegan Paul, 1978, p. ix.
18 S. Levitsky and D. Ziblatt, *How Democracies Die*, London, Viking, 2018, p. 7.
19 N. Clegg, *Politics Between the Extremes*, London, Vintage, 2017, p. 88. Adam Przeworski adds a shrewd comment on this pretence: 'Often no one knows what it is best to do, and governments do not know either. Governments are in the unenviable situation of not having the luxury to do nothing when they do not know what to do', *Why Bother with Elections?*, Cambridge, Polity Press, 2018, p. 125.
20 D. Runciman, 'Electoral reform and the constitution', in D. J. Galligan, ed., *Constitution in Crisis: The New Putney Debates*, London, I. B. Tauris, 2017, p. 18.
21 D. Runciman, *How Democracy Ends*, London, Profile Books, 2018, p. 5.
22 Przeworski, *Why Bother with Elections?*, p. 134.

3. Feminist Reflections on Representative Democracy

JONI LOVENDUSKI

Introduction

MOST DEMOCRATIC governments claim to support equality for women. None have so far achieved it. Probably equality is not deliverable, but its promise is part of both the attraction and standard defence of democracy. Failures result from fundamental biases of design. Such design failure was probably unavoidable if only because the establishment of representative democratic political institutions pre-dated women's political mobilisation. In common with other political systems, they were engineered for and by successive dominant groups of men aiming to build institutions to protect their power and privilege. The resulting arrangements are based on a relationship between public and private life that trapped women in the private sphere, where they are designated as others, as different, always as less than men. In these systems, women were first treated as chattel, as dependents, as minors, and more recently as a minority, despite constituting more than half the population. In short, efforts by women to get political equality fail because the operating institutions of representative democracy are inappropriate to accommodate ascribed and real differences between women and men.

Defining democracy

Normally when we think about democracy we think both about the ideas and the institutions, often without particularly acknowledging that they are different. The ideas raise expectations of inclusion and equality. Historically, the set of ideas around democracy became more complicated as struggles to establish, protect and be included in it have developed. So too did the political systems which accumulated an array of institutions of decision making and accountability. Ideas about what democracy is, and how it is defined may be placed on a continuum from a fairly minimal arrangement for choosing leaders to complex systems involving freedom, rights, accountability, equality, representation and security. The ideas are expressed in institutions such as legislatures, elections, political parties, constitutions and laws, judiciaries, executives, the separation of powers and freedom of the press and of expression. Contemporary democracies are political systems, sets of institutions that claim to guarantee and protect the

Published by John Wiley & Sons Ltd, 9600 Garsington Road, Oxford OX4 2DQ, UK and 350 Main Street, Malden, MA 02148, USA

agreed ideas. This is an ideal type. In practice, embedded in the structures that we know as democracies are the privileges of elites who are protected from their responsibilities.

How we define democracy is itself an issue. Sometimes reduced by analysis to no more than a system of decision making, in practice the way it is understood determines who is included and excluded and how it is controlled. Democracy is self-government of the people, historically practised in the ancient world via assemblies in relatively small city states. The people were men and the method, apparently, was direct. It was inefficient and by today's standards, not that democratic. Although citizens ruled through a process of frequent and lengthy meetings, the citizen body was very limited and its freedom to participate dependent on the work of women and slaves who were not citizens.

This essay hence concentrates on representative democracy, which I define simply as a governing system in which politics are organised around an elected assembly. The standard account of the evolution of contemporary representative democracy is that assemblies developed rapidly from the late eighteenth century to become central constitutional institutions. They became legislatures in which representatives were elected from larger territorial units to govern in the name of the people. Most representative democracies have become steadily more complex and at the level of voting and legal citizenship, more inclusive. During the twentieth century universal suffrage was completed by the enfranchisement of women and the working class in a number of states. Thereafter, women were in theory eligible to become representatives, but always on the basis of institutions founded before they were citizens or, in the case of the UK, were legal persons.

While women are eligible to vote and hold elected office, they are not thought to be central to democratic arrangements. Drude Dahlerup notes that only one of the sixty questions used by the Economist Intelligence Unit's Democracy Index deals with women (the number of women in parliament), while other indices ignore women's position or subsume it within the treatment of minorities.[1] Indices such as Freedom House and Human Rights Watch are similarly restricted and gender blind. These are not oversights; rather they reflect long-established priorities and arrangements. Only recently was feminine inclusion and presence acknowledged to be an issue. And that inclusion and presence has tended to be very narrowly defined, largely restricted to participation in elections as voters, candidates and elected representatives. As in the political institutions that the indices track, women are afterthoughts, not considered to be fundamental elements of systems of representative democracy.

Any reading of the history of democratic thought reveals not only that its key proponents were men, but also that its vision was a masculine one. With few exceptions, the role of women was not addressed. And even where it was, as in the case of John Stuart Mill's 1869 essay, *The Subjection of Women*, such interventions were not later considered to be part of the canon. Drude

Dahlerup reminds us that even the standard textbooks by modern historians of democratic theory such as George H. Sabine's seemingly endless *A History of Political Theory*, a set text for generations of politics students, did not mention women or women's position once in its 948 pages, and overlooked Mill's study of women's subjugation.[2]

The entire institutional structure and culture now requires wholescale re-engineering if women are to be politically equal. While the initial exclusion of women may be understood in terms of the social conditions in which representative democracy emerged, the assumption of their absence had been built into its institutions.

Exclusion was not only a matter of specific electoral law, but also an assumption of the formal and informal rules of political institutions. The struggle for women's votes was motivated by a reasoning that saw voting as a mechanism of inclusion. From the early nineteenth century, feminists organised to claim rights, including legal personhood, education, employment, property rights and pretty much all the rights that some men then had. Advocates believed that with the vote would come the possibility to establish equal rights and opportunities for women and men. Yet the struggle was long and difficult, resisted at every turn by the beneficiaries of exclusion, the dominant group of men for whom the system worked and who would continue their resistance from within political institutions. The institutions that women were aiming to join were flawed, not only imperfect as democracy, but also so embedded with the dominant masculinities of the times that the very logic of appropriate behaviour privileged men and masculinity and excluded women and femininity.

The biases of democratic citizenship

Ironically, given the association of democracy with the promise of equality, its practical political arrangements are rooted in inequality. Carol Pateman explains how the social contract on which Anglo-American democracies are thought to be based is underpinned by a sexual contract that established men's political control over women.[3] Originally, it established the 'orderly access' of men to women's bodies, denied property rights to women and, most damagingly, denied them personhood under the doctrine of coverture which was part of British Common Law until the late nineteenth century. The sexual contract underpins patriarchy; it is unequal and imposed. Does this mean that democracy is necessarily patriarchal? For many feminists it does; it is an historical fact.

Ruth Lister extends Pateman's arguments to a consideration of citizenship, another foundation stone of democracy.[4] Observing that women stood outside the civil society to which they were linked by subordination and dependence, Lister draws attention to the way that the concept of the citizen in political theory and constitutional law is an abstraction, actually male but formally disembodied. This way of thinking was supported by the separation of private and public life, in which women in the private sphere were the invisible precondition of public life through the provision of care, reproduction and other unpaid work. The abstraction was possible because only male bodies were present in public life, a life which women could not enter. Women's eventual entry into public life necessarily exposed the role they played in private life and revealed that the body of the abstract citizen was male. The longstanding public invisibility of embodiment and of the private sphere is fundamental to the nature of political institutions in the old democracies. These are organised around men's lives and interests. Women cannot participate on the same terms as men because of their separate roles, their different bodies, and the assumptions that accompany them are not built into the institutions. Lister and Pateman are contributors to a more general feminist debate on the nature of citizenship and democracy. Over several decades, feminist scholars unpacked the gendered dimensions of citizenship, highlighting the different terms on which women and men were treated in state policy—for example on social benefits, pay, employment, and education—showing political equality to be a chimera, dependent on unacknowledged requirements of non-existent economic, social and individual equality. They visualised a model of citizenship that allows for diversity and accommodates women's bodies, allowing for pregnancy, parturition and menstruation.

In common with many of the radical movements of the 1960s, feminists wanted a reorganisation of political life more compatible with principles of equality. In what Kathleen B. Jones described as 'transforming citizenship into friendship', idealised notions of family and friendship informed ideas about political participation. Narrowly constructed and impersonal notions of citizenship based on functional ties and built under conditions of capitalist competition were rejected, to be replaced by affective relationships based on trust. The pursuit of instrumental goals would be replaced by the creative development of personality and sense of community. Idealistic though such conceptions may have been, they contain an understanding that citizenship in a woman-friendly democracy should be rooted in the experiences of women and men. To practice citizenship, women must transform themselves into certain kinds of men rather than participate as women.[5] However, regendering political institutions has eluded reformers. Moreover, even in theory, the solutions of more participatory democratic systems, of direct democracy that many feminists proposed, feature many of the same kinds of problems found in contemporary political institutions. As in the Greek city states, the participation would depend on arrangements that make time and resources to do politics available to citizens.

So, while many feminist theorists offer ideas of democracy that are transformative and egalitarian, most agree that the actual political systems of representative democracy not only permit, but directly secure male power and dominance. This is borne out by empirical evidence which shows that women are numerically under-represented in elected assemblies, that politics is practised according to male coded norms and rules, that vertical and horizontal sex segregation are consistent features of political hierarchies and institutions, that the public perception of politicians is highly gendered and that policies are biased in favour of men.[6]

Such contentions are a devastating critique of democratic political systems because they deny the possibility of equality and do not permit regendering without a seemingly impossible change in the relationships between public and private life. Equality between women and men (and indeed among women and among men) is a logical impossibility for institutions based on inequality and subjection. This raises a central question: can democracy actually enhance equality for women? Simplifying brutally, we can start to answer this question by tracking progress of women's claims for equality in democratic politics. At a minimum, we should find that over time women come to be treated equally as individuals, colleagues and citizens in public life. I use three examples to illustrate progress, or the lack of it: the experiences of sexual abuse that reflect the treatment of women as individuals; the presence of women in democratic legislatures; and the obstacles to policy change on issues of particular importance to women.

The treatment of women as individuals

Feminist assessments of women's position in democracies illuminate a set of power relationships based on differences between women and men. In general discourse, political actors are not discussed as embodied beings, while masculinity is assumed in discussions of politics which normally treat the citizen or candidate or representative as male, without addressing the implications of so doing. That indifference may be lifting. Recent developments in the UK suggest changes, albeit reluctant and ambivalent, in attitudes to sexual politics. As I began to draft this chapter, the *Financial Times* broke the story of the sexual abuse that was part of the Annual President's Club dinner at the Dorchester Hotel in London's Mayfair. This 'all male' event was organised to raise funds for charity. There were in fact women present as casual employees, who had been instructed to dress in a sexually enticing manner, to jettison their mobile phones and to sign secrecy contracts in order to work the event. These were measures designed to protect the privacy of the many prominent men in attendance. A considerable amount of sexual harassment and abuse took place at the Dorchester, ranging from propositioning the unprotected women to inappropriate touching, flashing, suggestive comments and so forth. There can be little doubt that those in attendance knew what kind of event to expect. The story was taken up throughout the press, broadcasting and social media. It generated numerous comments, expressing surprise that the *Financial Times* regarded it as a story at all. It was a story because the *Financial Times'* editors thought so, their reasoning influenced by the exposure of abuse in the film industry and especially the many accusations against the powerful Hollywood film producer Harvey Weinstein that preceded it. These in turn followed the publication of the Donald Trump 'access Hollywood' tapes and widespread protests by women after his inauguration as US president at the beginning of 2017. The opening months of 2018 featured almost daily press accounts of the sexual abuse of women and, unusually, some political heads rolled as a result of specific accusations. The allegations were not confined to private arrangements. They also targeted the core institutions of politics, including the House of Commons and political parties.

In the world of politics, sexism and sexual misconduct in the House of Commons are long-standing examples of male privilege. That privilege has frequently been protected by the leadership of political parties. For example, all three major parties blocked the attempt in 2012 to give the Parliamentary Committee for Standards the scope to deal with issues of sexual misconduct.[7] Frequently brought to public attention, as various allegations are reported, only recently have there been active efforts to change this culture and it remains to be seen whether the measures will actually amount to anything. MPs and parliamentary staff are under severe pressure to remain silent about such abuse. The consequences of confronting it were all too apparent, as the investigations into Lord Rennard, the Liberal Democrat Peer and chief executive of the party from 2003 to 2009, accused of sexual abuse of less powerful women in his party, showed. The investigation findings were fudged: an internal Liberal Democrat party enquiry found credible evidence for some of the allegations, yet it was deemed insufficient for criminal charges. The accusers were discredited, their careers ruined. Meanwhile, Rennard himself was briefly suspended from his party, only to be elected in 2015 as Lords' representative to its ruling Federal Executive Committee, a post from which he withdrew following protests in the party and an intervention by party leader Tim Farron. He remains in the party, where he is still influential, while many of the women who he mistreated have resigned.[8] Thus, both Rennard and his victims were punished or penalised, admittedly an improvement on the days when only the victims were punished. More recently, Defence Minister Michael Fallon, International Trade Secretary Mark Garnier, and First Cabinet Secretary Damian Green, were forced to resign as a result of sexual misconduct allegations. They too are still in their parties and in the House of Commons.

If we are now at a tipping point, it has been a long time coming. Almost a century after enfranchisement, women have been able to get everyday sexual abuse onto the political agenda. It may not stay there, but even assuming it does, we must still ask why it took so long. The answer is not that we have only just thought of it. Sexual abuse has been an issue for women's movements since at least the nineteenth century. It is a crucial impediment to women's political activism and, as such, a barrier to democratic politics.

Slow change: the presence of women in democratic politics

The proportion of women in senior decision-making positions grows only slowly, if at all. Globally in the ten years to 2018, the percentage of women ministers grew by 2 per cent, of senior women managers by 1 per cent and the proportion of women in senior posts in information and communications technology fell by 6 per cent. Slowness also characterises the rise in women's share of legislative seats. This highly visible measure of equality is relatively easy to track. The proportion of women in the national legislature of a country has become a standard measure of their political equality, used by academics and international organisations such as the United Nations (UN), the World Bank, the Organisation for Economic Co-operation and Development (OECD), and International Institute for Democracy and Electoral Assistance (IDEA) amongst others. It is a highly visible symbol of women's political status and a useful indicator of underlying political processes. An inspection of this measure shows long periods of stagnation after the first suffrage elections in the 'old' democracies—even in the exceptional Scandinavian states. By the end of the 1990s, progress in most of the old democracies was steady, if not spectacular. Meanwhile, many of the new democracies, which were often established with quotas of women legislators as part of their founding constitution, made rapid progress and were described as having a fast track to equality.[9]

From the first elections with universal suffrage, it took Sweden thirty-two years and Denmark forty-eight years to get more than 10 per cent of women in their legislatures. These were the frontrunners. For the Netherlands, the figure was sixty years, while for the majoritarian systems of the USA, the UK and Australia, it took sixty-nine, seventy-two and ninety-three years respectively.[10] Thereafter, the numbers increased more rapidly, but as of 2018 only thirteen states have ever crossed the 40 per cent threshold of women's presence in the national legislature. Of these, only the four Nordic countries are classified as fully democratic in the Economist Intelligence Unit Democracy Index.

So, even after decades of struggle and despite significant progress, women are not yet politically equal in democratic states. They are rarely present in legislatures in proportion to their numbers in the population, their issues are rarely given legislative priority. Moreover, in terms of political representation, democracy does not seem to deliver for women. At the beginning of 2018, only one of the top five countries in terms of the presence of women in the legislature is a democracy and in only two countries, Rwanda and Bolivia, neither of which are democracies, are women more than 50 per cent of legislators.

At the beginning of this century, it was plausible to argue, as Pippa Norris and Ronald Inglehart did, that gender equality and democratisation were linked and that the proportion of women in the legislature was good evidence of that link. There was something in their claims. The data on women's presence in national legislatures show growth both in the proportion of women and in the number of legislatures. Between 1945 and 1985 the number of legislatures worldwide rose from twenty-six to 136 and the percentage of women deputies in them rose from 3 per cent to 12 per cent, falling slightly by 1995 when women were 11.6 per cent of 176 legislatures. By 2005, women were 15.9 per cent of 184 parliaments and by 2015 women were 22.1 per cent of 188 national legislatures.[11]

Although the number of democracies did increase over the period, many of the new legislatures were not in democratic systems or were in 'less' democratic systems. If we think in terms of different levels of democracy, then the pattern changes. Drude Dahlerup has demonstrated that there is no correlation between levels of democracies as measured by standard indices and levels of women's political representation as indicated by the presence of women representatives at national level.[12] But measurements do illuminate some dimensions of women's status in different political systems. As mentioned above, there are numerous indices that attempt to rank and track democratic systems. These should be read in conjunction with various gender indices that attempt to measure, rank and track women's equality. The questions raised by this process are tricky. Meaningful comparison of different political systems requires some agreement about which are more and which are less democratic. Some 193 countries have elected parliaments or legislatures on which most of them base more or less plausible claims to be democratic. In short, the evidence is messy, complicated by the fact that assembling it requires confronting a still widely accepted public–private divide that obscures power relations between women and men.

The democracy indices on the whole start with political institutions and restrict consideration of the status of women to suffrage and political candidacy. They do not consider the underlying private spheres of inequality that pretty much determine access to the public spheres of work and politics. By contrast, the gender equality indices start from the social position of women and treat political inclusion as a part of that, one of many variables. Moreover, taken by itself, although the presence of women in the national legislature is a useful pointer and the tables of representation produced by the Inter-Parliamentary Union (IPU) are a valuable resource, many of the listed countries are not actually democracies.

Analysis of the available data shows that highly rated democratic institutions are not a reliable predictor of women's representation. The top five countries for women legislators at national level in 2018 were Rwanda at 61.3 per cent, Bolivia 53 per cent, Cuba 49 per cent, Nicaragua 47 per cent and Sweden 43.6 per cent.[13] While the top ranking countries in the Economist Intelligence Unit Democracy Index do relatively well in terms of women's presence in legislatures, they are not among the highest ranking legislatures in terms of the presence of women, as the table below shows.

Country	Economist Intelligence Unit Democratic Index ranking	% women MPs	Ranking in IPU table of percentages of women legislators in 193 countries, December 2017.
Norway	1	41.4%	10
Iceland	2	38.10%	18
Sweden	3	43.6%	5
New Zealand	4	38.3%	16
Denmark	5	37.4%	22
United Kingdom	14	32% (HC)	39
United States of America	21	19.4% HR 21% Senate	99

We can also assess how rankings of democracy map onto international gender equality indices. The annual UN Human Development Report routinely includes a gender equality index. Its top five ranked countries in 2015 were Switzerland, Denmark, the Netherlands, Sweden and Iceland, only one of which is in the top five of the Inter-Parliamentary Union list of proportions of women in legislatures (IPU rankings were 35, 22, 26, 5, 18 of 193).

Analysing the status of women in representative democracies is an enormous undertaking, raising questions about presence and outcomes that make sense only in comparison to the many types of democratic and other political systems and to other points in history. Political inequalities between women and men are not only protected by centuries of tradition and powerful institutions, they are rooted in private life, in arrangements designed for reproduction and the preservation of property and so on, and seemingly in biological certainties whereby sex is binary, motherhood is a natural phenomenon, but fatherhood more of a rational, legal construct, until recently difficult to prove, but always important to the social order.

The main advantage of democratic systems for feminists is that they afford opportunities for mobilisation that in turn afford opportunities to bring women's issues to the political agenda. This is an important consideration but, as we have seen, one that works pretty slowly and against consistent resistance. Nevertheless, feminists have acted to reshape democratic practices in mobilisations and interventions at international, national and local levels. Frustration with slow progress has generated repeated mobilisations to secure women's political inclusion. Feminists have struggled not only for women's presence in legislatures, but also to place the promotion of women's interests on political agendas.

Substantive representation: women's policy agendas

Struggles for policy influence and representation (or presence) are intertwined. Feminist demands for institutional innovation range from the establishment and empowerment of equality committees and commissions to provision for mandatory quotas of women representatives in political institutions. Over decades of activism, new layers of organisation have been inserted into established structures and new processes inside organisations have been designed to secure the position of women's advocates. The interventions have led to some reshaping of institutions. Political parties have changed their candidate selection rules, practices and institutions. Interest groups have extended their agendas. Governments have altered systems of rules about campaign finance that penalised parties when they did not present women candidates to electorates. Government departments have been required to 'gender mainstream' their policies and feminise their establishments and government itself has become more feminised in both membership and issue concerns. The issues ranged across the public and private spheres, taking in equal pay, gender-based violence, reproductive rights, equal opportunity, family law, education, social benefits and political representation itself.

The changes are well illustrated by two examples: the movements to establish quotas of women candidates and legislators, and use of direct action, including the creation of alternative institutions to draw attention to the lack of accountability to women that characterises so many supposedly democratic political institutions. While the quotas campaigns targeted institutional reform, direct action claiming accountability to women either bypassed or subverted established institutions to draw attention to women's demands and to raise public awareness of women's claims.

The introduction and implementation of quotas of women political candidates nicely encapsulates aspects of both descriptive and substantive political representation. The quotas movement was a massive challenge to the rules of the game, as they upset long established power relationships that determine who decides who are political representatives. Feminists gradually persuaded equality advocates that the only way to increase women's political representation was to mandate it. This process of persuasion involved a significant power struggle that is still not settled in many countries. In terms of practice, the issues are about power. The power to select is valued by party leaders and members and has long been an arena of political struggle. In the old democracies, that struggle is mainly located in the political parties. While in general, parties of the left have been more responsive than parties of the right, both were sites of continuing struggle. The process is well illustrated by the British Labour party where, from the 1970s, successive party debates took place on the issue of equality of women's political representation. Concessions were won piecemeal as the party first agreed that there should be at least one woman on each constituency shortlist from which candidates are selected, building up gradually until the party agreed that there should be all woman shortlists in selected constituencies, thus ensuring a woman would be nominated there. As the policy was implemented, it became clear that the allocation of shortlists must take account of how likely the party

was to win the seat in question, as it was much easier to persuade constituencies that had no chance of winning the seat to take on an all-woman
shortlist. The method of candidate selection gradually changed to accommodate higher and higher targets of women in the parliamentary Labour party.
Resistance was a continuing feature of the implementation process, ranging
from refusal to implement the policies to more subtle means of undermining
the intentions of the quotas. For example, opponents ridiculed the policies
and the women who came forward. A common strategy of opponents was
to shortlist women who were inexperienced and would not be nominated,
even when experienced and qualified women were available. Legal challenges were made to the policy, which was suspended between 1995 and
2001 when a fall in the number of women MPs led to the passage of the Sex
Discrimination Political Candidates Bill that made the use by political parties
of quotas of women candidates legal, though it did not require it. In France,
the quota debate was similarly protracted but there, the solution was to set
targets sanctioned by financial penalties delivered via party finance laws
and the disqualification of electoral lists that did not meet the targets. Thus,
key mechanisms were different, reflecting different political institutions. In
both countries, it was not enough simply to nominate women: they had also
to be elected. These are examples of change in one of the core institutions of
a democratic system brought about by conscious and wilful feminist intervention. Even so, in both countries there was fierce and protracted resistance
to the implementation of the quotas.

We can expect resistance to any policies that challenge the gendered order.
Whilst there are many difficulties in identifying women's political interests,
there is general agreement that some issues are of particular concern to
women. These include the gender pay gap, sexism, childcare, gender-based
violence, reproductive rights and political representation itself. Yet, public
policy debates about these issues were not framed in terms of women's
rights or sex equality. For example, equal pay and opportunities policies
were framed as a matter of business efficiency, while violence to women
was framed in terms of family policy or child protection. These are examples
of what Judith Squires calls rhetorical entrapment whereby the frames used
to argue effectively for a policy result in a dilution and redirection of a policy away from the purposes for which it was proposed.[14] Such processes
reduce women's benefit from the policy by undermining their autonomy
and, yet again, raise the question of how accountable are democratic political
institutions to women.

In its narrowest procedural sense, the idea of accountability has implications
for inclusion and responsiveness and is therefore of concern to feminists. The
institutions of accountability are mechanisms that secure account-giving by
representatives and holding to account by the represented. Accountability,
therefore, is the overarching principle through which the political agenda, laws
and policies are kept aligned with citizen's views, opinions and interests. The
power to hold decision makers to account is thus crucial. Feminists seem to

lack access to the most common institutions of accountability. In general, elected representatives tend not have a clear mandate about how to act concerning women's issues and interests. As a consequence, women are not explicitly considered to be a group to whom decision makers should be accountable. Even though women are the majority of the population, they are required to organise and act politically on their issues from the position of the marginalised outsider.

The way the electoral system works not only masks the elitist and gendered bias of the political agenda, it also conceals the fact that formal accountability is mainly to the dominant groups in society, in this case privileged men. It is so precisely because of the way that their interests shaped and shape political institutions. Even though tools such as equality committees, equal opportunities commissions and equality ministries were established to secure attention to women's issues, these tend to be weak and underfunded, marginal to accountability processes, and forced to rely on strategies that result in assimilation. To date, they do not provide women in society the means to secure effective accountability. Moreover, they are tilted towards educated white working women whose policy interests most coincide with the dominant elites, leaving stranded the concerns of poor and uneducated women and women of colour, and precluding the possibility of meaningful social equality.[15]

Quota advocates were able to work within political parties because they showed how parties could benefit from appealing to women voters. They were able, against considerable resistance, to take part in the political process. But many issues that are of importance to women are not amenable to institutional interceptions—precisely because the relevant decision making is not treated as a matter for public debate. This goes back to the arguments about the sexual contract and the invisibility of embodiment and the private sphere discussed above. The public world does not easily accommodate issues about reproductive rights and gender-based violence, yet routine policy decisions have a huge impact on women's experiences.

The whole official apparatus of accountability so beloved of democratic theorists is in practice littered with the obstacles that protect insiders. Feminists have responded by claiming accountability to women mainly from outside the formal institutions. Feminist organisations and movements operate to make claims for women, in this sense securing a form of accountability that operates via public perceptions. They bypass representative institutions and processes by shifting the arenas in which issues are raised and discussed. Hence, in their search for power to hold the political system to account, feminists are denied effective access to the formal political institutions, if only because they were designed to protect other interests. They therefore seek alternative ways to mobilise in civil society in order to demonstrate their political needs, to mobilise opinion and bring external pressure to bear. Often direct action strategies are used in conjunction with the creation of alternative institutions. Examples are innovations such as rape crisis lines and women's refuges that later become incorporated into official policy. Such tactics, while not exclusive to feminists, have been used since the earliest waves of feminism. Think, for example, of the suffrage demonstrations, or about the French manifesto of 343, in which 343 prominent and difficult to prosecute women claimed, in a manifesto published in the news magazine *Le Nouvel Observateur* (now known as *L'Obs*) on 5 April 1971, to have had an abortion—an effective intervention in the French abortion legalisation debates of the time. Other examples include the Reclaim the Night marches of the 1980s in Europe and the USA, the Everyday Sexism Project website and the various hashtag campaigns including #MeToo and #TimesUp. In 2017 and 2018, there were women's marches across the globe protesting inequality, sexual harassment and abuse. Women in politics provide other examples. Recently, some feminists have taken to social media to subvert the masculine dominance of legislative institutions. Frustrated by inaction over complaints of sexual harassment in UK politics, women MPs, party activists and journalists have publicised their complaints about sexual abuse by male politicians and officials. In 2015, forty women political journalists in France published a manifesto decrying the sexism to which they were subjected in the course of their jobs. In 2017, some 140 women in California politics publicly announced widespread sexual harassment in the #WeSaidEnough campaign. There were similar campaigns in the US Congress and Senate. In the same year in the UK, #LabourToo began to collect testimonies of abuse faced by women in the party.[16]

Powerful, moving and influential, these are activities of political outsiders, evidence that on many issues of male privilege, women cannot rely on access to formal power to hold decision makers to account. They are forced to prompt accountability by other means.

Discussion: the masculine bias of political institutions

The examples suggest that women are still not citizens on the same terms as men. True, many groups of men lack access to the levers of political power, but it is not simply because they are men. Their bodies do not disqualify them from political activity or consideration. Disqualifiers for men are mainly about class and territory, barriers that women also experience. While women can become representatives and do achieve success in changing public policy in their favour through various means, they face additional obstacles simply because of their sex. The successes have not brought equality with men; they have been a long time coming and they always fall short of what is needed.

Thus, after decades of struggle, successive generations of women have not achieved political equality, even in the most democratic states. No set of institutions, including those with inclusion mechanisms such as quotas designed to ensure women's representation, guarantees the equal presence of women in democratic decision making. While things are not as bad as once they were, improvements have been slow. Change is impeded by resistance built into the institutions. Once in positions of power as representatives, women find themselves facing agendas that include issues of policy that will greatly affect women and also their other constituents. There will be established ways of dealing with the decision processes, including conventions, rules, patterns of alliance and coalition building that have proved to be effective over time in the institution. Mostly, the interests of constituents, including women constituents, are best served by playing by the rules, mobilising logics and frames that are part of the institutional culture, thus reinforcing the logic of the institution.

Women therefore face two obstacles in their quest for equality. First to make progress, they are required to play by rules of the established order. As they learn and use the rules, they become assimilated, weakening their ability to pressure for change. Second, their goals are not achievable without comprehensive system change. Indeed, change is not actually enough. What is needed is a paradigm shift whereby roles and institutions are reimagined and re-engineered. While feminists have offered transformative ideas about democratic politics and challenges to male privilege which provide a vision of democratic equality, such visions are challenges to the dominant group, are alien to the hierarchical cultures of politics, and almost impossible to put into practice. Thus, women's advocates are required to settle for relatively limited regulatory innovation in institutions that are well able to preserve their systems of domination. It is doubtful that sufficient institutional change to permit women's political equality has been, or can be achieved, in the face of such deep rooted political masculinity. It is not clear what, if anything, women should do about it.

We should not be surprised. The notion that the presence of women would automatically bring any necessary institutional adjustments so that women could take their place and perform their duties as representatives has repeatedly been shown to be false. And so, it continues. As more democracies were founded, versions of the old institutions were borrowed, sometimes apparently subconsciously, complete with their inbuilt masculine biases. Even in the case of newly created institutions designed with sex equality in mind, the rules and habits of practices from elsewhere contaminate the new arrangements. Thus, the equalities advocates among the founders of the Scottish Parliament were disappointed to see adversarial Westminster habits and ways of doing politics soon establish themselves at Holyrood.[17] An apparent naturalness of masculine dominance is hardwired into our thinking and part of the DNA of our organisations.[18]

The feminist struggle for women's inclusion came late in the day for democracies. Women sought inclusion in imperfect institutions that were designed to represent particular types of men and were imbued with the norms of dominant masculinity. In order to be included, incomers were required to mobilise according to well established practices that were designed to protect and insulate insiders. Inclusion entailed continuing power struggles in which the most successful strategies risked assimilation. In short, democratic institutions based as they were on agreements about exclusion and inclusion, already had inbuilt structures of resistance that could be and were mobilised against women.

Conclusions

Representative democracies vary; they feature diverse institutions and practices that have changed over time. The position of women in these institutions has also changed. The presence of women in democracies is contextually sensitive; some institutions are more women friendly than others. But research shows that no combination of institutions is both necessary and sufficient to ensure equality of political representation. Such variables as democratisation, the overall level of political development, the extent to which the culture of a country or region is egalitarian or secular, the degree of women's labour market participation and inclusion—and in the brokerage occupations in particular, the presence of women in public leadership, levels of political conflict and stability, the type of electoral system, the use of quotas of women, the type of party system, the type of party organisation affect but *do not fully explain* the level of women's political representation.[19]

Does democracy enhance equality for women? The answer is that the idea of democracy does but its institutions may well not. Nevertheless, feminists have benefitted from strong democracy. Arguably, the very existence of the feminist movement depends on its basic guarantees. While claiming inclusion, rights and policy preferences, feminists draw on their rights as citizens to make fundamental criticisms of democratic theory and practice and demand major reforms to its institutions.[20] Many feminists adopt democratic rhetoric to claim that their movements enhance democratic politics by virtue of the fact that they seek inclusion of more than half the population.

This discussion of women's political status in democratic systems is necessarily partial, but I am confident that the mixed and sometimes depressing picture it presents is broadly accurate. On one hand, women have made real progress in the institutions of the most democratic states. This progress has permitted institutional reform and political change that is supportive of further improvements in equality as decision makers mandate quotas of women on company boards, equal pay audits and promotion opportunities in the private sector. On the other hand, progress has been resisted, delayed and distorted in institutions that have not adapted effectively to the inclusion of women. Only recently, the World Economic Forum extended its prediction of the end of the economic gender gap from 2133 until 2234. On some indicators, more democratic systems have been slower than their less democratic counterparts to include women and women's concerns, although in more autocratic systems, inclusion may be more likely to be only symbolic.

The conceptions of politics that feminists proposed in the citizenship and difference debates of the 1980s and 1990s were advanced to support transformative goals of autonomy, self-regulation and diversity that could be realised only by probably unsustainable forms of intensive participation and direct democracy. Can democratic institutions be reformed such that they are equally hospitable to women and men? Or, especially now, when democratic institutions so often seem ineffective, should women put their considerable political energies to more productive use? Can democracy be re-gendered or must we start all over again incorporating feminist theories of political transformation into a newly imagined political system? Would such a re-gendered system be a recognisable variant of today's representative democracies? Could it bring the 'transformation of citizenship into friendship' envisaged by feminists in more optimistic times.

The political institutions that are labelled democratic were designed to accommodate divisions of territory, religion, class and ideology, all of which cross-cut gender. These differences have not gone away, but the assumptions about gender relations on which they are based are no longer accurate. Similarly, electoral systems are not designed to represent women as a group and representatives are not accountable to women. A further complicating problem is that while women's status as a group with some common interests arises from their bodies, they are (as are men) diverse and have conflicting interests as well. It is not difficult to see that any reformed system would be very much more complicated and potentially much less aggregative than any existing representative democracy. Here we have a problem—not of democracy, but of politics, which works better to aggregate demands when divisions are fewer. Although equality is a potentially unifying concept, the struggles to achieve it generate fragmentation and competition among different groups in what rapidly turns into a zero-sum game.

I have described a pattern of improvement. There is no doubt that legislatures have changed their practices in response to demands by women representatives.[21] I am, however, reluctant to conclude that a tipping point has been reached, for two reasons: first the pace of change is slow, particularly in the old democracies; second, the resistance has been and continues to be fierce. I am not even certain the pattern of very slow improvement will continue. That progress can be halted and reversed is evident in the recent restrictions on access to abortion in Poland and the USA. In addition, the structures of masculine dominance are intact and they remain well supported by an array of political institutions. A good example is the media treatment of Boris Johnson and Diane Abbott during and after the 2017 UK general election. Both were and are controversial characters, but while criticism of Johnson concentrated on his haphazard buffoonery, which may or may not be a suitable source of amusement, Abbott was and continues to be routinely subjected to appalling levels of sexist and racist abuse. Such abuse against women politicians is widespread. In the wake of the murder of

Jo Cox in 2016, many women MPs reported receiving routine abuse via Twitter and other social media.[22]

Why then should feminists support democracy? The standard answer is that it permits access to some of the resources needed to mobilise for change. Another answer is that there is no choice. Although we are not in a good place, we probably have no place else to go. But the current configuration of political arrangements is not guaranteed. More generally, while voter suppression, attacks on the judiciary, intolerance of minorities, increased violence all figure in recent assessments of democratic health, the continuing inequality of women has little purchase in the overall assessment made by watchdogs such as the Economist Intelligence Unit, Freedom House and Human Rights Watch—all organisations that are currently reporting serious threats to democracy. It seems that the relative absence of women is not thought to be much of a problem.

Moreover, democracies are steadily being displaced and their institutions outmanoeuvred by other kinds of organisations that are barely controlled by governments. It may be time to concentrate on what is coming next. Global corporations such as Amazon, Google and Facebook are assuming control of large parts of our lives. All the evidence is that they are, at best, very slow to prioritise ridding their companies of sexism; at worst, they are sexist organisations, many of whose senior employees take some pride in the exclusion and mistreatment of women.[23] As the division between public and private life gradually collapses, and as supposedly democratic political institutions continue to be unequal even as they are under increasing threat, are the structures of Silicon Valley a more urgent challenge for feminists than the difficult project of reforming democracies? If so, the challenge will be much the same as it is in representative democracies. The exclusion of women at the founding stages has likely produced institutional biases that require root and branch destruction followed by significant institutional re-engineering before sex equality is possible.

Notes

1 D. Dahlerup, *Has Democracy Failed Women?*, Cambridge, Polity Press, 2018, p 24.
2 Ibid., p. 5.
3 C. Pateman, *The Sexual Contract*, Cambridge, Polity Press, 1988.
4 R. Lister, *Citizenship: Feminist Perspectives*, Basingstoke, Macmillan, 1997.
5 For a full discussion of these debates see K. B. Jones, 'Citizenship in a woman-friendly polity', *Signs: Journal of Women in Culture and Society*, vol. 15, no. 4, 1990, pp. 781–812.
6 Dahlerup, *Has Democracy Failed Women?*
7 M. L. Krook, 'Westminster too: on sexual harassment in British politics', *The Political Quarterly*, vol. 89, no. 1, 2018, pp. 65–72.
8 J. Swinson, 'Sexual harassment: a chance for change', *Medium*, 19 November 2017; https://medium.com/@jo_swinson/sexual-harassment-a-chance-for-change-1e87a9db1581 (accessed 27 July 2018).

9 D. Dahlerup and L. Freidenvall, 'Quotas as a "fast track" to equal representation for women', *Feminist Journal of Politics*, vol. 7, no 1, 2005, pp. 26–48.

10 Dahlerup, *Has Democracy Failed Women?*, pp. 36–37.

11 Inter-Parliamentary Union, archive; http://archive.ipu.org/english/home.htm (accessed 24 February 2018).

12 Dahlerup, *Has Democracy Failed Women?*

13 In the 2017 Economist Democracy Index of 167 states, Rwanda ranks at 134th place, Bolivia at 90th, Cuba at 131st, Nicaragua at 106th and Sweden at 3rd.

14 J. Squires, *The New Politics of Gender Equality*, London, Palgrave, 2007, pp. 146–151.

15 J. Squires, 'The constitutive representation of gender: extra-parliamentary representations of gender relations', *Representation,* vol. 44, no. 2, 2008, pp. 187–204.

16 Krook, 'Westminster too'.

17 F. MacKay, 'Nested newness, institutional innovation and the gendered limits of change', *Politics and Gender*, vol. 10, no. 4, 2014, pp. 549–571.

18 M. L. Krook and F. Mackay, *Gender, Politics and Institutions*, London, Palgrave Macmillan, 2014.

19 S. Childs and J. Lovenduski, 'Representation', in G. Waylen, K. Celis, J. Kantola and L. Weldon, eds., *Oxford Handbook of Gender and Politics*, Oxford, Oxford University Press, 2013, pp. 489–513; K. Celis and J. Lovenduski, 'Power struggles: gender equality in political representation', *European Journal of Politics and Gender*, forthcoming.

20 A. Phillips, *The Politics of Presence*, Oxford: Clarendon Press, 1995; I. M. Young, *Inclusion and Democracy*, Oxford, Oxford University Press, 2000.

21 S. Childs, *The Good Parliament,* House of Commons Library, 2016; http://www.bristol.ac.uk/media-library/sites/news/2016/july/20%20Jul%20Prof%20Sarah%20Childs%20The%20Good%20Parliament%20report.pdf (accessed 27 July 2018).

22 M. L. Krook, 'Politics as usual?: Rising violence against female politicians threatens democracy itself', Democratic Audit UK, 8 August 2017; http://www.democraticaudit.com/2017/08/08/rising-violence-against-women-in-politics-threatens-democracy-itself/ (accessed 20 March 2018).

23 E. Chang, *Brotopia: Breaking Up the Boys' Club of Silicon Valley*, London, Penguin, 2017; L. Mundy, 'Why is Silicon Valley so awful to women?', *The Atlantic*, April 2017; https://www.theatlantic.com/magazine/archive/2017/04/why-is-silicon-valley-so-awful-to-women/517788/ (accessed 19 March 2018).

4. Why is Democracy so Surprising?

DAVID RUNCIMAN

ELECTORAL POLITICS has been rife with surprises in recent years, most notably in the UK and the US. From the 2015 general election (which the Tories weren't supposed to win but did), through Brexit and the election of Donald Trump in 2016, and on to the general election of 2017 (which the Tories were supposed to win but didn't), event after event has confounded expectations. This essay will not try to rehash the reasons for any of these particular outcomes. Instead, I am interested in why we were so surprised, and what that tells us about the current state of democracy. I am also interested in a question that lies behind these others but rarely get asked: is being consistently surprised a good thing or a bad thing for democratic politics?

At one level, democracy is meant to be surprising. It is designed to allow the voters regular opportunities to thumb their noses at their masters, by returning them answers they did not expect. In its classical origins, the idea of democracy was built on a notion of randomness, through the election of public officials in a lottery. By deliberately employing chance in the allocation of political responsibility, ancient democracy was intended to prevent political elites from getting too comfortable with the status quo. If anyone could rule, then nothing should be taken for granted. Likewise, modern democracy has as one of its qualities the capacity to pick up on buried signals of popular discontent. Surprises can be welcomed insofar as they show that democracy is still attuned to subterranean rumblings of dissatisfaction that other regime types tend to miss. Democracies may not always come up with the correct responses to the challenges that they face. But by being open to sudden changes of direction, they are good at avoiding getting stuck with the wrong ones.

That said, modern representative democracy also requires some degree of consistency and predictability in order to function effectively. Elected representatives need to be able to anticipate the voters' wishes if they are going to be able to meet them. Moreover, modern democracy is not just a matter of electoral politics. It also depends on a bureaucratic and administrative machinery that has to plan for the future. That is very difficult if the future keeps changing overnight. Democratic politics ought to be open to the unexpected. But it can't forsake the expected altogether.

What helped make the recent surprises of British and American elections so raw is that they were literally experienced as overnight events. This was particularly true for anyone following the results in the UK. Because of the accident of the time difference, Trump's election, like the outcome of the general elections and the Brexit referendum, was only confirmed in the small hours of the morning. On each occasion, the unfolding drama cleaved to what soon became a familiar pattern. First, there were initial indications that

© The Author 2019. The Political Quarterly © The Political Quarterly Publishing Co. Ltd. 2019
Published by John Wiley & Sons Ltd, 9600 Garsington Road, Oxford OX4 2DQ, UK and 350 Main Street, Malden, MA 02148, USA

something unforeseen might be afoot (exit polls, early counts). Then, as other results came in, the picture became more mixed, and different commentators searched frantically for the snippets of evidence that might confirm what they thought should be happening. Finally, shortly before dawn, it became clear what had actually happened. Red-eyed after little or no sleep, and in some cases after tears, politicians, pundits and voters alike faced a new day that looked very different from the old one.

The extraordinarily condensed timeframe of these events—with political careers made and broken in a matter of hours—should not lead us to assume that this is the only way political surprises can happen, nor that these are necessarily the most significant ones. There is a case for saying that the biggest surprise of all in 2017 was the election of Emmanuel Macron as president of France. Seen in the broader context of recent French history, the emergence of the inexperienced former finance minister of the failed Hollande government as the popular saviour of France at the head of his own political movement was a truly astonishing turnaround. But there was nothing surprising about the night of Macron's election itself, because his victory against Le Pen was by then a foregone conclusion. The surprise was a slow-burn phenomenon, marked by a series of incremental upsets (including the scandal that did for Fillon's chances). Equally, the 2017 German election, which saw the vote share of the two main parties fall to historic lows, while the far right *Alternative für Deutschland* (*AfD*) entered parliament for the first time as their largest rival, was in its way just as out of the ordinary as anything that has happened recently in the UK or the US, even if nothing truly extraordinary happened on the night of the vote. It took six months to form a government afterwards. For a country as preoccupied with political stability as Germany, that too is a sign of the unexpected. Some surprises are to be measured by what doesn't happen, not by what does.

Yet the suddenness of the turnaround marked by the four electoral events I want to discuss here captures a particular feature of contemporary democratic politics: its capacity to take everyone by surprise all at once. One of the most remarkable features of recent British and US elections is that the winners appear to have been just as taken aback by the outcomes as the losers. Donald Trump was reported shell-shocked on the night of his triumph, as were many Brexiteers in the UK. Jeremy Corbyn wore a bemused smile of astonishment on election night in 2017, masked only by the fact that he had been looking somewhat bemused and astonished ever since his extraordinary election to the leadership of the Labour party two years earlier. Of course, not everyone was taken by surprise. We all know some people who saw these events coming. My mother repeatedly told me before the May 2015 general election that the Tories would win an overall majority, regardless of what the polls were saying, and she was right. I should listen to her more often. But almost no one saw *all* these events coming, and those who did were ignored by just about everyone else.

In each case, six distinct categories of participants were taken by surprise by the outcome—let us call them the six 'Ps'. Public, pundits, political scientists, pollsters, prediction markets and politicians all got it wrong. Perhaps we should not be so surprised by the failure to foresee the outcome in the first four cases. The public decides the result of elections, but that does not mean the public knows what it is going to do before it does it. It is often only when the people have spoken that the people discover what it is they wanted to say. Journalists and commentators have little incentive for calling correctly what will happen next in politics, at least relative to their incentive for saying something noteworthy. They are in the business of reporting and commenting on news, not of predicting it.

Political scientists are also not really in the prediction business. Their job is to make sense of what has happened. Nonetheless, many cannot resist making predictions based on formal models of their own devising and in the case of perhaps the most shocking result of all—the election of Trump as president—some of these models proved surprisingly accurate. They indicated that the Republican candidate, at that point in the economic cycle, should have a good chance of outperforming a Democrat tied to the incumbent. But they were no use before the event, because what almost no one could see was that these models applied even when the Republican candidate was Trump. Most political scientists, like most other commentators, could not see past all the things that made Trump unlike any other political candidate in modern history and, therefore, to their eyes, unelectable. The fact that many voters did see past those things and treated Trump simply as the Republican candidate who could defeat a despised Democrat simultaneously confirmed their models and at the same time made them worthless, because that was not something they could predict.

Polls have been getting elections wrong as well as right ever since modern polling was invented. In fact, each of these recent elections saw a few polls in the run up to the vote correctly predict the outcome, and the final divergence from the actual result taken from the average of all polls was not as great as in the greatest polling failures of the past (for instance, the 1992 British general election). The trouble, though, is that the accurate polls were impossible to spot amidst the plethora of less accurate ones, which meant that they did little to temper expectations. Many polls correctly foresaw the outcome of the 2016 US presidential election, in that they predicted a relatively comfortable win for Hillary Clinton in the popular vote (she ended up ahead by a margin of more than 2 per cent). What they did not capture was the possibility that Trump could nonetheless secure an equally comfortable win in the electoral college on just such a result. The gap between the broad-brush national picture and the way it played out on a state-by-state basis added to the element of surprise: what happened was not supposed to happen given what was expected to happen. The consequence was that organisations that drew on broadly accurate national polling data gave Trump almost no chance of ending up as president (the Princeton Election

Consortium notoriously gave him a less than 2 per cent chance of victory). Even the people who saw it coming did not see it coming.

Neither pundits, political scientists nor pollsters are strongly incentivised to make accurate forecasts: their primary customers—readers, students, newspapers—are often more interested in other things, including being told what they want to hear. I heard one prominent American academic who specialised in electoral politics but saw no chance of a Trump victory say after it happened that his students should go to the dean of their university and demand a refund, since he clearly did not understand what he was talking about. Yet in truth, students would be more likely to be offended by a professor who told them correctly that Trump might win and that he was fine with that than by one who told them incorrectly that Trump couldn't win and that he was fine with that instead. In the academy as much as outside, political preferences carry more weight than predictive precision.

Prediction markets, however, should be different. In prediction markets, there is no other incentive than getting it right. Nothing else is at stake except whatever is being wagered on the outcome. That is why, prior to these recent events, betting markets were held up as a better guide to the likely result than polling, punditry or academic prognostication. Having money at stake is meant to filter out sentiment. Nonetheless, on the day of each of the four votes in question, the actual result (a Tory majority, a Brexit win, a Trump win, no overall majority) was priced at about 15 per cent on the prediction markets, and in each case significant sums of money had been wagered on the outcome (nearly £120 million was gambled on the EU referendum, the largest sum ever staked on a non-sporting event in the UK). This means that while some people made large sums, equally large sums were lost by people who ought to know better. When something with a 15 per cent probability happens, it is surprising but not all that surprising: after all, it will come to pass roughly one in every seven times. But when four such events happen in a row, that is very rare indeed.

The combined probability of these four results, as priced on the day of each vote, was cumulatively 0.05 per cent, or 1 in 2000. It could be argued that this is a false statistic as it treats each event as independent when in fact there was some correlation between them: Trump did not call himself Mr Brexit for nothing. Yet what is extraordinary is that these were the market prices when the markets had the information about the earlier results to draw on, so any correlation was already factored in. Trump was given a 15 per cent chance on the day of his victory notwithstanding the Brexit result four months earlier. The Tories losing their majority was given a 15 per cent chance in 2017 notwithstanding the fact that the polls had got it so wrong last time round.

What explains this failure? It seems likely that the real correlation was not between the events themselves but between the people betting on the outcome. Feedback loops and groupthink were at work. In a world where information is so readily accessed and shared in real time, and where betting markets have been fed the knowledge that they are the best predictor of results, it is perhaps inevitable that punters should spend more time watching what other punters are doing than looking for outside sources of evidence. Just as financial markets are more broadly correlated than they have ever been—and therefore more vulnerable to massive corrections across the board—so too are betting markets.

At the same time, the people doing the betting on political events are drawn from a relatively narrow pool. The advantage that prediction markets are meant to have is that they derive their information—that is, their predictions—from the widest possible range of sources and without prejudice, given the relative anonymity afforded to participants. But political betting—unlike say betting on a major sporting event—remains a relatively niche activity. In each of these cases, a lot of the money being staked derived from the City of London. As a consequence, the betting markets and the financial markets were closely intertwined: prices in each tended to track the other. Moreover, the people working in large financial institutions are hardly representative of the wider population. They increasingly tend to be metropolitan and university educated, which places them on one side of the major dividing line in contemporary politics (to borrow David Goodhart's crude but effective shorthand, it makes them 'anywheres' rather than 'somewheres'). The truth is that although some gamblers predicted that Leave would win, few of the many millions of people who wanted Brexit and were intending to vote for it were also betting on it.

The fact that professional politicians were as surprised by these results as professional gamblers is striking because they should be equally strongly incentivised to want to know what is actually going to happen. Their careers, unlike in the case of journalists and academics, depend on their being able to predict what the voters are likely to do, or at least to anticipate it. Yet they too were often dumbfounded. Something similar appears to be true of the political class as of other professions: its members are increasingly cut off from many of the wider currents of public opinion. This may be because, to a greater extent than at any time in the past, politicians too come predominantly from only one side of the big political divides in democratic politics. Of course, that would not follow if the divides are characterised in purely partisan terms: the British Parliament and the US Congress are as divided, and in that sense as diverse, as the countries they represent. But in other respects, they are not diverse at all. There are many divides in contemporary democracy that increasingly transcend party politics.

One of the most significant is educational: levels of education attainment turned out to be among the best indicators of likely support for Brexit, for Trump, or for Corbyn. Whether or not someone went to university was a better independent indicator of voting patterns in both the EU referendum and the US presidential election than gender, income or age. That means that the UK Parliament and the US Congress are now massively unrepresentative assemblies, because higher education has become something close to a prerequisite for entry. More than 90 per cent of MPs in the current House of Commons are university graduates, whereas the majority of their con-stituents did not go to university (this is still true even of the 18–24 age group). Earlier routes into Parliament for those who didn't go to university —trade unions for would-be politicians on the left, or the army for those on the right—are now relatively closed off. Perhaps we should not be surprised that politicians seemed to have had the same experience of shock as many other professions following these election results: no matter how much they talked with and to each other, they were only ever hearing one part of the wider political conversation.

However, there is still a puzzle here. In the pursuit of an edge over their rivals, political campaigns and participants in prediction markets now have access to vast amounts of data, which give them more information than ever before about voter preferences and behaviours. Even if the groups doing the sampling are relatively closed off from alternative points of view, the groups being sampled are more accessible than ever. There is more known about how people vote, drawn from a wider variety of sources, than at any point in the past. Why does more information not lead to more predictability? Why does it not correct for professional bias? As the examples discussed above tend to show, the key issue is not so much the amount of new infor-mation available but, given the sheer volume, how it is filtered. People pre-dicting election results don't simply have more evidence to draw on. They have more evidence to pick from, and it is the picking that is the problem. That is where the bias comes in.

We also need to remember that this is a two-way process. It is not only that there is more information about how voters make their choices, but also that more information is available to voters as they make their choices. The public has access to vastly greater amounts of information at the same time as people trying to study or second-guess what they might do with it. And like the people trying to understand them, the voters get to pick and choose as well. So, this is not just a contest to see who is better informed. It is one set of filtered perspectives trying to make sense of another set of filtered per-spectives. The biases here do not cancel each other out. They add another barrier in the way of seeing what is really going on.

It is clear that both these processes—the greater availability of informa-tional choice and the greater extent of informational bias—are in part func-tions of how digital technology works. It is helping to create parallel worlds of information. This is often framed, and implicitly condemned, in the lan-guage of 'echo chambers', as part of a wider lament about the growing intol-erance and mutual incomprehension of our political discourse. But the divide may be more basic than that. What for some people is news is for other people not even happening. We don't simply discount what the other side is saying because we don't want to hear it; often, we don't even know they are saying it. A comprehensive study by BuzzFeed showed that during the 2017 British general election the most shared stories on Facebook coming from the Labour side were about fox hunting and the ivory trade. The most shared image was a picture of Theresa May juxtaposed with a dead elephant. People who were not sharing these stories and images were simply oblivious to them. They did not feature in coverage of the election in the mainstream media, and the Tories did not respond to this line of attack because they did not know the extent to which it was happening. Out of sight was out of mind.

There is an inevitable tendency to turn this growing gap between what different people see as news into evidence of something illicit. If some people are gravitating towards news sources that are not recognised by many of their fellow citizens, then it is tempting to think this news must in some sense be 'fake'. There is also a tendency to want to make it instrumental: news that only appeals to certain groups must be being deliberately targeted at them in order to manipulate their preferences. These concerns have come to a head with the revelations about the role that Cambridge Analytica may have played in the Brexit and Trump votes. 'Microtargeting' is now a shorthand for fixing the result, especially for those who didn't like the result in the first place. But as an explanation for why politics is so surprising, it does not offer much. First, if this were some deviously efficient new technique for skewing election results, then the winners ought to have been less surprised than the losers and that does not seem to be the case. Second, it takes too much agency away from voters. Of course, all of us are vulnerable to being swayed by effective advertising. But that does not mean that we are simply the tools in someone else's scheme. We choose the information that suits us just as much as we have it chosen for us.

What, though, does it mean to say that certain kinds of information 'suit' us? That simply raises the wider question of what people are doing when they decide to vote the way they do. Understanding individuals' motivations for voting remains a problem in the academic study of politics. There are, essentially, two rival accounts. One offers an instrumental explanation: we vote because we want to help make certain things happen (our side to win, its policies to be carried out). The alternative account makes the explanation expressive: we vote in order to convey who we are and how we identify ourselves (with our side, not with the other side). Neither is fully convincing. As a way of effecting change, voting is pretty ineffectual, not least because of the notorious problem that no single vote ever won an election of any significant scale, certainly not a referendum or a general election. In that sense, your individual vote makes no difference. And even if it did, the line between an election result and a desired outcome can be very attenuated. There are lots of ways someone might act in order to end the ivory trade, from campaigning to boycotting to sabotaging. Voting for Jeremy Corbyn is not obviously the one likeliest to succeed.

For that reason, such a vote can look more like an expression of the voter's identity and attitudes rather than his or her practical aspirations. Yet expressive theories also face a basic problem: going into a private booth to cast a ballot—and in many cases refusing to talk about it or even lying about it afterwards—is an odd way of trying to express your identity. Again, there are many better ways to do it. Moreover, many individuals' identities are nowhere reflected on the ballot paper, least of all in national elections, when the choice before them often seems remote from their personal experiences. In the last UK general election, many voters expressed themselves dissatisfied with having to choose between the two main parties, each lead by a relatively unpopular leader with dismal approval ratings. Aside from the passionately committed few, not many identify with either May or Corbyn. Yet in that election, the two parties combined vote share—at above 82 per cent—was higher than it had been for a generation. Turnout was up significantly as well. A lot of people voted for people they didn't much like.

Recent political science—notably the influential 2016 book *Democracy for Realists* by Christopher Achen and Larry Bartels—has sought to square this circle by characterising the primary drivers of voting behaviour as tribal loyalties. On this account, we vote out of a sense of belonging, which would help to explain, among other things, why for many Republicans the fact that someone like Trump was standing as a Republican counted for more than the fact that the Republican party had nominated someone like Trump. Tribalism can be understood as a mix of the instrumental and the expressive. Contributing your vote to the common cause of achieving a desired outcome can lead to good results for your tribe—perhaps in policy terms, certainly in power terms—and also be a means of expressing where you feel you belong. Tribalism captures what is often the strongest motivation for many voters, which is not what they want to achieve, but what they want to avoid. The sense of attachment to your own political representatives—many of whom will not come from your world at all—might be fairly thin; but the sense of detachment from the ones on the other side might nonetheless be total. Detachment may be understating it; for many voters the feeling comes close to loathing. Often, elections are less about who we want to win than who we want to lose.

But that raises another puzzle. If politics is tribal, with the sense that conveys of how hard it is to move people's preferences and how deep-rooted many of our allegiances are, why is it currently so surprising? Shouldn't tribalism make politics easier to predict? All you need to know is who belongs to which tribe. In fact, there are several reasons why tribalism feeds rather than tempers unpredictability in contemporary politics. First, though people are very hard to persuade to change sides, it may be far easier to persuade them to stay at home rather than voting at all. In an age of tribal politics, the key question is not who switches allegiance but who shows up on the day. Insofar as microtargeting affected the outcome of the US presidential election, it appears to have been particularly effective in persuading some Democrats from the Obama coalition—particularly young African–American men and young white women—not to turn out for Hillary Clinton, because she was not one of them. Trump won with fewer votes than Romney achieved in 2012. He won not because of who voted for him, but because of who didn't vote for his opponent. The mere fact of tribalism is little help in trying to predict turnout.

Second, we are less sure than we used to be who the tribes in our politics actually are. It is no longer just a question of party allegiance—least of all in referendums like the Brexit vote, where many of the key divisions transcended the two main parties. Turnout on that occasion was high, in part because millions of voters who did not normally see any point in voting at general elections found something here they could identify with. At the same time, we have by no means moved beyond party altogether. In the US presidential election, Republican tribalism—in the face of strong provocation from the 'Never Trumpers'—held together just enough to get Trump elected. In the 2017 UK general election the Labour tribe turned out to be much more united, and much more inclined to vote, than almost anyone had anticipated, including the Labour party itself.

Yet in this second case, the tribalism that motivated the vote was not purely party based. The age divide—primarily between those aged under and those over forty-five—was a large factor in shaping the outcome of the election, and some of that was tribal too: no one seeing the queues of young people turning out for Corbyn in university towns could be in any doubt that their sense of belonging was generational as much as it was party political. Education also creates its own tribalism, as was revealed by the Brexit vote, which showed a gaping divide between the university towns (which voted near uniformly for Remain) and most of the rest of the country. Educational tribalism is particularly hard to calibrate, because the educated usually don't recognise that they are a tribe. They are inclined to mistake their tribalism for superior knowledge, which they believe to be relatively dispassionate. That, of course, can make the tribalism worse for those on the other side. There is nothing more likely to reinforce a sense of distance and a commensurate sense of belonging than to be told that you don't belong with the clever people. The Brexit vote reflected some of that feeling too.

Tribalism is also harder to read because it may be more transient than it was in the past. This is the age of network effects, driven by digital technology, which means that individuals have reason to join in with the crowds they see forming in order to share the benefits of belonging. That can create powerful new kinds of identity that exist for a relatively short period of time. Part of the surprise about the ivory trade being such a big issue for many Labour voters in 2017 is that it almost certainly wasn't a priority for many of them before that election, even if it was something they dimly cared about. It was only when it became a vehicle for expressing anti-Tory (and specifically anti-May) sentiment that it proved irresistible for many voters, turning weak ties into temporarily strong ones. This could be called the age of pop-up tribalism: it is possible to create communities of belonging more quickly than ever in the past, though that also means they are less likely to persist. Knowing how the Labour message was communicated in 2017 is a poor guide for knowing what might happen in 2022 or beyond, because we cannot know for sure what will bring people together next time round. Having tried to learn the lessons of 2017, the Tories are currently making efforts for being seen to care about animals (Michael Gove has gone so far as to promise an animal-friendly Brexit)—that may turn out to be a case of shutting the stable door after the virtual horse has bolted.

One way to describe this new landscape is that voting is increasingly expressive—not so much of individuals' identities as of their desire not to have their identities taken for granted. What voters seem sometimes to be saying is: don't assume that my tribalism fits your definition of what counts as a tribe. I will find my tribe, and I don't need your permission to belong. The result is that politics has a deep capacity to surprise, because many of the conventional signals that marked what was and wasn't permitted by way of tribalism no longer seem to apply. When Donald Trump was caught bragging on tape about his right to grab and abuse women—'you can do anything'—most commentators, Republican as well as Democrat, supporters as well as opponents, assumed he had crossed some unspoken line between the acceptable and the unacceptable, as a result of which he had made himself unelectable. But many voters were no longer willing to follow those cues. More than that, plenty reacted against them, using the fact that another group of self-appointed arbiters was telling them what to do as a cue to reinforce rather than to rethink their sense of belonging. Put simply, voters seem less inclined than in the past to wait for permission before doing something surprising.

In describing the four most recent votes in the UK and US, I have not mentioned the one that preceded them, which had a less surprising outcome. The Scottish independence referendum, which ended up endorsing the status quo, conformed to the previous wisdom—previous, that is, to Brexit—that while voters might flirt with radical constitutional change, they tend in the end to revert to the devil they know. The Scottish referendum was a passionately charged affair, revealing deep-seated antipathies and strong feelings of belonging on both sides, and it generated an exceptionally high level of turnout (just under 85 per cent). Yet it produced the result all sides had expected. Why? The conventional wisdom—again until Brexit disproved it—was that 'Project Fear' had worked and enough Scottish voters had been spooked by the unknowns and economic risks to hold back from independence. Given what has happened since, that now seems unlikely. The week before the vote, with the independence campaign having taken a narrow lead in the polls, the leaders of the three main Westminster parties went to Scotland to pledge greater devolution come what may. That was not Project Fear (unless we include the sudden fear of defeat among the Westminster elite). It was Project Listen. The Scottish referendum was won by the side defending the status quo because in the very last week, its representatives stopped taking anything for granted. The Brexit referendum was lost because that lesson was not learned. Instead, Project Fear persisted till the very end. The Cameron/Osborne strategy was to keep insisting that it would be foolish to take such a big gamble. But many people no longer feel they need elite permission to take a surprising gamble. In fact, the absence of permission is what permits the surprise.

So, to return to the question with which I started, is the 'surprisingness' of contemporary democratic politics a good thing or a bad thing? There are many reasons to welcome it. That we are still capable of being so surprised is a strong indicator that democracy retains its capacity to pick up on otherwise unheard strains of public opinion. It means that political elites cannot take their superior knowledge, or their power, for granted. What's more, it means that politics is not boring. This is an important and easily overlooked consideration. We often say we want people to be more engaged with democracy. But nothing is less engaging than feeling the outcome is known in advance. Not knowing what will happen next is the best way of keeping people tuned in.

However, there are also reasons to think that this run of surprises, especially if it continues, is a danger sign for democracy. One is that it is not only the voters who have ceased asking for permission to do something surprising. Politicians are feeling increasingly liberated too. Neither Trump nor the Brexiteers were waiting to be told what the system permits. The same can be said for Corbyn. That approach worked as a campaigning tactic. But in government it is more dangerous. A permissionless politics that neglects or reacts against the conventional signals of what can and can't be done ends up making it very hard to get anything done. Trump is finding this out and so too are the more iconoclastic supporters of a hard Brexit. Frustration with a lack of tangible results, along with a desire to show that the reason for this failure is the refusal of the system to bend, can lead democracy alarmingly close to authoritarianism. Democratic politics needs recognised cues as well as the exhilarating moments when these are ignored. It is a system founded on randomness and at the same time a system built on shared expectations.

Surprisingness, or randomness, are never enough on their own. They need careful institutional framing to prevent them from becoming destructive, especially if we are to avoid the risk of boomerang effects, where one surprise leads to bigger surprises in return. The randomness of ancient politics only worked because it was framed by an elaborate institutional architecture designed to ensure that it remained an enhancement of democratic politics rather than a threat to it. Surprising politics needs robust institutions in order to thrive. Too many of our recent surprises are expressions of resentment with the institutions needed to make surprises workable. That does not mean they cannot be made to work. But we need to recognise that for every surprise that democracy throws up, there has to be a shared democratic framework to manage it. At present, given the extent of the mutual incomprehension that is driving the surprises, it is not clear we have one.

5. Constitutional Reform: Death, Rebirth and Renewal

VERNON BOGDANOR

I

DURING Victorian and Edwardian times, there was a lively debate on constitutional reform—on Irish Home Rule, on federalism, on the role of the second chamber, on the electoral system and on the referendum. This debate was part of a liberal and radical movement designed to improve the quality of democracy. It came to an end as a result of three developments: the 1911 Parliament Act, the Anglo-Irish treaty of 1921, and, ironically, the Representation of the People Act of 1918—the Fourth Reform Act.

The 1911 Parliament Act enabled a government, even if supported by only a minority of the voters, to secure its policy untrammelled by any significant check on the part of a second chamber. It ended the debate on the composition of the upper house, and on constitutional checks and balances. There was, admittedly, a preamble to the Act which implied that it was a mere interim measure, until there could be substituted 'for the House of Lords as it at present exists, a Second Chamber constituted on a popular instead of hereditary basis'. But the preamble then prudently went on to add, 'such substitution cannot be immediately brought into operation'. The preamble was not seriously intended. It was inserted primarily to mollify the Foreign Secretary, Sir Edward Grey, who was opposed to single chamber government, which he believed to be the likely consequence of the Act, and who favoured an indirectly elected upper house. However, few other Liberals shared his view. Having been thwarted by a hereditary second chamber, the Liberals were not about to create a more powerful obstacle to social reform in the form of an elected upper house which, because it enjoyed a degree of democratic legitimacy, would have been able to resist Liberal legislation more effectively than a hereditary upper house ever could.

Grey believed that the British people shared his opposition to single chamber government. But they appear to have been remarkably insouciant about it. There has been little popular demand either for democratising the House of Lords or for its abolition. Certainly, governments of the left have been loath to give the upper house greater legitimacy. Both the Asquith and the Attlee governments, the two most successful governments of the left in the twentieth century, concentrated on reducing the powers of the Lords, so as to make it more amenable to radical legislation, and refused to consider rationalising its composition. In the words of Richard Crossman, Leader of the House of Commons in Harold Wilson's Labour government in the late

Published by John Wiley & Sons Ltd, 9600 Garsington Road, Oxford OX4 2DQ, UK and 350 Main Street, Malden, MA 02148, USA

1960s, Labour's position was that 'an indefensible anachronism is preferable to a Second Chamber with any real authority', a position that he found 'logical but rather reactionary'.[1]

The second development which ended the debate on constitutional reform was the independence of Ireland, recognised in the Anglo-Irish treaty of 1921. This ended the debate on devolution and federalism in Britain for over fifty years, since that debate had arisen largely as an attempt to resolve the Irish question within the confines of the United Kingdom. Introducing the third Irish Home Rule bill in the Commons on 11 April 1912, Prime Minister Asquith had declared that it was 'the first step, and only the first step in a larger and more comprehensive policy'; while, at around this time, Winston Churchill, as a Liberal Cabinet minister, toyed with the idea of restoring the Heptarchy by dividing England into regions as part of a quasi-federal reconstruction of the constitution. Such a scheme, some believed, might resolve the Irish problem by yielding symmetrical devolution in a form that would satisfy those who objected to Ireland being given an exceptional status; and it might also satisfy Ulster Unionists who, so some believed, could be reconciled to Home Rule if only Ireland were not treated differently from the rest of the United Kingdom. But the debate on federalism was somewhat artificial, except perhaps in Scotland, precisely because it was in large part a by-product of attempts to resolve the Irish question. It was always unlikely that those living on this side of the Irish Sea would countenance a massive constitutional upheaval merely to placate Irish nationalists.

In 1919, a conference on devolution was established under the chairmanship of the Speaker of the Commons, James Lowther. But the issue was no longer of much political interest, and the conference got nowhere. In his memoirs, Lowther wrote, 'The discussions had been of great interest, as they often raised recondite and sometimes difficult questions of Constitutional lore and law, but all along I felt that the driving force of necessity was absent.'[2] That 'driving force of necessity' had been given by Ireland, which was about to leave the United Kingdom. Devolution now seemed irrelevant. Winston Churchill was to write mischievously that the two supreme services which Ireland rendered to the Empire were her accession to the Allied cause at the beginning of the war and her withdrawal from the Imperial Parliament at the end. Some, admittedly, continued to argue for Scottish Home Rule, but the onset of the depression made it appear an irrelevant piece of constitutional tinkering which could do nothing to resolve deep-seated economic and social problems.

The 1918 Representation of the People Act—the Fourth Reform Act—served to end the debate on electoral reform for over fifty years. It did so by establishing the first past the post system as the norm for parliamentary elections, with the exception of the four multimember university seats, where the single transferable vote was adopted. The retention of first past the post was ironic, since the Speaker's Conference, which had preceded the reform, had unanimously recommended proportional representation for 211 of the larger borough constituencies out of the total of 569 borough constituencies. In the smaller borough constituencies and in the counties, the Conference recommended, by majority vote, the alternative vote system.

Decisions on electoral systems are generally defended and attacked on grounds of high principle, but determined largely by perceptions, whether accurate or not, of party self-interest. In 1918, it seemed to many that party self-interest dictated electoral reform. It was generally assumed that the post-war scene would see the development of a more fluid multiparty system. The Liberals were divided between supporters of Lloyd George and supporters of Asquith. The Conservatives were divided between supporters and opponents of the Lloyd George coalition. The rising Labour party was threatening the Liberals from the left; and few predicted in 1918 that Ireland would no longer be sending MPs to Westminster, so making hung parliaments less likely. On the right in 1918, there were fears, absurdly exaggerated though they now seem, of the revolutionary dangers of a Labour government elected with a majority in the House of Commons on a minority of the vote. What better way to prevent it than by proportional representation?

It might have been expected that the coalition government, led by a Liberal, Lloyd George, would have been only too happy to give effect to the unanimous recommendation of the Speaker's Conference for proportional representation. But Lloyd George was opposed to it just as Gladstone, Asquith and most other Liberals had been when the Liberals had seemed the natural party of government. Lloyd George regarded proportional representation as 'a device for defeating democracy, the principle of which was that the majority should rule, and for bringing faddists of all kinds into Parliament'.[3] The proposal for proportional representation in the larger boroughs was indeed the only unanimous recommendation of the Speaker's Conference, which the Lloyd George Cabinet rejected. Even so, in the first vote in the Commons on reform, an amendment proposing proportional representation was defeated by just eight votes. Around two-fifths of the Liberals voted against it. There can be little doubt that, if Lloyd George had given a lead, or if the Liberal party had voted unitedly in favour of it, proportional representation would have been carried.

Lloyd George remained opposed to proportional representation for a few more years. In 1922, however, the Asquithian or independent Liberals became the first political party to adopt it in its manifesto, though Asquith had, as Prime Minister, previously been unsympathetic. But, by the time of the 1923 election, which the Liberals fought as a reunited party, proportional representation had disappeared from the manifesto, since Lloyd George would not countenance it. In April 1923, indeed, he had refused an invitation to speak at the annual meeting of the Proportional Representation Society, now the Electoral Reform Society. But, in 1924, Lloyd George declared that he now favoured the second ballot system and, once it had become clear that the Liberals had become the third party in the state, he lamented his failure to have supported proportional representation as Prime Minister. In 1925, C. P. Scott, editor of *The Manchester Guardian*, reported that 'George evidently felt that he had made a great mistake. 'Some one ought to have come to me', he said, 'in 1918 and gone into the whole matter. I was not converted then. I could have carried it then when I was prime minister. I am afraid it is too late now.' But, of course it was not the general principle which needed explaining to him, but its special application to the interests of the Liberal party.[4] Lloyd George could not have foreseen in 1918 that a political earthquake was about to relegate the Liberal party so that it became the third party in the state.

Lloyd George's rejection of proportional representation in 1918 had a paradoxical and tragic consequence for the Liberals. In the 1920s, the Liberals were opposed both to socialism and to tariff reform, the main Conservative policy for dealing with unemployment. The majority of the British people almost certainly agreed with them in their opposition to socialism and tariff reform. So, the Liberals were aligned on policy with the majority of the British people. Yet, the effect of the first past the post system was to exclude them from government. Paradoxically, the Labour party conference in 1918 had come out in support of the single transferable vote at a time when the largest portion of the Liberal party in the Commons was against it, though Labour did not include it in its election manifesto. Confusion, muddle and division on the left not only allowed the Conservatives to dominate the interwar years, it allowed them also to dictate the rules of the electoral and constitutional system, rules which were to give them a great advantage in the struggle for power.

There was a flicker of interest in electoral reform during the period of the second minority Labour government from 1929 to 1931. There seems to have been an agreement between Labour and the Liberals that Labour would introduce the alternative vote in return for the Liberals maintaining the government in office for the time needed to overcome the delaying power of the House of Lords—two sessions under the provisions of the 1911 Parliament Act. A bill providing for the alternative vote did indeed pass the Commons, but it was met with wrecking amendments in the Lords. Before the Commons could deal with these amendments, the financial crisis had intervened and Labour was replaced by a National Government which was returned with a landslide majority in the general election of 1931. The Liberals had lost their leverage and no more was heard of the alternative vote. But, in any case, this system seemed an artefact, a poor substitute for proportional representation which the Liberals now favoured but which neither Labour nor the Conservatives were prepared to concede. The alternative vote seemed to have little popular support. In 1930, one opponent of the system reminded the House of Commons of what Oscar Wilde had said of Whistler —that he had no enemies but was cordially disliked by all his friends. The same was true of the alternative vote in 1931 and was to be so again in

2011, when a referendum on this electoral system was held, in which it was defeated by a two to one majority on a derisory turnout of 42 per cent.

It is a paradox that the 1918 Act, which enfranchised more new voters than any previous reform act, both in total and as a proportion, ended the debate on improving Britain's democratic system for over fifty years. For, apart from the brief flurry of interest on the alternative vote, constitutional issues fell off the agenda of British politics. Expectations of a multiparty system proved false, and the interwar years saw a movement towards a two-party system, with Labour replacing the Liberals as the main party of the left. The multiparty elections of 1922 and 1923 proved but a transition to the new dispensation, although they yielded some odd outcomes. In 1922, the Conservatives, against expectations, achieved an overall majority of seventy-three on just 39 per cent of the vote, while, after the 1923 election, Labour was able to form a minority government on just 31 per cent of the vote.

The two major parties were perfectly content to avoid constitutional issues. The Conservatives were in power, either alone or in coalition, for almost the whole of the interwar period. They saw no reason to tamper with the system. Labour, though in opposition, assumed that it would be in power sooner or later, and appreciated that it could use the sovereignty of Parliament to push through radical and much-needed social and economic reforms. That had indeed been Ramsay MacDonald's view before the 1914 war. He had been instrumental in ensuring that Labour, almost alone amongst European social democratic parties, had come out in opposition to proportional representation in 1914.[5] At Labour's 1926 party conference, George Lansbury, leader of the left, in defending first past the post, admitted that 'the majority of the decisions under the present system had worked for the other people', but added, 'if they were wise, they could now make it work for themselves', as of course the Attlee government was to do after 1945.[6] Both parties, therefore, for their own contrasting reasons, supported the system which came to be characterised by Lord Hailsham in the 1970s as one of elective dictatorship.

II

The debate on constitutional reform, then, came to an end in the 1920s. But it revived in the 1970s. Why did it revive?

The first reason was the return of the Irish question to British politics following the troubles in Northern Ireland at the end of the 1960s. This led both Labour and Conservative governments to come to the conclusion that the Westminster Model could not work in that part of the United Kingdom. This Model presupposed alternating or potentially alternating majorities. But, in Northern Ireland, the conflict was between two rigidly tribal communities, with the Unionists enjoying a permanent majority. It was much easier to cultivate the extremes than the middle ground and alternation in power was highly unlikely. For this reason, successive British governments of both political colours proposed constitutional innovations to meet the special conditions in Northern Ireland—such as power-sharing, proportional representation and a Bill of Rights—which they would not have dreamt of introducing for the rest of the United Kingdom. In 1973, Britain's first regional referendum was held in Northern Ireland—the border poll—and it provided something of a precedent for the national referendum on Europe which was to be held in 1975.

The early 1970s saw the introduction of an even more momentous issue into British politics than the return of the Irish question: the issue of Europe. In 1973, Britain entered the European Community, precursor of the European Union. But the Labour opposition rejected entry on 'Tory terms' and demanded a referendum, which was duly held in 1975, and resulted in a two to one majority for remaining in the Community.

What was the rationale for Britain's first national referendum? It was that, while the decision to enter the European Community was clearly of major importance, the voters had not been given the opportunity of giving their view on whether Britain should or should not join it. That was because, in the 1970 general election—the last before entry—all three major parties had been in favour. This meant that there was no way by which an elector could indicate by her vote that she was opposed to entry. It was not possible, therefore, for the government that took Britain into the Community to claim that it enjoyed a mandate for entry. The party system was not working effectively on the European issue as an instrument of democratic choice.

But there was a second reason for the referendum. For, even if the party system *had* been working effectively, many felt that a decision made by Parliament alone on so momentous an issue would lack legitimacy. Edward Short, Leader of the House of Commons, told the Commons in March 1975, 'The issue continues to divide the country. The decision to go in has not been accepted. That is the essence of the case for having a referendum.'[7]

It is a weakness in the doctrine of parliamentary sovereignty that some decisions are so fundamental that a decision by Parliament alone is not sufficient to secure legitimacy for them. They need also endorsement by the people. That is the case not only with continued membership of the European Community, but also with a decision by one part of the country—Northern Ireland or Scotland—to secede, a decision to devolve legislative power, and a decision to alter the electoral system. All of these decisions are held to require validation by referendum.

The Northern Ireland Constitution Act of 1973, since reaffirmed by both Conservative and Labour governments and by the Good Friday Agreement of 1998, has provided that only the people of Northern Ireland in a referendum, and not Parliament, can deprive Northern Ireland of her membership of the United Kingdom. Since then, as well as decisions on membership of the European Community/European Union, there have been referendums on Scottish independence, the transfer of legislative power downwards through devolution, and on a new electoral system.

There is a clear rationale for such a requirement. MPs are given authority by the people to legislate, but not authority to transfer the powers of Parliament—either upwards to the European Union, or downwards via devolution—nor to alter the electoral system by which representatives are chosen. Locke, in his Second Treatise of 1689, declares that 'The Legislative cannot transfer the power of making laws to any other hands. For it being but a delegated power from the people, they who have it cannot pass it to others.' Voters, it might be said, entrust MPs as agents with legislative powers, but they give them no authority to transfer those powers or to make radical alterations in the machinery by which laws are to be made. Such authority, it may be suggested, can be obtained only through a specific mandate, that is, a referendum. The referendum, then, gives us a form of constitutional protection, perhaps the only form possible in a country without a codified constitution in which Parliament is sovereign. It provides a safeguard against major constitutional changes which the people do not want. It is the people's veto. It prevented devolution to Scotland and Wales in 1979 and devolution to the regions in 2004. It may also have prevented membership of the euro zone at a time when the Blair government, enjoying a huge majority in the Commons, favoured it. For Labour had committed itself to a referendum before entry. The referendum on the euro, however, was never held, since every single opinion poll showed that a majority of the British people were opposed to it. The referendum is now ejecting Britain from the European Union against the wishes both of government and of Parliament.

Some liberal-minded people find themselves uncomfortable with the doctrine of the sovereignty of the people. They use arguments against it similar to those deployed by nineteenth-century conservatives opposed to the extension of the franchise. Jean Rey, ex-President of the European Commission, speaking in London on 17 July 1974, deplored the coming referendum: 'A referendum on this matter consists of consulting people who don't know the problems instead of consulting people who know them. I would deplore a situation in which the policy of this great country should be left to housewives. It should be decided instead by trained and informed people.'[8] Some liberals have become elitists, berating the voters for seeking to use their democratic rights. Yet the high turnout of 72 per cent in the Brexit referendum in 2016—the highest since the 1992 general election—offers a striking illustration of democratic commitment on the part of the British people; and, if the majority do not wish to remain in the EU, it would be wrong, surely, for Britain to remain in the EU.

At a seminar at King's College, London, held shortly after the Brexit referendum, the Professor of European Law, Takis Tridimas, declared that it was the most significant constitutional event in Britain since the Restoration in 1660. For the referendum showed, or perhaps confirmed, that on the issue of Europe, the sovereignty of the people trumped the sovereignty of

Parliament. In the referendum, Britain voted, against the wishes of Parliament and government, to leave the European Union.

Admittedly, the 2015 European Union Referendum Act had provided that the referendum should, by contrast with the referendum on the alternative vote held in 2011, be advisory and not binding. Nevertheless, the government had agreed in advance to be bound by the result. A sovereign Parliament could not be so bound, but, as the Leader of the House of Commons, Edward Short, had declared in the House of Commons in relation to the 1975 Referendum Bill, 'one would not expect honourable members to go against the wishes of the people'.[9]

Brexit, therefore, is coming about not because government or Parliament want it, but because the people want it. Government and Parliament feel themselves required to do something that they do not wish to do. That is a situation without precedent in our long constitutional history. The majority of the Cabinet which proposed the withdrawal bill were Remainers; so were the majority in the Commons, and even the majority of Conservative MPs; while the majority in the Lords for Remain was, almost certainly, even larger than the majority in the Commons. In the conflict between a supposedly sovereign Parliament and a sovereign people, the sovereign people have triumphed. Europe, therefore, has been responsible for the introduction of a new principle into the British Constitution—the principle of the sovereignty of the people.

These two issues then—the return of the Irish question and the introduction of the European question into British politics—brought constitutional issues back to the political agenda. But there was a third issue: devolution. That was primarily a result of the success of the Scottish National Party (SNP) in the two general elections of 1974 and the threat which it posed to Labour. In the October 1974 general election, the SNP gained 30 per cent of the Scottish vote, becoming the second strongest ethnic minority party in western Europe. Admittedly, under the exigencies of the first past the post electoral system, it won just eleven out of Scotland's seventy-one seats, but it was second in a further forty-two seats, including thirty-five of Labour's forty-one Scottish seats. Were the SNP to advance further, it would seriously compromise Labour's chances of forming a government. In the 1970s, therefore, Labour proposed devolution in Scotland and Wales, but its proposals failed to win sufficient support in referendums held in 1979. In 1997, however, Labour, under Tony Blair, held referendums which did secure majority support, and devolved bodies were accordingly established in Scotland and Wales, as well as in Northern Ireland under the provisions of the 1998 Good Friday Agreement. But devolution served to raise, once again, problems which had tormented the Liberals before the First World War. Was it a genuine half-way house between the unitary state and separation, or would it prove a mere slippery slope to separation; and could asymmetrical devolution survive the lack of constitutional logic—for few in England sought devolved bodies of their own to complement devolution in the non-English parts of the United Kingdom? Few were prepared to campaign for Churchill's Heptarchy. Disraeli had once said that England—perhaps he meant Britain—was governed not by logic but by Parliament. That proposition is now open for testing. Indeed, the question of whether devolution will yield a stable constitutional settlement in Scotland remains, at the time of writing, highly uncertain.

But it was developments in the electoral system which arguably had the most profound effect on bringing the constitution back into British politics. In the February 1974 'Who Governs?' election, called by Edward Heath to seek a mandate for firmer action against the striking miners, the voters returned the first hung parliament since 1929; and for the first time also, since 1951, the 'wrong' party won the election, since Labour, with four more seats than the Conservatives, had over 200,000 fewer votes. The Labour party won 301 seats on just over 37 per cent of the vote and formed a minority government, while the Conservatives, having won 297 seats on nearly 38 per cent of the vote, went into opposition. But the Liberals, who secured just over half the vote of each of the two major parties—19 per cent, nearly one-fifth of the vote—won just fourteen out of 635 seats in the House of Commons. In the October 1974 general election, the Liberals were again grossly under-represented winning just thirteen seats for 17 per cent— around one-sixth—of the vote. The SNP, as we have seen, was also under-represented.

The two general elections of 1974 cast doubt on two of the conventional presumptions concerning the British electoral system. The first was that Britain had a geographically homogeneous two-party system rather than a territorially diversified one. That presumption was difficult to sustain when, in both elections, only around 75 per cent of those voting had supported one of the two major parties, and 30 per cent of Scottish voters had supported the SNP, while Northern Ireland had moved outside the British party system entirely, and returned no MPs from the Labour or Conservative parties. The second presumption was that the first past the post system would always produce 'strong government' which was equated with a working majority for a single party. But the February 1974 election had failed to yield an overall majority, while the October 1974 election had yielded a majority of just three for Labour, insufficient to sustain a majority government for the whole of a five-year Parliament. By 1976, indeed, the government's majority had been eroded through by-election losses and defections, so that from 1976 to 1979 there was once again no overall majority for the government in the House of Commons. It is hardly surprising that proportional representation became once again a live political issue. It was no longer supported only by the Liberals who could be accused of special pleading, but by a large tranche of establishment opinion, and in particular by many in the business community, distressed by the 'adversary politics' of alternating Labour and Conservative governments which, so they believed, led to economic uncertainty and made it difficult for companies to plan ahead with any assurance.

Proportional representation also came to be supported by some Conservatives, primarily on the 'wet', anti-Thatcher wing of the party, who feared the depredations of a left-wing government elected on a minority of the popular vote. They did not believe that Margaret Thatcher could win an overall majority on her own; and they feared that, even if she did, she would lack the authority to tame the trade unions. Some in the Labour party were also to become more sympathetic to electoral reform, not when Labour was in power from 1974 to 1979, but during the long years of opposition. By then, however, it was too late. For the debate on proportional representation was largely stilled by the four election victories won by the Conservatives between 1979 and 1992, two of them—in 1983 and 1987—with landslide majorities.

More recently, however, it has again become apparent that the first past the post electoral system might no longer be capable of yielding stable single-party majorities. The last three elections—in 2010, 2015 and 2017—have yielded respectively a hung parliament, a small Conservative overall majority of eleven, felt by Theresa May in 2017 to be inadequate to yield sufficient authority for the Brexit negotiations, and a hung parliament. The failure of the system to produce working majorities is due to long-term tendencies first charted by the psephologist, John Curtice.[10] He has noticed the long-term decline in the number of marginal seats over the last sixty years. If a marginal seat is defined as one in which a swing of 5 per cent from one major party to another would cause the seat to change hands, the number of such seats has almost halved—from 166 in 1955 to 89 in 2017. In consequence, a larger swing than in the past is now needed for a major party to win a seat from the competing major party; and a party needs a larger lead in votes than in the past to enjoy an overall majority. In 1955, Sir Anthony Eden's Conservatives had a 3.3 per cent lead over Labour. That yielded a majority of fifty-eight seats. But, in 2010, David Cameron's Conservatives had a 6.9 per cent majority over Labour which did not yield an overall majority at all; while in 2015 a Conservative lead of 6.5 per cent yielded a narrow majority of just eleven, and in 2017 a Conservative lead of nearly 2.5 per cent again failed to yield an overall majority. Hung parliaments, therefore, have become much more likely than in the past. Moreover, although the 2017 election seemed to restore the two-party system, with 84 per cent voting for one of the two major parties—the highest percentage since 1979—fifty-three seats were won by third parties. This was, admittedly, the lowest number since 1997, but nevertheless higher than at any election between 1945 and 1992. Perhaps, therefore, the elections of the second decade of the twenty-first century will resurrect the debate on electoral reform which has been in abeyance since the debacle of the alternative vote referendum in 2011.

Electoral reformers, while they did not succeed in securing change at Westminster, did secure proportional representation for all elections in Northern Ireland other than Westminster elections, for elections to the devolved legislative bodies in Scotland and Wales, for elections for the Greater London Assembly, elections to the European Parliament, and for local elections in Scotland. First past the post, therefore, survives only for Westminster elections and local government elections in England and Wales. Perhaps proportional representation has become, like the incoming tide, a force which it will be impossible to resist.

Tony Blair's Labour government, elected in 1997, was not unsympathetic to proportional representation. Indeed, it established an 'Independent Commission' to consider it under the chairmanship of Roy Jenkins, who was known to be in favour. But the Blair government was unwilling to implement the recommendation of the Commission for a limited degree of proportional representation; nor was it willing to call a referendum on the issue. On other constitutional issues, however, the Blair government was more radical. It inaugurated a great period of constitutional reform, establishing directly elected legislative bodies in Scotland, Wales and Northern Ireland, Britain's first directly elected mayor in London, a Human Rights Act, the removal of all but ninety-two of the hereditary peers in the House of Lords, creation of a new Supreme Court separate from the House of Lords, and freedom of information. These reforms have made Britain a much better-governed country than it was before 1997. But they have not fulfilled the hopes of constitutional reformers, for a main aim of the reformers was not just to secure better government but to renew British democracy. That aim has not been achieved. The reforms have done little to increase popular engagement with politics, nor to check popular disenchantment with politicians, a disenchantment that reached record levels with revelations of the expenses scandals in 2009.

III

Since the 1980s, the British people have made great strides towards citizenship in the economic sphere and in their relationship with public services. Under the premiership of Margaret Thatcher in the 1980s, citizens were encouraged to become home owners and owners of capital. By the time her premiership ended, there were more shareholders in Britain than trade unionists. Under the premiership of John Major in the 1990s, citizens were encouraged, through the provisions of the Citizen's Charter, to demand higher standards in public services and they were given the right to redress when these standards were not met. Yet those same citizens were expected to remain passive in their political lives, restricted to voting on relatively infrequent occasions at general elections, while, between elections, they were expected to trust elected representatives to make decisions on their behalf. The *forms* of representative government seemed no longer congruent with the political *forces* of modern Britain. Margaret Thatcher had opened up the economic system, and John Major had opened up the public services. But the constitutional reforms of the Blair government had not opened up the political system. It is, however, hardly possible to expect a citizen who is encouraged to be independent and self-reliant in her economic dealings and in her dealings with the public services not also to demand a more active role in the political system as well. In a perceptive Fabian pamphlet written as long ago as 1992, entitled *Making Mass Membership Work*, Gordon Brown argued that 'In the past, people interested in change have joined the Labour party largely to elect agents of change. Today they want to be agents of change themselves.' It was no doubt this sentiment which encouraged the great increase in membership, particularly noticeable amongst younger voters, for Jeremy Corbyn's Labour party after 2015.

The reform programme of the Blair government did little to meet these new popular aspirations. Most voters, particularly voters living in England, would remain unaffected by them. A voter in England would probably not want devolution, for there is comparatively little demand for either a new layer of regional government nor for an English parliament. A voter in England, while she might welcome the Human Rights Act, would hope never to have to use it or to seek redress from the courts. So, if she were to ask 'What difference has constitutional reform made to me?' it would be difficult to come forward with a convincing answer.

The trouble is that the constitutional reforms of the Blair era led to a sharing of power amongst the elite, so putting an end to Lord Hailsham's 'elective dictatorship', but they did little to transfer power from the elites to the people. The reforms could be seen, cynically perhaps, as an exercise in which the officer class decided how it would re-apportion the spoils. Power has been redistributed away from politicians at Westminster, towards politicians in Scotland, Wales and Northern Ireland, towards life peers in the House of Lords, towards directly elected mayors in London and in some other local authorities, and towards judges; but it has not been redistributed to the people. Power has been redistributed sideways but not downwards.

In 2007, Gordon Brown's government produced a Green Paper entitled 'The Governance of Britain' which contained an important section entitled 'Improving direct democracy'. 'In the past', the Green Paper declared, 'individuals and communities have tended to be seen as passive recipients of services provided by the state. However, in recent years, people have demonstrated that they are willing to take a more active role and that this can help improve services and create stronger communities.' The government proposed, therefore, to begin a consultation process on such matters as the introduction of citizen juries and on giving citizens the power to ballot, that is, call for referendums, on local spending decisions. The Brown government was moving, albeit tentatively, towards the introduction of new elements of direct democracy into the British political system.[11]

This development was, of course, aborted by Labour's defeat in the 2010 general election. Nevertheless, the next phase of constitutional reform should involve an injection of direct democracy into the British political system. Perhaps the prime target for such an injection should be local government. For local government ought to be government by the people, lay people, ordinary citizens, rather than by professional politicians. That was certainly the view in the late nineteenth century in the great age of local government reform. In 1894, following the Local Government Act establishing elected parish councils, a Continental lawyer, Josef Redlich, summed up what he hoped the outcome would be. He believed that 'England has created for herself "Self Government" in the true sense of the word—that is to say, the right of her people, to legislate, to deliberate and to administer through councils or parliaments elected on the basis of popular suffrage—And this is the root of the incomparable strength and health of the English body politic.'[12] Local government badly needs to became `Self Government' once again.

Yet today, local government has become far removed from Redlich's inspiring vision. Indeed, so attenuated is it as a result of the depredations of governments of both left and right that it has become almost a marginal element of the British Constitution. Part of the reason for this is the excessive dominance of political parties in most local authorities. Indeed, given the trend towards backbench rebellion in the Commons, party discipline is probably tighter in many local authorities than it is at Westminster. It is a paradox that the fall in party identification over the past fifty years has coincided with entrenchment of the political parties in local government. Many councillors are seen, in consequence, as emissaries of their parties, members of the political class, representing not 'us' but 'them'. That is why local government found it so difficult to attract the popular support which would have enabled it to resist the pressures of centralism.

Admittedly, turnout rates for local elections are low. That may be in part due to the transfer of powers away from local authorities. But there are, nevertheless, striking indications of an unsatisfied demand for participation. Around 40 per cent of us belong to a voluntary organisation, while around 3 million 18–24 year-olds, the very generation that in the past seemed least likely to vote, volunteer every year. As the 2016 referendum showed, the democratic spirit in Britain is healthy, but it badly needs institutions of direct democracy in which it can be expressed. Local government is a prime arena for experiments in direct democracy. The Local Government Act of 2000 provided that 5 per cent of electors in England and 10 per cent in Wales could require a referendum on replacing the traditional council model with a directly elected mayor. But the result was disappointing. There were just fifty-seven referendums, only twenty-three of which resulted in endorsement of a directly elected mayor. Turnout for the referendums was low, typically around 30 per cent. While there is still a case for extending the power to call a referendum to other local government matters, it cannot be said that this power has so far done much to increase the salience of local government. Something much more radical is needed.

That more radical innovation might be found in the principle of sortition —selection by lot. That principle was first adopted in fifth-century Athens, a direct democracy, which chose its office-holders by lot. But there is no reason why the same principle should not be adapted to a modern representative system. It is perfectly feasible to extend participation in a modern democracy, and to ensure that such participation need not be the exclusive province of the better-off and the better-educated. A small proportion of councillors—say 5 per cent or 10 per cent—could be selected randomly by lot from the electoral register. Participation, by contrast with jury service, would be voluntary in that those selected could refuse to serve, but most of those selected would probably be willing to do so. That would increase the representation of the young and of members of ethnic minorities, groups markedly under-represented in most local authorities. Those selected in this way would be genuine independents. They could decide what was best for their communities without being beholden to party. For these councillors, membership of a local authority would become a valuable form of civic education with beneficial consequences for the quality of our democracy. Like most other democracies, we in Britain have hardly begun to utilise the potential of the ordinary citizen. What better place to begin than with local government, the Cinderella of our political institutions? That, surely, is the best arena for the next phase of constitutional reform.

In 1918, the Representation of the People Act paved the way to universal suffrage. But it legitimised a system in which the role of the people was fundamentally passive. One hundred years later, it is clear that the age of pure representative democracy is coming to an end and that representative institutions need to be supplemented by the instruments of direct democracy if they are to retain the confidence of an increasingly educated and sophisticated electorate. In 1918, the greatest threat to democracy lay in the fact that it did not embrace the whole community. In 2018, the greatest threat to democracy lies in the fact that it does not *engage* the whole community. The greatest threat to democracy comes from a passive electorate, one that has ceased to concern itself with public issues. John Stuart Mill says somewhere that we learn to swim or cycle not by reading books about swimming or cycling, but by doing them. Similarly, we learn about democracy, not by reading about it, but by doing it, by making decisions for ourselves on matters of public policy. The task of constitutional reformers today is to make true self-government possible by developing mechanisms of direct democracy to complement our increasingly ossified representative system.

Notes

1 Quoted in M. Taylor, 'Labour and the Constitution' in D. Tanner, P. Thane and N. Tiratsoo, eds., *Labour's First Century*, Cambridge, Cambridge University Press, 2000, p. 169.
2 J. W. Lowther, Viscount Ullswater, *A Speaker's Commentaries*, London, Edward Arnold, 1925, vol. II, p. 271.
3 T. Wilson, ed., *The Political Diaries of C. P. Scott, 1911–1928*, London, Harper Collins, 1970, 3 April 1917, p. 274.

4 Ibid., 13–14 November 1925, pp. 484–5.

5 This anecdote hardly counts as historical evidence, but the historian, Michael Brock, once told me that the great R. C. K. Ensor, author of the magnificent volume in the Oxford History of England series, *England 1870–1914*, and a member of the Independent Labour party before 1914, had told *him* that Ramsay MacDonald had confided that, although before 1914 the first past the post system was disadvantageous to Labour, one day Labour would be the majority party and then it would benefit from the system. That was why MacDonald had persuaded Labour to reject proportional representation.

6 'Report of the 26th annual conference of the Labour party', 1926, p. 273.

7 *House of Commons Debates*, 11 March 1975, vol. 888, col. 292.

8 Quoted in M. Arnold-Forster, 'EEC Beyond Housewife's Ken', *The Guardian*, 18 July 1974, p. 8.

9 *House of Commons Debates*, vol. 888, col. 293, 11 March 1975.

10 See, for example, the table on p. 32 in J. Curtice, 'How the electoral system failed to deliver—again', in J. Tonge, C. Leston-Bandeira and S. Wilks-Heeg, eds., *Britain Votes 2017*, Oxford, Oxford University Press, 2018.

11 It is believed that Gordon Brown hoped, if returned in 2010, to mark the 800th anniversary of Magna Carta in 2015 by producing a codified constitution for Britain.

12 Cited in B. Keith-Lucas, 'Parish councils: the way ahead', The Fourth Mary Brockenhurst Lecture, Devon Association of Parish Councils, 1985, p. 1.

6. Three Types of Majority Rule

ALBERT WEALE

I am always hearing about the Middle Classes. What is it that they really want? Can you put it down on a sheet of notepaper, and I will see whether we can give it to them?[1]

UK POLITICAL history since 2010 has provided us with three examples of how the principle of majority rule can operate in a democracy: 2010 produced coalition government; 2015 a return to the norm of single-party government; and 2017 a minority government. Each illustrates a particular type of majority rule. Theoretically, majority rule captures the value of democratic fairness, but its seeming obviousness disappears once political competition involves more than two alternatives. The traditional Westminster system skirts around this problem by making the relevant majority the parliamentary one, without the need for parliamentary majorities to rest on electoral majorities. The principle of a double majority is that governments should rest both on parliamentary and on electoral majorities, a principle illustrated by the pattern of German coalition governments. However, even in such systems there may be no overall majority position. The principle of the issue-by-issue majority is exemplified in Nordic democracies, in which minority governments need to secure *ad hoc* agreement on particular elements of their programme. It is possible to combine these principles and this possibility is illustrated by a putative reform of the UK House of Lords.

A UK trio: 2010, 2015, 2017

Three elections; three results; three parliaments varying in their party balance: three types of government. Three types of majority rule.

The 2010 election produced a hung parliament, with no one party holding an overall majority of seats in the Commons, leading to a Conservative–Liberal Democrat coalition government, the first in the UK since 1945. In 2015, the UK reverted to its familiar type with one party holding a majority of parliamentary seats, and with the Conservatives able to form a single-party government. The 2017 election produced another hung parliament and the government exhibited yet another form: a minority government dependent on a small party, the Democratic Unionists, for confidence and supply, but without the assurance that it could carry the whole of its programme during its term of office.

Occurring within seven years, these three examples illustrate the different ways in which the principle of majority rule can be interpreted. A typical pattern of government formation in the UK is exhibited in 2015: one party

Published by John Wiley & Sons Ltd, 9600 Garsington Road, Oxford OX4 2DQ, UK and 350 Main Street, Malden, MA 02148, USA

gains a majority of seats in parliament on less than a majority of votes in the election, with the Conservatives holding just over 50 per cent of the seats on the basis of 37 per cent of the popular vote. This pattern conforms to the traditional view of majority rule in the UK. On this view, majority rule means government by the party that can secure a majority of seats in the legislature whether or not it has secured a majority of votes in the country. Indeed, no single-party government in the UK since 1935 has rested on an absolute majority of the popular vote. Instead UK governing parties are elected on a plurality of the popular vote, a plurality being the single largest group of voters. So in general, and as exhibited in 2015, UK government is majoritarian with respect to parliamentary support, but pluritarian with respect to popular support.

Contrast this familiar pattern with that of the coalition government between 2010 and 2015. The Conservatives and Liberal Democrats held 56 per cent of the seats and between them shared 59 per cent of the popular vote. The governing parties were majoritarian in respect of both their parliamentary and their popular majorities. This pattern illustrates a second interpretation of government by majority rule, which might be called the double majority principle. In a system of double majority rule, governments with a majority status in the legislature should also command majority support among the electorate. If we are looking for an empirical example of this type of government formation, Germany by and large exemplifies this pattern.

The 2017 minority government illustrates a third understanding of majority rule. A minority vote among the electorate gives rise to a minority of seats for the leading party in parliament. Support for the government continuing in office lies with a small minor party, but without the guarantee that the governing party can secure its full political programme, any item of which will depend upon an *ad hoc* parliamentary majority in order to pass. Majority rule therefore works issue-by-issue. Majority rule does not mean the rule of a party that secures a majority in parliament or the country, but instead amounts to majority decision making on an issue-by-issue basis. In the UK this pattern of majority rule is rare, but it is exemplified by minority governments in the Nordic countries where no one party or coalition of parties can guarantee to secure its programme across the full range of policies and where governments negotiate their polices on a case-by-case basis.

The key to understanding the logic of these different forms of parliamentary government is to be found in the way they combine a principle connecting voters to parliaments and parliaments to governments. Differing combinations are widely used in the literature on comparative politics to define different types of democracy.[2] The combination of an electoral plurality and a parliamentary majority gives rise to the classic Westminster understanding of democracy. The combination of electoral majorities and parliamentary coalitions yields representational or consensus democracies, a familiar type in much of western Europe. The combination of an electoral plurality and a parliamentary plurality gives us the Nordic pattern in minority government. Table 1 maps the three UK cases by this two-by-two typology.

Table 1: Relation of popular vote to legislative outcome

		Popular Vote	
		Majority	Plurality
Legislative Outcome	Majority	2010 Coalition	2015 One party
	Minority	Null. 1951 Close	2017 Minority

Table 1 also includes a theoretically possible fourth type of majority rule, namely one in which a party with a popular majority of the vote secures only a minority of seats in a parliament, whilst a party with a minority of the votes holds a majority of the seats. There are no actual examples in the UK of this pattern, but the general election of 1951 comes closest with the Labour party securing 48.8 per cent of the vote, a higher share than the 48 per cent gained by the Conservatives, but with Labour having only 47 per cent of the seats compared to the Conservative's 51 per cent. Had Labour piled up even larger majorities in its safe constituencies in 1951, it is possible that there would have been Conservative government with an electoral minority and a parliamentary majority.

The three-way gyration of government types in the UK over seven years is a consequence of the operation of its electoral system in a situation in which there is significant third party support among the electorate. Whatever the benefits and costs for the UK political system of such gyrations, their advantage for the analyst is that they provide vivid and real-life examples of important theoretical possibilities. If we are rethinking democracy, we ought to begin from first principles, but we also ought to bear in mind the various ways in which those principles can be worked out in practice. The sequence of elections since 2010 shows us that different understandings of majority rule are not merely matters of abstract theoretical speculation, but correspond to different ways of thinking about the foundations of democracy.

What is so good about majority rule?

To be a democrat is to be a majoritarian. For many people this is true by definition. After all, the principle of majority rule seems to provide an obvious solution to the problem of how to make a common decision when a group of people have to act together, but differ in their views as to what should be done. If the members of a sports club have to decide between two ways of spending money—say painting the outside of their building or refurbishing the bar—then an obvious way of making the decision is to take a vote at the annual general meeting and go with the majority decision. In relation to collective decision making, the majority principle is what Schelling called a prominent solution.[3] Prominent solutions seem obvious in some way. In wage bargaining 'splitting the difference' is a prominent solution; in the sale of tickets for a concert 'first come, first served' is a prominent solution. Prominent solutions are the first type of solution that comes to most people's minds when thinking about such problems. (How many people, for example, would suggest a 52:48 split in wage bargaining?) In a similar way, taking decisions by a majority vote when there is a need to determine a common course of action in the face of disagreement is so widespread in many contexts, that its value seems obvious.

As well as being obvious, the majority principle also captures the idea of fairness. Because the majority principle takes decisions only by reference to the numbers favouring one side rather than another, it captures the principle of the equality of participants. When the sports club makes its decisions by majority rule, the poorest member's views weigh as heavily as the richest member's views, just as the views of the newest members count as much as the views of the oldest members. The principle of majority rule is no respecter of persons. Neither is it biased towards particular types of alternatives, for example the status quo compared to a new proposal. For these reasons, the principle of majority rule is democratically fair. It counts everyone as one and no more than one, whilst also being responsive to the preferences of those voting. Indeed, in meeting these conditions, the principle of majority is unique. It is the only rule that satisfies them all.[4]

This combination of customary familiarity and democratic fairness is the principal reason for thinking that decisions made in accordance with the majority principle rule are legitimate. Notice that this legitimacy is a procedural legitimacy. Those who favour majority rule as the obvious solution to resolving differences of political view do so because of its responsiveness to the choices of those involved in the decision, independently of the outcomes to which the rule gives rise. You can think that a particular majority decision is wrong, short-sighted, based on widely held misconceptions, or just crass. But whatever you think about any particular decision, you can still think that in the general run of political decision making, the majority principle is the right one to follow.

What are the implications for our understanding of government if we adopt this principle of democratic fairness? An important implication is that through electoral competition, governments should be responsive to, or at least constrained by, the preferences of the median voter. If we imagine voters lined up from left to right in terms of their attitudes, then the median voter sits mid-way between the two extremes. Typically, median voters will form a group whose members share similar political opinions. This does not automatically mean that median voters are centrist in terms of their political attitudes. If public opinion is tilted strongly to the right or strongly to the left, then the median voter will be found to the right or left of centre. However, given the distribution of public opinion in most democracies, median voters will generally be found at the centre of the distribution of opinion and often not too far from the status quo. So, they may favour some tax cuts or some tax increases, but they are unlikely to favour the sort of slash and burn economics associated with the bonfire of regulation or be sympathetic to revolutionary attempts to build the New Jerusalem on earth within two parliamentary terms. They are quintessentially an enlarged version of Harold Macmillan's middle classes.

Democratic fairness also puts a brake on the projects of passionate minorities who occupy government office. The less responsive a government needs to be to the median voter, the more freedom it will have to pursue ideologically inspired goals through policies that would otherwise be punished by opposition from median voters. For example, if a party only needs around 40 per cent of the electorate's support in order to gain a majority in parliament and form a government, then the effective pivotal voters will be found around that 40 per cent mark, and the party's policy programmes and campaigning will be aimed at that group, irrespective of what median voters think. Avoiding this drift away from the centre does not strictly require that in order to gain a parliamentary majority at least 50 per cent of the popular vote is required. The gravitational pull of the median voter will be exercised in elections in which two parties are dominant, with each competing for a winning share of the popular vote. If third party interventions are small in scale, then neither of the two dominant parties will need a 50 per cent share of the vote in order to gain a parliamentary majority, but they will need something close.

In short, the procedural justification for the majority principle as a principle of democratic legitimacy is that it captures a basic sense of fairness among citizens. It does not give disproportionate weight to one group or type of voter relative to others. This virtue will carry over to parliaments if governments depend upon majorities that themselves capture the views of the median voter.

One doubt often raised about the procedural justification for majority rule is prompted by examples in which unconstrained majority rule seems to lead to tyranny and oppression, as with segregation in the southern states of the USA in the first part of the twentieth century or the Nazi seizure of power in Germany in 1933. In fact, in each of these cases there are grounds for arguing that it was the suppression, rather than the empowerment, of majorities that was the main problem. In the US south, great efforts were made to exclude African–Americans from the vote, and true majority voting required the imposition of federal standards on electoral administration after 1965. In 1933, the National Socialists gained their largest share of the vote at around 44 per cent, but their decisive seizure of control came with their abuse of the emergency powers granted after the *Reichstag* fire. However, even if we allow that the untrammelled operation of majority rule can lead to tyranny, so that certain political and civil rights need to be protected from its scope by counter-majoritarian institutions, there is still a large area of public life that will fall within the domain of majority rule, including those cases where a political decision is needed to resolve dilemmas that are thrown up by conflicts among rights.[5]

In any case, the main challenge to the obvious fairness of majority rule comes not from any potential conflict between majority preference and individual rights, but from the difficulties of understanding the meaning and implications of the majority principle when a choice has to be made between more than two alternatives. The difficulties can be illustrated by reference to the case of the sports club having to decide on priorities for maintenance and improvement. If, instead of two possible projects, there is a third alternative, for example re-turfing a pitch as an alternative either to refurbishing the bar or painting the outside, there may be no overall majority in favour of any one option. In this case, the club could adopt the plurality interpretation of the majority principle and adopt the alternative that garners the single largest number of supporters, or it could try some exhaustive ballot system and ask its members to vote on each alternative pitched against the two others. The result of the second type of procedure need not coincide with the plurality preference, particularly when one alternative is favoured as second-best by a large number of people in addition to those for whom it is first best. The sports club will have to decide which procedure is the fairer of the two without either being obvious.

One important cause of an increase in parties—and thus of more than two-party competition—in democracies is the rise of issues that cannot be thought of in simple left–right terms and so have the potential to divide party supporters who are otherwise united in left–right terms. The gyrating forms of UK governments since 2010 arise from the presence of a significant third force in party competition, whether that be the Liberal Democrats or the Scottish National Party. In the present context, it does not matter if we assign the rise of these forces to social and economic change or to the skill of political entrepreneurs in picking on and promoting those issues known to be disruptive. In terms of understanding the meaning of the majority principle, the existence of political contests that are three-way, or even more than three-way, poses significant problems for the meaning of majority rule and, therefore, of its legitimacy. The problem is how to define the equivalent of a majoritarian procedure in circumstances in which an absolute or near-absolute majority does not emerge, given that there is no simple 'either/or' pair of alternatives. In other words, the challenge to the legitimacy of majority rule comes from having to provide a fair way of making party and policy choices in situations in which political pluralism has increased. What might be the meaning of majority rule in those circumstances? There are at least three options: the Westminster system, coalitional government, or government in accordance with the principle of the issue-by-issue majority.

The Westminster system

In the UK, governments normally enjoy a majority in parliament without the need to gain a majority of votes in an election. The Westminster system therefore is typically majoritarian in respect of parliament–executive relations, but pluritarian with respect to voter–parliament relations. Although voter-parliament and parliament–executive relations are logically distinct dimensions of democracy, the Westminster combination is often justified by a single rationale. If the purpose of an election is to have 'strong and stable' government, then a pluritarian electoral system will usually produce that end. It does this by reducing the incentives for third parties to form and by raising the barriers of success once they do form. The parties for whom it is easiest to jump those barriers are those which are geographically concentrated, like the nationalist parties, or those which adopt a localist strategy, as the Liberal Democrats and their predecessors have done. However, in the nature of the case, geographically concentrated political forces find it hard to establish the scale of presence that the two major parties have. Moreover, if accountability is an important value, then it can be argued that pluritarian democracy achieves that goal. With one-party government, there are fewer opportunities for blame-shifting by governments. Blame-shifting clearly occurs particularly at the beginning of the parliamentary term, when incoming governments can attribute all the problems to their predecessors and all the successes to themselves. Over time, however, blame-shifting becomes increasingly implausible, and certainly if a party wins successive elections, it becomes virtually impossible. No one but the Thatcher government was responsible for the poll tax, just as no one but the Blair government was responsible for the Iraq war. And everyone knew it.

From one point of view, this line of argument suggests a tension between the value of accountability and the value of majority rule. Someone in favour of strong and stable government seems to be in favour of clarity of blame-attribution over the requirement to secure majority support in the population at large. Provided one is majoritarian at the parliamentary level, it seems to matter less that one is pluritarian at the electoral level. From another point of view, however, clarity of accountability might be said to provide an incentive for responsiveness to the views of electors. Only a relatively small change in party preference among the electorate will produce a large change in the balance of seats in parliament. In this way, it might be argued, governments have an incentive to be particularly responsive to voter concerns. On this account UK governments are responsive precisely because they typically rest on less than an absolute majority of the popular vote.

Of course, this supposed virtue may be turned on its head. If UK governments are peculiarly sensitive to relatively small changes in popular support, that can lead them into a pattern of chop-and-change policy making. A long-standing critique of the Westminster system is that its adversary politics underpinned by the electoral system induces frequent and counter-productive swings in public policy. The tendency of the electoral system to magnify relatively small swings in votes to relatively large changes of seats leads to a damaging politics of see-saws in government policy.

The argument also prompts a larger question about accountability. One way of thinking about the principle of accountability is to see it as bringing together two requirements on agents responsible for making decisions.[6] The first is the requirement to explain and justify those decisions. The second is the requirement to be liable for sanction. Single-party government, however, provides little incentive for questioning and deliberation in the making of legislation, even when that legislation turns out to be unpopular in electoral terms and indeed could have been predicted to be unpopular. Moreover, the sanction mechanism is weak. The principle of ministerial responsibility is fiction not fact; many of the problems of policy show up long after governments have left office; UK governments often rush through legislation and policy without the opportunity to deliberate on problems; and few governments are confronted with the need to negotiate with other parties. Before the Thatcher governments of the 1980s, some of the problems of one-party government were mitigated by conventions aimed at cross-party consensus, for example the use of royal commissions and committees of enquiry, as well as retaining a strong policy analysis capacity in the civil service. But those practices no longer exist.

These developments mean that it is hard to put too much weight on accountability. In its deliberative dimension—the aspect of accountability that is concerned with explaining and justifying policy choices—the mechanisms for governments to seek out a broadly acceptable view are weak under the Westminster system. In its sanctions dimension—the aspect that is concerned with providing an incentive for governments to seek out those broadly acceptable views—the practice is weak or non-existent. Ministers do not resign for failure or have left office by the time that failure becomes manifest. And an election covers a multitude of sins.

So, it is hard to argue in practice that the virtues of accountability are so clear and obvious that they should outweigh the disadvantages of giving power to a party that secures only a plurality of the vote. Of course, it is not necessary to insist that a governing party secures at least 50 per cent of the popular vote before it can claim some majoritarian legitimacy. If a party secures, say, 48 per cent of the vote with no other party within 5 per cent, then one can argue that, given the inevitable presence of some third party, this is as close to the median mandate as one can get in practice. However, as the plurality support for a single party in government falls below 48 per cent, the sense of legitimacy weakens. For myself, I find the sweeping Thatcher reforms with large parliamentary majorities resting on a share of the popular vote that never rose above 44 per cent illegitimate in terms of majority rule, but others may judge differently. However, when a plurality falls below 40 per cent, it is hard to say that a government rests on anything but a minority. When a government secures a parliamentary majority with only 37 per cent of the popular vote, we are clearly in the territory of minority rule, with all the dangers that brings.

Note that this argument is not the same as the argument that was often made under the Thatcher government, namely that the then government was opposed by the majority. It might look as though a government having a parliamentary majority with a plurality of the vote is equivalent to the theoretical case suggested by the 1951 result, namely a popular majority securing only a parliamentary minority. If the Thatcher government's electoral plurality led to a parliamentary majority, is that not the same as saying that the opposition's electoral majority has only secured a parliamentary minority? But the two are not mirror image cases. It is true to say that the Thatcher government could have been defeated by an opposing majority if that majority had been united into one force. But it never was. In fact, what the Thatcher governments faced were opposing minorities, of roughly equal size, represented by Labour and the Liberals/Social Democrats, but each smaller than the minority that supported the Conservatives. The situation was one of opposing pluralities, not of a single electoral majority deprived of its rightful parliamentary share of seats.

If one is going to defend the Westminster system, given the principle of majority rule, one either has to show that the principle of accountability does actually provide a way of securing responsiveness to the views of a majority or that the virtues of accountability trump those of majoritarian responsiveness. Either of these claims seems hard to uphold. A third alternative is to say that one should not be too literal about the principle of majority rule and that some plurality short of a strict majority is still a good enough practical approximation. Whilst that may seem plausible for governments resting on, say, 48 per cent of the popular vote, it becomes increasingly implausible the further support for the government falls away from that figure.

Double majority government

Double majority governments require both a parliamentary and an electoral majority. It is no accident that of post-1945 governments in the UK, the 2010 coalition has been the only government to satisfy the double majority requirement. Outside those increasingly rare cases in which two parties dominate the electoral landscape, it is hard for a single party to secure enough popular support for it to be able to command an absolute majority in the country, even if the party can secure a majority in the legislature. In consequence, the double majority principle favours coalition government. It does not follow, however, that legislative majorities produced by coalition always rest on popular majorities. German coalition governments sometimes rest only on parties that between them have less than 50 per cent of the popular vote, for example the 2009 coalition that rested on only 49 per cent of the popular vote.

Yet, the German experience also highlights the distinction between Westminster majoritarianism and coalitional majoritarianism. In 2009, the German Christian parties won around 34 per cent of the popular vote, not far short of the 37 per cent that David Cameron's Conservatives had in the UK in 2015. Yet, in Germany the Christian parties were nowhere near forming a parliamentary majority, whereas Cameron's Conservatives had a good working majority. Even if, strictly speaking, coalitional majority governments do not always rest on a popular majority, they will always come close to doing so, given that the electoral system produces roughly proportional results. In that sense they gravitate towards median voters.

However, the system of coalitional majorities also exemplifies the complexity of majority rule. Elections can throw up results in which there are potentially large numbers of alternative coalitions. Consider the German election result of 2017, in which there were six parties, counting the two Christian parties as one, elected to the *Bundestag*. These were, with their share of seats in brackets, the CDU/CSU (35 per cent), the Social Democrats (21 per cent), the Alternative for Germany (13 per cent), the Free Democrats (11 per cent), the Left (10 per cent) and the Greens (9 per cent). From this array of parties, and if, quite contrary to fact, there were no constraining factors, there are, in principle, a large number of minimal winning coalitions, that is to say coalitions involving combinations of parties in which the withdrawal of one party would turn the coalition from being winning to losing. Of course, neither the Alternative nor the Left were acceptable coalition partners for the two leading parties (or for one another), but were we to assume that these constraints did not operate, there would be eleven possible minimal winning coalitions given the results. With real world constraints in operation, there were only two possible minimal winning coalitions: the 'Jamaica' coalition, involving the Christian, Green and Free Democratic parties, that Angela Merkel sought to form after the September 2017 elections, and the grand coalition between the Christian and Social Democratic parties that Merkel eventually negotiated. Although each of these coalitions can be validly called a majority coalition, the policies that they would be likely to follow could be significantly different from one another.

Remember that the justification for majoritarianism was that it provided for a fair reconciliation of the balance of opinion among a group of citizens in a situation in which there were different and incompatible views about what should be done collectively. The key idea is that government policy is responsive to, or at least constrained by, the preferences of the median voter. Yet, in what sense is the government constrained by the median voter when it is made up of one type of coalition that could be very different in composition and policy orientation than another coalition that might have governed? The double majority condition, which at first sight seems to impose quite tight constraints on which governments can form, seems in practice to allow for different coalitions that are quite diverse in character.

However, any sense of arbitrariness at this point would be misplaced. When there are potentially quite different coalitions that might be formed out of a given electoral result, this is normally a sign that parties are being elected to parliament on the basis of very different appeals to electors. In particular, it suggests that some electors care strongly about some issues, whilst others care strongly about other issues. As a result, parties will be elected for different reasons. A green party may secure as many votes as an anti-immigrant party, or an anti-free trade party as many as a libertarian party. In forming any coalition, therefore, it may be necessary to combine opposites, but such opposites can be defined in different ways.

In a simple one-dimensional political world, in which the main political forces line up on a left–right spectrum, the coalitions that are likely to form are ones that will be centrist and compatible with one another in policy terms. However, when more than one dimension of political conflict is in play, intelligible connections between parties may not exist. Much depends on how close in the two or more dimensions the parties are, in a situation in which it is possible for parties to be close in one dimension and far apart in another. For example, low tax parties can differ from one another on such topics as immigration or social morality, making a joint coalition hard or impossible. There may be no simple answer to the question of how close to the median voter a governing coalition is. It is not that different and incompatible minimal winning coalitions fail to encompass the median voter. It may simply be that there is no one median group of voters seen from all points of view. No group is median with respect to the left–right spectrum, social morality, the environment, national unification or immigration. There is no single centre taking all these dimensions of policy together. Yet, while there may be no median voter seen from all points of view, there will be median voters seen from the point of view of any one policy dimension. This leads naturally to the issue-by-issue majority principle.

The issue-by-issue majority

Suppose that the median group can only be identified with respect to particular policy issues. There will be a median voter on tax issues, on environment, on migration, on social morality and so on. Suppose also that parties campaign, making some of these issues a point of specific concern. If a sufficient number of voters prioritise some particular concerns over others, and so are drawn to specific parties, then proportional representation electoral systems will give those parties seats in the legislature. Yet, just as with the electors, there may be no party in the legislature that is the median for all dimensions of policy. For each dimension of policy, however, there will be median parties. The way is opened up for issue-by-issue coalitions, in which parties vote together on some issues and against one another on different issues. For example, in Denmark in the 1980s, a conservative government secured its measures on financial and economic affairs with support from opposition parties, but conceded to the alternative 'green majority' made up of governing and non-governing parties on environmental policies.[7] The combination of policies that resulted were therefore fiscally conservative, but environmentally progressive.

This pattern of policy making is one that is typical of minority governments in the Nordic states, in which some parties will support others in office, without entering the government themselves, and in which legislation is passed by *ad hoc* coalitions on particular issues of policy. For example, between 1945 and 2011, over three-fifths of governments in Norway were minority governments; in Sweden the figure is over 70 per cent; and in Denmark nearly 90 per cent. Indeed, in European countries in general, minority governments are common around a third of the time.[8] Such governments have to make compromises on their budgets and legislation, just as the 2017 Conservative government had to promise the Democratic Unionists extra spending in Northern Ireland, and had to recoil from proposed legislation on fox hunting and grammar schools.

The principle of majority rule exhibited in these types of systems is one in which *ad hoc* majorities on different issues get their way without there being any one majority that ends up with the combination of polices that it favours. Indeed, it is easy to show with issue-by-issue majority voting that one can theoretically end up with a situation in which no one favours the combination of policies that emerge from a sequence of votes. Nonetheless, there is a clear sense in which there is majority rule, even if the composition of the majority varies by issue. Of course, it may be said that there are some issues that are intrinsically connected together so that the separability of issues that issue-by-issue voting will be limited in scope. For example, fiscal conservatism may be combined with environmental progressivism, since the first concerns taxation and public spending and the second regulation, so that the policies for one can be reasonably separated from the policies for the others. However, within a fixed public budget, it is not possible fully to isolate the priority given to one spending commitment from the implications for other spending commitments. This may be one reason why public spending is typically higher in Nordic democracies than elsewhere, because issue-by-issue voting leads to pressure to relax the budget constraint. The same logic was nicely illustrated in the UK in 2017, when the Conservatives, having campaigned on the claim that there was 'no magic money tree' to increase public expenditure suddenly found that there was such a tree, worth £1bn, and it grew in Northern Ireland.

The crucial condition that makes issue-by-issue voting possible is a separation of questions to do with the continuation of the governing party or coalition in office from questions about matters of particular legislation. Whether a parliament grants confidence to a government to continue in office is a different matter from whether a parliamentary majority can be mustered for the political programme of that government. The implication is that parties in government will not be able to secure the passage of their whole programme, because they cannot muster a sufficient majority in parliament on all issues. However, minority governments can still *govern*. They can propose measures, they can implement agreed policies, they can conduct foreign affairs and so on. What they cannot guarantee is that they will get their way on particular matters of policy and legislation. In this respect minority governments and their conventions of majority voting are at the opposite end of the spectrum from governments in Westminster systems.

Second chambers

So far, I have discussed these three interpretations of the majority principle on the assumption that they characterised mutually exclusive political institutions. Since the three different ways of thinking about majority rule correspond to different ways of classifying democracies, there is an obvious logic to this assumption. However, recently Steffen Ganghof has drawn attention to the fact that this assumption is an over-simplification, since it implicitly makes the role and operation of second chambers redundant in our understanding of democracy.[9] By ignoring second chambers, we risk neglecting the possibility of combining different principles of majority rule in one functioning system. In particular, Ganghof argues that democracy is best served by separating the functions of maintaining the executive in office on the one hand and passing legislation on the other, and that these two functions can be allocated to different houses of parliament. He shows that something like this system is approximated in the Australian Commonwealth, as well as in the Australian states of New South Wales, South Australia and Tasmania. Ganghof himself suggests that these systems combine the clarity of responsibility associated with the Westminster system with the responsiveness to the plurality of interests and values associated with issue-by-issue majoritarianism.

If one transposed this logic to the UK, it would provide a clear basis for reform of the House of Lords. If the Commons continued to be elected on the current first past the post system, then a government would be formed from whatever party or parties commanded a majority in the Commons. However, a reformed House of Lords could be elected by a highly proportional system. It could be denied the power to pass a vote of no confidence in the government, as is effectively the case now, but it would be able to vote down measures proposed by the government if those measures could not command majority support in the chamber. In effect, this is to turn the existing Salisbury convention on its head. The Salisbury convention means that the Lords will not veto legislation that had been promised in the manifesto of the governing party. By contrast, were the Lords to acquire the power to reject legislation that could not command a majority in the second chamber, the government of the day would have to craft its legislative proposals in such a way that it could reasonably anticipate sufficient cross-party consensus to secure passage of the legislation. It would replicate in two-chamber form some of the features of the single-chamber Nordic systems. The House of Lords would become a house of laws.

I do not mention this possibility to advocate it (though I do think it has merit). There are many detailed questions that would have to be considered, even to entertain the prospect. Where does the right of initiative lie, do the terms of office of the two chambers coincide or not, what arrangements have to be made for joint activities by both chambers, would there be a danger of legislative deadlock? Moreover, there may be other calls on the function of a second chamber, as there are in Germany in institutionalising the federal system. However, the idea of separating the role of parliamentary chambers in respect of their confidence and their legislative functions does offer a workable example of the way in which two types of majority rule could be combined. It also provides a way in which some of the objections to the practice of so called 'accountable' government in the Westminster system could be met. Even if the sanctions part of accountability remained weak, the deliberative part would be enhanced. Different types of majority may complement rather than compete with one another.

Conclusion

The principal justification of majority rule is that it provides a fair way of coming to a common policy when people disagree. In situations in which only two alternatives are in play, that democratic fairness is relatively easy to observe. However, where there are three or more alternatives seriously involved, there are different types of majority rule each with their own distinctive characteristics. The three very different types of government that the UK has had since 2010 illustrate the different ways in which majority rule can be institutionalised in the face of electoral pluralism. People often ask in these circumstances what is the right way for finding the majority. But this is to pose the wrong question. We should not imagine in situations of political pluralism that there is a majority hidden but struggling to come out as the will of the people—like the proverbial thin man trying to get out of the fat one. What is needed instead are fair and open ways of institutionalising political negotiation among different groups in a way that embraces an incentive towards encompassing different interests and opinions. Coalition government, issue-by-issue voting in minority government and two-chamber government in which one chamber is purely legislative, all provide ways in which this can be done. If this sounds like empowering minorities that majorities might emerge, there is neither irony nor contradiction in that claim.

Notes

1 Note from Harold Macmillan to Michael Fraser, the director of the Conservative Research Department, February 1957.

2 A. Lijphart, *Patterns of Democracy: Government Forms and Performance in Thirty-Six Countries*, New Haven and London, Yale University Press, 1999; G. Bingham Powell Jr., *Contemporary Democracies. Participation, Stability, and Violence*, Cambridge, Mass., Harvard University Press, 1982.

3 T. C. Schelling, *The Strategy of Conflict*, Oxford and London, Oxford University Press, 1960.

4 K. O. May, 'A set of independent, necessary and sufficient conditions for simple majority decision', *Econometrica*, 20, 1952, pp. 680–684.

5 R. Bellamy, *Political Constitutionalism: A Republican Defence of the Constitutionality of Democracy*, Cambridge, Cambridge University Press, 2007.

6 M. Bovens, 'Analysing and assessing accountability: a conceptual framework', *European Law Journal*, vol. 13, no. 4, 2007, pp. 447–468.

7 M. Skou Andersen, 'Denmark: the shadow of the green majority', in M. Skou Andersen and D. Liefferink, eds., *European Environmental Policy: The Pioneers*, Manchester, Manchester University Press, 1997, pp. 251–286, at p. 265.

8 T. Saalfeld, *Executive–legislative relations in Europe*, Abingdon, Routledge, 2015, table 20.2.

9 S. Ganghof, 'A new political system model: semi-parliamentary government', *European Journal of Political Research*, vol. 57, no. 2, 2018, pp. 261–281; S. Ganghof, S. Eppner and A. Pörschke, 'Bicameralism as semi-parliamentarianism', *Australian Journal of Political Science*, vol. 53, no. 2, 2018, pp. 211–233.

7. Rethinking Political Communication

ALAN FINLAYSON

'CONTENT', is hardly something contemporary political culture could be said to lack. Political news, opinion and disputation fill newspapers and broadcast media. Platforms such as Facebook, Medium, Reddit, Twitter, podcasts and YouTube have given rise not only to new kinds of political participation, participants and audiences, but also to new genres of political argument and expression. The last decade has therefore seen an extraordinary and far-reaching transformation of the volume, sources and the styles of political communication. The effects of all this on our democracy are, at present, definitely mixed. More information has been met by more misinformation. The increased speed of reporting on politics has decreased the span of attention and the time for reflection. Expanded participation in political discussion has also improved opportunities for those who want to exploit free speech for sectarian advantage (or to abuse it for their own amusement).

The freedom and the capacity for people to think for themselves is—it goes without saying—a source and a goal of democratic politics. That necessitates, in turn, the freedom and capacity to express those thoughts publicly, to take part in formal and informal discussion and debate about political decisions, and to argue over the quality and nature of economic and social life. It does not follow, however, that just any political talk whatsoever is necessarily and always good for democracy. Mendacity, stupidity and flippancy can manifest in political speech as much as any other, and like bad currency they drive out of circulation the tokens of good communication. It is therefore tempting to see in contemporary political communication a problem of inflation—too many people, saying too much, too loudly or, as Plato put it when complaining of the Athenian Assembly, 'shouting or hammering their disapproval and approval, grossly exaggerated in either case, of the things that are said and done'. That temptation is to be avoided. Our choice is not between acquiescence to elite authority on the one hand, and acceptance of our cacophonous public sphere on the other. If we refuse that choice we can instead turn our attention to thinking carefully about how contemporary communications technologies are changing the ways in which we experience and take part in democratic politics.

Such re-thinking is necessary because technologies of political communication do not simply reflect or transmit political ideas and opinions. They give shape to thinking and are the means by which we 'educate, agitate and organise'. But different means of communication make possible different kinds of answers to the questions of who will be educated, what will agitate them and how they will be organised. Digital media are new and still rapidly evolving, but they have already changed the kinds of ideas that can

Published by John Wiley & Sons Ltd, 9600 Garsington Road, Oxford OX4 2DQ, UK and 350 Main Street, Malden, MA 02148, USA

have currency in our political culture, and the ways in which people apprehend, respond to and use them. They have intensified an ideological 'culture war' and given new life to paranoid and conspiratorial thinking from the daft (such as flat earthers) to the wicked and sinister (anti-Semites and neo-fascist monarchists).[1] Yet digital communication has also expanded the range of people who can play an active part in the refinement of our collective political intelligence, feeding creativity, enhancing political education and giving rise to new kinds of dynamic and adaptive political alliance. The challenge is to work out—through conceptual reflection, practical action and experiment—how best to agitate, educate and organise with these new tools, to develop new rhetorical styles and strategies, and to plug these into structures and processes of political organisation and struggle in ways which can enhance democratic freedom and the capacity to exercise it.

In what follows, I first consider how political communication is today commonly thought of by progressives as a problem. While acknowledging the seriousness of this problem, I argue that the way we frame it means that we risk succumbing to the anti-democratic temptation which just wants the noise to stop. Such a framing hinders our understanding of new media and the search for answers to the question of how to speak well and loudly about radical democratic politics today. I therefore introduce a way of understanding politics and communication which I hope helps us think things through better, consider some of the challenges posed for us by the political culture of social media, and look at some examples of the ways it is being successfully used by new kinds of political actors emerging from the right.

The problem and the question

Early enthusiasm for the 'digital public sphere' has—in the face of insurgent populisms across Western democracies—given way to a feeling among many liberal and radical democrats that the public sphere is in total crisis. Expressions of that feeling tend to focus on three broad sets of issues. The first of these is the way social media have enabled those with most resources to leverage undue and unaccountable influence on the public sphere. Of particular note here are widely publicised allegations—such as those involving the company Cambridge Analytica—that well-resourced and cynical political campaigns have been able to access and use psychometric data derived from social media in the design of political advertising targeted at precise segments of the population. In addition to giving the few an unfair advantage over the many, two problems are usually highlighted: that such communications are unjust because they are manipulative, cleverly appealing to the emotions in a way that suppresses individuals' rational reflection; that the use of 'dark ads', seen only by those they are aimed at, enables political actors to bypass the public sphere and the scrutiny, debate and rebuttal that might be generated there, thus allowing all kinds of propaganda and incitement to spread unquestioned. The latter concern overlaps with the worry that social media create 'bubbles' in which we see, hear and read only that which reinforces our current beliefs, ceasing to engage in the kind of reflexive revision of beliefs considered essential for rational democratic deliberation. What unites all these concerns, then, is their underlying sense that the public sphere is becoming dominated more than usual by irrational ways of thinking.

A second and related area of concern, is that of 'fake news'. This label is attached to different phenomena. One of these is false stories created with the intention of misleading people. Examples here include Russian government-sponsored 'troll farms' of the kind that are the subject of indictments by US Attorney General Robert Mueller in his investigation into interference in the 2016 US presidential election. These consist of people paid to cultivate social media profiles and then insert into blog posts and online discussions, particular news stories, political opinions or other claims in a twenty-first century version of Nixon's 1950 'whispering campaign'. Another kind of 'fake news' is political 'clickbait', websites and stories created with the simple goal of generating web traffic and thus advertising revenue. Examples include the work of young entrepreneurs in Veles, Macedonia who, during the 2016 presidential election, created websites with misleading names such as NewYorkTimesPolitics.com, on which they published pro-Trump 'news' articles that they assiduously circulated on social media, generating a decent income.[2] What unites the set of concerns about 'fake news' is the view that the public sphere is being corrupted by communication with an instrumental goal—political or financial advantage—rather than the ethical goal of increasing public understanding and honestly searching for the common good.

A third and final set of issues concerns the extent to which unregulated online communication enables or even encourages speech which exceeds the limits of what a democratic commitment to discussion and debate can tolerate. Platforms such as Twitter, Facebook and Reddit have been urged —and in some cases required—to remove users whose communication is threatening or aggressively prejudiced: racist, sexist, homophobic, transphobic and so forth. That there is a lot of this about is undeniable. Abuse of women politicians on Twitter, for example, is well documented.[3] It is also clear that while some of this kind of harassment is indicative of the attitudes of a few individuals, some of it is planned and implemented as part of a political strategy.[4] The core concern here is two-fold: that such speech actions are harmful in themselves, a kind of assault, and that their goal or effect is to prevent some kinds of people from participating in public discussion and debate. Social and cultural inequalities are thus reproduced in the political public sphere which, rather than being a space where citizens meet as equals, becomes a means of sustaining that inequality.

Charges of irrationality, instrumentalism and inequality are, then, at the core of the progressive critique of contemporary political communication along with proposed remedies: the revision of electoral law so that it can better control campaign activity; more effective regulation of social media companies by, for example, treating them as news organisations; new protections and means of legal redress for victims of harassment.

While the power of psychometrics is over-stated, there need be no doubt that social media are increasing the spread of falsehood, encouraging the unchecked declaration of untenable opinion, and are a means for widespread harassment. Regulatory and legal remedies are certainly required. But we do need to pause here. The way these problems and remedies are often framed tends to construe them either as intrusions into an otherwise fair and free public sphere or as undermining the ongoing effort to build one. That is to say, critique is guided by an idealised version of the public sphere that was the product of a particular form of democratic organisation reliant on print and some kinds of broadcast media. Accordingly, it tends to assess the new by measuring how far it departs from the old, and to demand regulation which can make the new be more like the old. New forms and styles of political communication are considered as breaches of the current rules, leading to a search for ways to enforce the rules better and for new rules to cover new infractions. Is this adequate for grasping and responding to our current situation? Is there not a risk that in thinking the new in the terms of the old, we end up adopting a position that is reactive and defensive in ways that disable us from seeing what is really happening and working out how best to respond? I see two problems in particular. The first is practical: that while we check the rule book and propose revisions, our opponents are busy winning by breaking the old ones and are in effect writing the rules for a new game of their own devising. The second is conceptual: the focus on managing the overall culture of political communication means that we are not thinking about how to do it, that is, how to adapt to a changing political culture, and how to develop and use new technologies to create new forms and styles of rhetoric and argumentation in ways that increase democratic capacity. We are assuming that we are hegemonic, that nobody could seriously or sincerely contest the way in which we think the public sphere and politics should work, and we are letting that assumption do our political and ideological work for us. It isn't working.

To be clear, none of this is intended to encourage complacency about the irrationality, instrumentality and inequality produced and sustained by some parts of our culture of political communication. On the contrary, these must be acknowledged as both ethical and legal challenges, but also as a pressing *political* problem, which is to say, one that concerns the forms taken by power and the ways in which it can be wielded and contested. In addition to thinking about how to stop others wielding that power, we need to think about how to wield it ourselves. We have to think about how to act not only *on* the digital public sphere but *within* it, in ways that can defeat manipulation, promote factual and rational analysis and defend our people from attack.

An analogy might help here. The extension of the franchise in 1918 was not just a quantitative change in British elections. It transformed how British politics took place and what it was concerned with. It was an 'amendment' to the constitution which transformed the significance and value of other parts of that constitution and their relationships with each other, changing the ways in which publics were formed and connected to government, how political parties worked, the relationship of Commons to Lords, the kinds of political demands that were counted as legitimate, the scope of rights and thus also the extent of state action. How people thought about and engaged with politics changed irrevocably. Anyone doing politics in the old way was overwhelmed. Those that survived did so by developing new kinds of rhetoric, new ways of speaking to people, and new venues through which to do it. My concern is that our critique of emerging tendencies within contemporary political culture is not adequate to the scale of the transformation underway, and that we risk being so far on the wrong side of history that in the future it will be us whose 'strange death' will be the topic of scholarly debate.

Changes in the technologies and uses of communication alter the 'constitution' of political society. The expansion of online platforms has changed who takes part in political debate, how they take part and what they think they are doing when they are doing it. That isn't just an amendment to the established way of doing things. It is a change in the relationship of communication *to* political institutions and practices and thus a change *in* them too. The question for political analysis is how to understand that change—how people's relationship to government and politics is being altered, how politics is becoming something different from what we thought it was. The challenge for progressive political practice is not the restoration of things to the way they were, but the development of platforms, styles and strategies for working in this new context—in ways which not only enable us to defend past gains and check opponents, but also to find potential for enhancing democratic capacities.

Communication, party and people

If we reframe the problem in this way, then the questions we have change too. In addition to asking why something is being allowed to happen, and what can be done to prevent it, we also ask for a thicker understanding of the relationship of communication technologies to politics. A starting point for that is a typically provocative 2007 essay by Regis Debray, in which he proposed that political movements are an ensemble of three things: people, institutions and 'tools of transmission'.[5] In the case of socialism, those people were members and supporters of the working class, brought together in institutions such as parties, trade unions, corresponding societies and workingman's associations, linked to a physical infrastructure, including buildings, in which, as Debray puts it, one could access 'a library, newspapers, evening classes and lectures' and where archives of previous classes, debates and discussions were kept. The 'tools of transmission' were newspapers, pamphlets and books, a vibrant print culture linked to a powerful oral culture of rallies, speeches and congresses, songs, stories and sermons. In combination, these constituted a movement and its thinking into which people could be inducted, learning where it had come from and where it might go. It also gave rise to a vocabulary and a language—ways of describing and analysing social and political conditions, concepts to help grasp them critically and forms of presentation and argument for communicating that understanding persuasively.

People could learn that language, use and share it and in doing so were not only describing a politics but also being part of its development. For socialism, the printed word in the form of the pamphlet, the book and the party newspaper was not only a means of distributing an ideology but also the embodiment, and the means to an enactment, of its core propositions: equality, collective self-organisation, liberation. The cheap and readable pamphlet educated readers otherwise excluded from education and was allied to lectures, seminars, discussion groups and debates affirming that everyone could understand the world: that the worker was a thinker, that anyone could talk, argue and decide about politics, and that the division between mental and manual labour could be overcome. All this was, of course, also the way in which the movement could coordinate people in political struggle. Tools of transmission allied to institutions such as the party and the union could turn people out on streets or on strike, could direct their action and deliver their vote, leading to change in the institutions of government and economy. The party newspaper, for example, mixed propaganda with the dissemination of news and the presentation of an analysis, 'transforming', in Debray's words, 'a conception of the world into small change, a philosophical system into everyday slogans' and enabling individual energies to be integrated with the practice of party and political leadership.

So deeply was the high-water mark of socialist party politics associated with this kind of print culture that Debray thinks it could not survive when media systems developed from a means of transmitting ideas into a commercial mass market for images. He has a point. In the UK, the party newspaper, the caricature of *Socialist Worker* aside, is a thing of the past. Notably, *Labour Weekly* closed in 1987, the same year that Labour ran a widely applauded but unsuccessful 'professional'—meaning media-driven—election campaign centred on promotion of the personality of the party leader. The rise of twenty-four hour news and the beginning of the shift from print to digital, triggered a transformation of party communications that was also a change in the form of the political party. The (always fraught and contested) communication of information about society up and down, from the grassroots of a movement to its leadership, was replaced with the identification of 'public opinion' via the opinion poll and the focus group. The public was no longer conceived of primarily as a body of citizens, but as a collection of individuals making up an audience. This was not simply a change in cam-paign practice. It was a change in ideology, a replacement of the ideal of the self-organising citizen seeking to increase and exercise collective power with that of the individual consumer, weighing up each party's 'offer', expecting efficient and effective 'delivery'.

In this context, the dissemination by a party of information and ideology to a mass membership came to seem a waste of time and a misdirection of energies better aimed at cultivating rigorous message discipline and the arts of 'news management'. That was itself a way of adapting to a voracious media and to a political culture in which, as the sociologist Jeffrey Alexander puts it, the public sphere is not so much a forum for rational deliberation as a public stage.[6] That stage, he argues, hosts performances (sometimes con-tentious) of ongoing 'social dramas' which publics assess in light of past and present performances, their shared repertoire of recognisable plays and parts, controversies and characters which performers (be they party leaders, celebrity activists or columnist commentators) must play or be made to play: the bold reformer, risking it all to go up against orthodoxy; the teller of truths that others dare not tell; the loyal and reliable hand who will do what is needed in times of trouble; the tough guy ready to take on the bad guys; the Machiavel; the jester; the traitor; the solider; the nanny; the wise owl. Political campaigns place such figures within larger historical 'narratives' that dramatise answers to questions about who we think 'we' are and what we think is happening, and into which politicians try to cast themselves as grand protagonists. Consider, for example, Boris Johnson, in the summation of the BBC live debate on the EU referendum calling for our 'Independence Day'.[7] These were the words of a fictional American president, from the film of the same name, the drama of a people recalling their foundation myth as preparation for their final conflict against mute and monolithic aliens. In evoking this performance, Johnson, consciously or not, cast Brexit as a par-ticular sort of heroic drama which, despite its postmodern blurring of national cultures, fiction and reality, resonated with those willing and able, perhaps needing, to recognise themselves in that call for national re-creation and renewal.[8]

Politics has always had a dimension of dramatic spectacle. But the chang-ing stages on which it can play out have changed the way the narrative unfolds. The period of televisual broadcast politics—characterised by tight news management and focus on leadership personalities—peaked in the 1990s and gave rise to a form which still dominates the theory and practice of the main broadcast and print media outlets. In them, the character of the proper, reasonable and reliable politician is quite tightly circumscribed, and political journalists are like expert theatre critics who interpret the play for us and tell us who is acting well, performing properly, and who is not. Today, however, that division of labour is falling apart. In the last decade, to take one example, what started as 'below-the-line' comments in online newspapers have developed into genres such as the political blog, enabling all sorts of people to become opinion columnists, bypassing editorial gate-keepers and even finding self-employment as pamphleteers and polemicists. Thomas Clark, an English tutor based in Yorkshire, blogs under the name Another Angry Voice. During the 2017 election campaign, two of his articles were in the top three most shared online—far in excess of anything from the newspapers.[9] Blogs like Clark's—along with larger sites hosting multiple authors such as Guido Fawkes and Westmonster on the right, The Canary and Evolve Politics on the left—increase the number of stages upon which politics goes on show and the range of roles which political actors can play and be recognised as plausible. That undermines the 'vertical integration' of the political 'marketplace' so assiduously developed by the 'cartel parties' and their official supporters in the news media.[10] Avant-garde and retro-revivalist performances that once seemed way, way off-Broadway, with no chance of an audience, provincial companies that would never get a booking in the urbane theatres of a cosmopolitan capital, can now all find an audi-ence, grow it, amplify it and help it to recognise itself.

However, the break-up of the cartels of political culture—of their mono-poly on what counts as right-thinking—and the fragmentation of electorates, is not the most significant development. What internet politics invites above all is the self-abolition of the audience. Everyone, anyone who wants it, is invited onto the stage. Via the social media platform of our choice, each of us can play a role, however small, in the social dramas of our time. That is what is most changing, and will continue to change, the way we understand our relationship to politics and to democracy.

The form of the content

If Debray is correct and part of the success and value of the culture of nine-teenth-century socialism was the way it included people within a culture of egalitarian self-education then, surely, the means for inclusion and knowl-edge distribution afforded by digital culture provides an opportunity for the re-creation of what was lost in the age of the broadcast image. However, that is to reckon without the ways in which online platforms encourage a culture of competitive and acquisitive individualism. Onscreen the world is a series of things for me to open, close, delete and move at will. I can arrange the things upon it just as I please; I can watch a political speech, pausing, rewinding, switching between it and a commentary upon it, my own writing about it, my email, my Twitter timeline. The things of the world I have accessed via the computer become objects, defined by the rela-tionship to me that I give them (with anything unexpected or undesired, experienced as an intrusion into my space, to be expelled or blocked imme-diately). Perhaps this is one source of the sadism that too often characterises online behaviour. 'If the movie screen always directs toward', writes the media theorist Alexander Galloway, 'the computer screen always directs away. If at the movies you tilt your head back, with a computer you tilt in.'

In the legend told by Plato in *Republic* the Ring of Gyges makes the wearer invisible, posing the question of how virtuous we would be if we thought we could never be seen, caught and punished. Online, Galloway argues, the legend is inverted: 'The computer is an anti-Ring of Gyges. The wearer of the ring is free to roam around in plain sight, while the world, invisible, retreats in absolute alterity. The world no longer indicates to us what it is. We indicate ourselves to it, and in doing so the world materializes in our image.'[11] That is to say, the computer lets us dress the stage, design the lighting, so that we appear as we think we want, and with the house lights up the world beyond the stage is hidden from view.

That individualisation of experience is given a further impetus by the ease and speed with which digital platforms convert communication into forms of capital which they invite us to accumulate. Through liking, following, sharing, upvoting and so on, the value of what we say can be measured in social or cultural capital (and in how much we have or lack compared to others). Blogs and YouTube videos can easily be converted from cultural into money capital through advertising or through the patronage of followers via systems such as Patreon. The civic goals of communication are (yet again) cut across by a commercial imperative which demands novelty and distinction.

For these reasons, digital communication tends to promote a political culture in which self-expression predominates over and, indeed, decomposes collective political ideologies of any kind. Online, the heroic (and its counterpart of the comic) performance of self-expression, the declaration and demonstration of a place on the stage (wherever that is and no matter how small), is a dominant register of political discourse. Those of us whose work gives us some little access to very minor roles on the main stages of the public sphere should not feel we have the right to judge those putting on a show of their own. There is a democratic dimension to this, there is empowerment and there is a strongly egalitarian aspect to the individual citizen having the chance to argue against the politician, the professional pundit or the professor. The problem is that it comes to seem as if self-expression is the goal of public political discourse, as if just saying stuff is an achievement in itself without need of a connection to a political movement, a plausible political demand or a strategy for persuading others to support it.

Indeed, digital culture erodes the distinctiveness of political thought and action. To speak at a political meeting is to do something different from what one is doing when speaking generally. To write a letter to a newspaper used to involve a specific effort and sometimes a distinct form of address. Online, the way we interact as citizens is indistinguishable from the way we deal with email, pay bills, communicate with family, joke with friends. Some platforms, such as Twitter, are simultaneously and often indistinguishably, work, citizenship, brand-building, socialising and private life. One of the causes of conflict online (and sometimes of public and official scandal) is that statements of an 'everyday' nature shared between friends have the same appearance as statements made in an organisational or official capacity. The former can then be taken to have the seriousness, the moral or political significance, of the latter, while people in their official role can hide their politics within an everyday mode of discourse. What is lost here is recognition of the fact that when we do democratic politics, we are doing something distinct. It is not work, leisure or shopping. It is where we become something other and more than ourselves, where self-interest develops beyond itself, beyond even our natural social interest in the company and recognition of others, such that we are concerned for what is in the interest of all, for the good of what is in common.

It is in this part of our post-democratic political culture that the populist right has prospered. It has grasped that the power of the medium lies in the fact that it allows a kind of political communication that is the opposite of that encouraged by broadcast media. The latter invite forms of address aimed at the broadest range of people, at an imagined entire public. This leads us to look for instances of the typical—'Mondeo man', 'soccer mom', 'Worcester woman'—and to appeal to them by showing that we recognise their typicality, affirming that they are the norm, that what they want is what all should want, and that our policies will meet their needs. But, online we can create our own profile, striving to believe in its atypicality, and looking for the audience that will applaud it. It may seem paradoxical given that part of the populist argument is that we should think of ourselves as first and foremost one part of a people, a nation or a race and that we should accept and conform to the natural impositions of our biological sex, but online the radical right appeal to people on the basis that they are atypical, beyond the mainstream and part of a counter-culture. They invite and enable people to think of themselves as individuals who eschew orthodoxy and think for themselves, sceptical about the pronouncements of the officials in government, media and universities. Indeed, the core of their critique of liberalism is that, in their telling, it demands that we conform to our social identity, our class, race or gender. Supporters are enabled and encouraged to demonstrate, to perform, their rejection of such liberalism and to enjoy what one Trump-supporting meme calls 'liberal tears'. Indeed, the way in which he affronts liberal sensibilities is central to the appeal of Trump. It gives supporters vicarious pleasure to see him take down liberals a peg or two, an attitude so convinced that it is natural, normal and given. A related meme mocks liberals for relying on the argumentative technique of asserting 'the current year', that is, when somebody says something to the effect of 'it's 2018, how can you say, think, do this, how can this be allowed to happen?' The point is to expose the extent to which liberalism takes for granted its own hegemony even as it denies it, and in so doing to show to potential converts that what claims to be generous-minded universalism is in fact the expression of a particular cultural interest.[12]

This is part of a much more extensive phenomenon. Three brief examples will have to suffice: Jordan Peterson, the Canadian psychology professor, now world famous self-help author, critic of gender politics and left-wing academics, and advocate of the mythical re-enchantment of the world; 'Sargon of Akkad', real name Carl Benjamin, a thirty-eight year old who lives in Swindon, describes himself as a classical liberal, mostly agitates against feminists, and who achieved infamy for abusive and unrepeatable comments directed at the Labour MP Jess Phillips;[13] Paul Joseph Watson, a thirty-five year old from the north-east now based in London and working for the world's finest purveyors of conspiracy theory and nutritional supplements, InfoWars. Until recently, Peterson was not widely known outside Canada and certain parts of the internet; Benjamin and Watson are largely unknown to those over forty who don't share their politics (unless condemned to make a deliberate study of it). Why should we know about them? Consider the numbers. 'Sargon' has 785,000 subscribers to his YouTube channel. To put that into context, *Newsnight* has just over 198,000 (which is 150,000 more than the Labour party). His most watched video has been viewed 2.8 million times. The most watched Labour party video has been seen 667,000 times. Peterson has just over 1 million followers on YouTube; his video *Identity Politics and the Marxist Lie of White Privilege* has been viewed by 1.1 million at the time of writing (and he is estimated to earn between $19,000 and $79,000 from supporters via Patreon).[14] Watson has 1.2 million subscribers, and videos viewed as many as 12 million times. His June 2016, rhythmically rhetorical performance, *The Truth About Brexit*, has been viewed 753,000 times.

The videos these three make are not short, pithy pellets of multimodal propaganda. Watson's often last ten to fifteen minutes; *The Truth About Brexit* is a twenty minute speech, mostly delivered direct to the camera; Sargon's regular feature *This Week in Stupid* runs for thirty minutes to an hour. At the start of 2018, over half a million people watched him engage in a live online debate with the North American fascist Richard Spencer, for over four and a half hours. Peterson's diatribe against identity politics is a lecture which runs for over 2.5 hours. Each of these prolific (and perhaps verbose) ideologues links the curious viewer to a much larger political–intellectual ecosystem including other videos, extensive subsidiary discussion, debate on Reddit and other forums, and further reading ranging from history books and evolutionary psychology to various shades of conservative, right-wing and far right political theory. It is a large and dynamic arena of international ideological production which includes events offline—conferences, conventions and lectures. In July 2018, Peterson debated with the celebrity atheist Sam Harris and the professional anti-immigration conservative Douglas Murray at the O2 Arena in London. Tickets cost from £60.00 to £210.00 and it was billed by the promoters as 'the Woodstock of live speaking and debate'.

Sargon, Peterson and Watson belong to different fractions of this 'new, new right', and each exhibits a different political style (from Watson's populist sensationalism to Peterson's performance of academicism), but they share in common a mode of political self-dramatisation: they are individuals who will think the unthinkable, and say the unsayable, eschewing what they present as the merely fashionable or intellectually orthodox, suffering bravely the blows and the persecution of their enemies. That persona is a key part of their rhetorical strategy, an ethos of sober realism, and a demonstration of their ideology according to which the world is tragic and painful, civilisation is in decline, we are beset by decadence and barbarism, all a good man can do is stand on his own two feet, think for himself and defend that which is his—his identity, his property, his family (his nation, his people, his race).

But, crucially, what these performers do is more than simply tell people what to think. They also show them how to think in a particular way. Much of their content consists of polemical critique and analysis—sometimes at great length—of what they consider to be the errors and idiocies of their opponents. They demonstrate how to argue against these and offer a broad-based analysis of what is wrong with the world, who made it wrong, and how to make it right for yourself. In that sense they are educative, turning 'a conception of the world into small change, a philosophical system into everyday slogans'. They give their audience things to think with and things to do—ways of reacting against the world they believe to be unjust (such as pointing out every use of the 'current year'). This, then, is a way in which people, institutions and tools of transmission are assembled today.

Conclusion

Just as there is a means of production before any particular thing is produced, so there is a means of political communication which gives rise to particular acts of communication. And, like the means of production, the means of political communication creates 'definite social relations' between people, organising them in relation to each other and to their own political activity. Digital communication is affecting politics at this level. It isn't just a new way of doing an old thing, but a change in what can be done and what value it has. In altering the stages, scripts and dramas with which we perform our politics for each other, it is also altering what people know (or think they know) about politics, and how they feel about it. It has shifted the context against which they perceive themselves and their aspirations, the questions they ask and the kinds of answers they are prepared to entertain, the propositions and their proofs which give shape to what is politically thinkable.

Twenty-first century political communication builds on the 'personalisation, informalisation and dramatisation' which characterised *fin de siècle* political journalism by enabling everyone to do it for and to ourselves. That might involve nothing more than recirculating (sharing or retweeting or reposting) content; it might mean building on it, clarifying and extending it, in online forums or on Facebook; it could involve making a response video on YouTube or memes of one's own; it might be linked with a public meeting, a march or a campaign. In this world, the successful political performers will be those giving people something they can use—a script (ideas, arguments, slogans) that they can take up, adapt, improvise upon. The most successful of all will connect this to an ideological proposition, giving people the chance to perform an identity which makes them part of the historical drama: a spear-thrower in the last-ditch fight against the barbarians within or without; digging the foundations for the rebuilding of the empire; a member of the chorus chanting the name of the leader who came out of the wilderness. Those who can do this will, in the future, prosper politically. Those who cannot will be have no place on stage.

It is not sufficient to respond to this by arguing for new forms of governance for communication. Building higher walls will not protect the twentieth-century agora. Those walls have already been breached. The pressing question is: why is the left not very good at developing its own popular, polemical and participatory media? It has its tribunes, of course, on sites such as The Canary, and the success of Momentum is in part down to a sophisticated understanding of how to use digital media effectively to educate, agitate and organise and of how to link it to real-world events, including those focused on political education, such as the conference fringe events organised under the banner The World Transformed.[15] But the left and Labour are still predominantly signed-up to the party of print and its key performers are people of the press and publishing. Owen Jones, for example, has a YouTube channel (107,000 subscribers) and the content is primarily an adjunct to his journalism, often involving interviews with politicians and similar in style to mainstream broadcast media.

There is no left-wing equivalent to Sargon, Benjamin or Watson. Perhaps that is a good thing. The left should not ape the right by becoming an aggressive alt-left, purely polemical or busily producing its own fake news (although clearly that is a temptation to which some might succumb). But it is necessary to develop means of overcoming the reduction of political communication to misinformation, brand-building and self-declaration disconnected from policies, programmes and parliaments. Doing so requires recall of the political culture of the nineteenth-century left, recreating ways to resist the individualising tendencies of digital political media as presently constituted, and giving rise to a politics of participation in the construction of collective political intelligence. That cannot be done until we appreciate that political communication is not now solely, or even primarily, reducible to political marketing to promote a party, a policy, or a programme, to a general electorate. It must also be an appeal to particular audiences, those who want more than 'delivery' and who want to learn how to take part in the broader 'culture war' underway. That may mean reactivating genres of old —a twenty-first century version of the Fabian *Facts for Socialists* perhaps— providing resources for understanding and argument rather better than declaring it the current year. It means not being afraid of ideological argument, bringing forward the ethical and philosophical claims which underpin the policies we advocate, letting debate and dispute be seen as good things, part of how we apply ourselves to the problems of the present. Above all it requires us to show how all of this must be tied to a political movement, requiring discipline of thought and speech and awareness that we stand, not only for ourselves, but also for each other, and against those who would harm our friends and take our democratic politics from us.

Notes

1 For an overview of thinking into the cultural context behind this politics, see L. Rensmann, 'The noisy counter-revolution: understanding the cultural conditions and dynamics of populist politics in Europe in the digital age', *Politics and Governance*, vol. 5, no. 4, 2017, pp. 123–135.

2 See also S. Subramanian, 'Inside the Macedonian fake-news complex', *Wired Magazine*, 15 February, 2017.

3 Just one example is A. Dhrodia, 'We tracked 25,688 abusive tweets sent to women MPs—half were directed at Diane Abbott', *New Statesman*, September 2017; see also The Fawcett Society campaign 'Reclaim the Internet'; https://www.fawcettsociety.org.uk/reclaim-the-internet (accessed 8 August 2018).

4 S. Murdoch, 'HNH explains...Trolling and the alt-right', HopenotHate.com, 10 October 2017, https://hopenothate.com/2017/10/10/hnh-explains-trolling-alt-right/ (accessed 8 August 2018).

5 R. Debray, 'Socialism: a life cycle', *New Left Review*, vol. 46, July-August 2007.

6 J. C. Alexander, 'Cultural pragmatics: social performance between ritual and strategy' in J. Alexander, B. Giesen and J. Mast, eds., *Social Performance: Symbolic Action, Cultural Pragmatics and Ritual*, Cambridge, Cambridge University Press, 2006; J. C. Alexander, *The Performance of Politics: Obama's Victory and the Democratic Struggle for Power*, Oxford, Oxford University Press, 2010.

7 BBC News, 'EU referendum: Davidson and Johnson close great debate', 21 June 2016; http://www.bbc.co.uk/news/av/uk-politics-eu-referendum-36590539/eu-referendum-davidson-and-johnson-close-great-debate (accessed 8 August 2018).

8 For a larger study of these kinds of 'citations' and performances see J. Atkins and A. Finlayson, '"...A 40-year-old black man made the point to me": anecdotes, everyday knowledge and the performance of leadership in British politics', *Political Studies*, vol. 61, no. 1, 2013, pp. 161–177.

9 R. Booth, 'DIY political websites: new force shaping the general election debate', *The Guardian*, 1 June 2017; https://www.theguardian.com/politics/2017/jun/01/diy-political-websites-new-force-shaping-general-election-debate-canary (accessed 8 August 2018).

10 On the theory of the cartel party see R. S. Katz and P. Mair, 'Changing models of party organization and party democracy: the emergence of the cartel party', *Party Politics*, vol. 1, no. 1, 1995, pp. 5–28.

11 A. R. Galloway, *The Interface Effect*, Cambridge, Polity Press, 2012.

12 This particular strategy of the right precedes the digital era and was well used and developed by North American radio hosts and columnists throughout the 1980s and 1990s. Sam Chambers and I explored it, through the case study of one

especially sectarian commentator in 'Ann Coulter and the problem of pluralism: from values to politics', *Borderlands*, vol. 7, no. 1, 2008.

13 On the deep and intimate connection between the online right and opposition to feminism, see A. Kelly, 'The alt-right: reactionary rehabilitation for white masculinity', *Soundings*, issue 66, 2017, pp. 68–78.

14 This wide estimate is taken from a Patreon funded site, Graphtreon; https://graphtreon.com/creator/jordanbpeterson (accessed 8 August 2018).

15 J. Elgot, 'Momentum building in Brighton as grassroots group goes mainstream', *The Guardian*, 24 September 2017; https://www.theguardian.com/politics/2017/sep/24/momentum-brighton-labour-party-conference-the-world-transformed (accessed 8 August 2018).

8. Protecting Democratic Legitimacy in a Digital Age

MARTIN MOORE

'ELECTION campaigns are communications campaigns', the University of California political scientist, Bruce Bimber, wrote in 2014.[1] During a campaign, a candidate presents his or her case for why they ought to be elected and, depending on how well they and their party present their case, gains or forfeits enough voters' support to win or lose office. Barack Obama became best known as 'the great communicator', after the success of his *Yes We Can* Presidential campaign in 2008.[2] By contrast, Hillary Clinton's failure to win in 2016 was blamed on her inability to communicate a simple compelling message to the US electorate.[3] Theresa May, who managed to lose the Conservative party's parliamentary majority following a sterile and wooden election campaign in 2017, cemented her nickname as 'the Maybot', in John Crace's cruel but apposite portmanteau.

As our communication between one another has become more and more digital, so has our politics. In 2017, the total number of internet users surpassed half the population of the world. In many democracies more than three quarters of the adult population are online. In the UK, nine in ten adults use the internet regularly. Of these, more than three quarters use social media, many of them for over ninety minutes a day (meaning, in practice, using a combination of Facebook, YouTube, WhatsApp, Twitter, Instagram, Snapchat, Google+ and Pinterest). Amongst these services, the social media goliath is Facebook. More than half the UK population used Facebook regularly in 2016.[4] For 18–29 year-olds, 90 per cent of whom have a Facebook profile, the service has essentially become a social utility (even as they migrate to other social media services they keep a presence on Facebook). Nor are people simply communicating with one another online; they increasingly find their news and information there as well. Three-quarters of Britons consume news online and four in ten use social media for news.[5]

Campaigns follow voters, and as voters have shifted online, so too have campaigns. We saw this first in the US, back during the presidential primaries in 2004, but since then this has mushroomed and spread across the world. For the 2016 presidential election in the US, candidates spent $1.4 billion on online advertising.[6] This does not include what each spent on gathering data and on digital campaigning more broadly. In the UK, 2015 was the first election in which a party devoted a significant amount of its resources to data-driven social media campaigning. The Conservatives spent over £1.2 million on Facebook alone.[7] The following year both the Leave and Remain

Published by John Wiley & Sons Ltd, 9600 Garsington Road, Oxford OX4 2DQ, UK and 350 Main Street, Malden, MA 02148, USA

campaigns focused heavily on digital, with the director of Vote Leave, Dominic Cummings, claiming that theirs was 'the first campaign in the UK to put almost all our money into digital communication'.[8] By the 2017 UK general election, all parties—and associated campaigners—were dedicating much of their time and money to digital campaigning.

Political campaigners themselves even appear to be convinced that campaigns are now won and lost through the strategic use of personal data and digital platforms. After the 2015 UK election, Jim Messina, strategy advisor to the Conservative campaign, said that Facebook was 'the crucial weapon'. Labour insiders agreed, according to reports in the *Financial Times*, saying they were sure the 2015 UK general election was secured through Facebook. Similarly, in 2016, immediately after the Brexit referendum, the funder and joint leader of Leave.EU, Arron Banks, wrote that 'The use of big data for the first time in any election in the UK left Leave.EU [with] a massive advantage [over] both official campaigns.'[9] In the US, Brad Parscale, the digital director of the 2016 Trump campaign, told CBS that 'Twitter is how [Trump] talked to the people, Facebook was going to be how he won.' Jennifer Palmieri, communications director for the Hillary Clinton 2016 campaign, said that Facebook was 'the most powerful communications platform the universe has ever seen'.[10] Nor is it just major parties that are benefiting. In Italy, Matteo Salvini, the leader of the far-right Northern League which leapt to the third largest party in the 2018 elections, said after the results, 'Thank God for the internet, thank God for social media, thank God for Facebook.'[11]

This could simply be seen as a natural evolution of political campaign communication. Just as print was superseded by broadcast, so broadcast is being superseded by digital and social media. 'Political parties have always sought to target voters,' Giles Kenningham, the Conservatives' director of communications for the 2015 election wrote, 'whether that be through door-to-door canvassing or direct mail. The parties are simply moving with the times.[12] Yet many have preferred to see digital developments in more revolutionary terms. During the Arab Spring in 2011, protestors in Tahrir Square held up handwritten cardboard signs thanking Facebook. At that point they, and many others, saw the internet and social media as inherently democratising. Five years later, following the Brexit vote and the election of Donald Trump, many people judged the internet and social media to be equally influential, but saw it as disruptive and destructive of democracy rather than the reverse.

Every major change in communication has provoked exaggerated hopes and fears about its political effects. 'Modern means of communication', H.G. Wells wrote in the *New York Times* in the 1920s, '... have opened up a new world of political processes. Ideas and phrases can now be given an effectiveness greater than the effectiveness of any personality and stronger than any sectional interest'.[13] It is only natural that in periods of rapid transition, when changes in communication enable shifts in power, people should be both excited and anxious. As people become more accustomed to new forms of communication, as one generation passes to the next, so some of these anxieties will subside, and some of the fears will be proved excessive or groundless. Already, for example, there is evidence that people who are active on social media may be exposed to more sources of news rather than less, contrary to what the filter bubble thesis would have us believe.[14] Emerging academic studies also question the extent to which false or invented news could have affected the result of the US election.[15]

Yet, it is possible to point to a number of specific areas in which digital communication and data-driven campaigning do appear to circumvent and challenge existing democratic principles and protections. If left unaddressed, these will necessarily reduce the legitimacy of elections and referendums. This is not to suggest that there are not many other issues raised by the rise and rise of the use of data and digital platforms in politics, but simply to focus on those areas where it is already possible to see discrepancies between what democratic protections aim to achieve, and what digital politics allows. These areas are not particular to any one democracy, though given the important distinctions between democratic processes and laws in different countries, the chapter will focus on one country—the UK—and reference other examples where applicable.

This chapter identifies five areas where democratic protections, built up in Britain over the last 150 years, appear threatened by digital communication and data-driven campaigning. These five are: protecting the secrecy of your vote; protecting voters from undue influence; maintaining a level playing field between different candidates; preventing elections from being bought; and enabling people to better assess the credibility of political claims based on where they come from. In each case, it will sketch out how these protections developed, why they are important to democratic legitimacy, and why they are threatened by the use of personal data and dominant digital platforms.

It is rare that an academic paper becomes infamous, but that is what happened to one published in 2013 that describes how 'easily accessible digital records of behavior' can be used to predict, with a startling degree of accuracy, all sorts of personal characteristics and attributes.[16] One of these is political affiliation. Based on people's Facebook 'likes', Michel Kosinski and his colleagues could predict, with 85 per cent accuracy, whether someone in the US would support the Democrats or the Republicans. Three years later, after the election of Donald Trump in 2016, the use of Facebook data to target voters would erupt into a global scandal. Yet, as the authors noted, we now all leave such copious digital traces that Facebook 'likes', while particularly revealing, are only one of many potential points of reference. In addition to which, subsequent research has found that far from needing large quantities of personal information, a small number of key data points can be enough to indicate political preference. A 2017 academic study, for example, found 'that even a single selective Facebook like can reveal as much about political voter intention as hundreds of heterogeneous likes'.[17] Inferring people's political affiliations from their digital traces may even be unnecessary given how many of us now advertise our allegiances openly online. We do this by, in some cases, making it explicit in one of our many online profile descriptions, or by signing petitions aligned with a particular cause, or adding a badge to our profile picture.

Most campaigns now go far beyond just trying to gauge people's political affiliations or activities, gathering information on everything from our consumer habits, our media consumption, and our social attitudes. Cambridge Analytica boasted that it had 5,000 data points on over 200 million Americans. Another US firm, i360, claimed to have 1,800 unique data points. The Republican National Committee and the Democratic National Committee have databases which, according to Daniel Kreiss, a leading scholar of digital politics in the US, 'have over 900 points of data on every member of the electorate'.[18] In the UK, prior to the 2016 referendum vote, Vote Leave ran a football competition with a £50 million prize, expressly in order to collect the personal details of hard-to-reach voters. Once collected, cleaned, organised and analysed, a campaign will use this data to decide which voters to target, how, and with what. It gives them far greater knowledge about individual voters than those voters have about the campaigns themselves.

This information asymmetry, which gives campaigns the ability to predict political preferences and attitudes, jeopardises the principle of voter privacy. A secret ballot was introduced in Britain after 1872, in order to prevent intimidation, bribery or treating of voters. Up to that point, many votes had been held at hustings in the centre of town. A table would be set out, surrounded by a gaggle of electoral personnel, within an enclosed wooden structure. As voters approached to register their vote with the clerk, they would often 'be applauded, heckled, blocked and even beaten up by hired thugs; effigies could also be tossed their way'. Violence and intimidation were endemic to Victorian elections. In the six elections of 1857 to 1880 there were 181 recorded 'episodes of disorder'. Bribery was similarly common. In 1867, J. E. Reeves writes, the standard price for a vote was £10. As was 'treating', or plying voters with drink and free food to win their allegiance. There are even recorded instances of 'cooping' when large numbers of voters were abducted and prevented from voting.[19] Charles Dickens, in *The Pickwick Papers*, describes an election in the fictional constituency of Eatanswill in the 1830s, where one agent had locked voters in the coach-house 'to prevent our getting at them' the opposing agent tells Mr. Pickwick. And 'even if we could,' he says, 'it would be of no use, for they keep them very drunk on purpose. Smart fellow Fizkin's agent—very smart fellow indeed.' After the Ballot Act of 1872, voters could come to an individual decision, in the privacy of a polling booth (modelled on a system used in Australia). This did not stamp out bribery and intimidation, but made it harder and, in combination with the Corrupt and Illegal Practices Act a decade later, reduced it to a level that meant much greater legitimacy for individual electoral contests. Private polling booths subsequently became the norm in democracies across the world.

Personal data collection and analysis, and the ability to predict how someone will vote, subverts the secret ballot. Knowing someone's political allegiance, the extent to which they are politically active online, and lots of other personal information, can be extremely useful to campaigns. It can enable them to identify who might be the key voters who could swing the election or referendum. It can indicate what factors might help them decide not only who to vote for, but whether to vote at all. It can enable them to better tailor their communications to fit with each voter's priorities, personal preferences, predilections, prejudices, and sensibilities. In the lead up to the 2015 UK general election, the Conservatives identified Liberal Democrat supporters in the south-west as the 'soft underbelly' of the centrist vote. Not only were these voters disappointed with the LibDem performance in the coalition government, they were—the Conservatives discovered—particularly anxious about the possibility of a future coalition between Labour and the Scottish National Party (SNP). The Tories then fed this anxiety by targeting these voters with Facebook advertisements playing up the potential of a Labour–SNP coalition, and the danger of letting this happen by voting for the LibDems. 'Vote LibDem and this will happen', one Facebook ad read, with a picture of Nicola Sturgeon, Ed Miliband and Alex Salmond in front of 10 Downing Street, 'Vote Conservative to stop it'.[20] These ads could have the twofold effect of dampening the LibDem vote and boosting the Conservative vote.

Intimate knowledge of each voter has also revived the potential for voter suppression campaigns. Knowing people's political allegiance and political activity can be as helpful in identifying those who might be discouraged from voting, as those who might be encouraged. The Trump campaign admitted that in 2016 it ran three voter-suppression campaigns in order to depress the turnout of idealistic white liberals (Bernie Sanders supporters), young women (who were angered by the behaviour of Bill Clinton), and the black vote (on the basis of comments Hillary Clinton made about black males in the 1990s).[21] The campaign could identify the individuals it thought would be most susceptible to these arguments thanks to its hoard of personal data, and reach them directly thanks to digital delivery platforms.

Of all the digital delivery platforms available up to 2018, Facebook—and its subsidiaries Instagram, WhatsApp and Messenger—most directly threaten the principle of voter privacy and best enable undue influence to be exerted on voters. This is partly because of the platform's astonishing reach—it had 2.2 billion active users in 2018—but also because of the tools it makes available to campaigns and campaigners. Most of these were originally designed for commercial rather than political use, though came to be used for both. The use of 'dark posts', for example, was a service Facebook introduced in 2013 to enable companies to test different ads on similar audiences to see which performed better. It is a practice common in marketing, called A/B or multivariate testing. Facebook was able to offer a particularly powerful service thanks to its reach and automation. Companies could test thousands of different versions of advertisements, see which ones were more effective, and evolve them accordingly. This same service was then used by Trump's digital campaign director, Brad Parscale, to deliver upwards of 50,000 advertisements a day to voters, each one adjusted according to how people responded. Since these posts were 'dark', they were only visible to three individuals or organisations: the political candidate or party, Facebook, and the intended recipient. To everyone else, they were invisible. It was therefore impossible to know the extent to which political messages were consistent or contradictory, accurate or misleading, fair or false. Facebook, and other digital platforms, provided a host of other services, from 'custom audiences' to 'lookalike audiences', intended to enhance the precision and effectiveness of commercial advertising, which were then similarly adopted by political parties and candidates.

The power of Facebook advertising tools, many of them only introduced since 2012, meant they quickly became one of the primary means by which political campaigns communicated with voters. It helped that campaigns were not constrained on social media in the same way they were elsewhere (such as the prohibition on broadcast political advertising in the UK). In the ten weeks prior to the 2016 EU referendum, the official leave campaign, Vote Leave, sent over one billion targeted digital ads, the majority via Facebook.[22] During the 2017 UK general election campaign, eight UK parties spent around £3 million directly on Facebook—with the Conservatives alone spending £2.1 million.[23] Yet, as with the messages sent during the US election campaign, we know about only a tiny sample of these advertisements, and these thanks chiefly to the efforts of civil society groups and news outlets to crowdsource ads from their recipients. We know, for example, that the Conservatives sent many targeted ads which personally attacked Jeremy Corbyn. We know that the Labour party targeted ads at specific demographics, such as middle-aged women. And we know that the Liberal Democrats sent ads to particular geographic areas encouraging people to vote tactically.[24] We do not know if any these campaigns deliberately sought to suppress voter turnout, if any were deliberately misleading, or if any sought undue influence over particular voters.

Knowing someone's political sympathies, and being able to reach them directly via digital platforms, can also enable undue influence of a rougher and more intimidatory kind. In what may be compared to Victorian mob violence prior to elections, cybermobs and 'organised brigades' can bully, harass and attack people online whose views they disagree with. This happened frequently during the US 2016 presidential campaign. Research by the US Anti-Defamation League found that in the year up to the end of July 2016, at least 800 journalists received one or more of 2.6 million anti-Semitic tweets. Many of these came from a limited number of Twitter accounts and were directed at Jewish journalists, and prompted by comments criticising

Donald Trump or the Trump campaign.[25] Attacks on individuals or groups during the campaign were often collective and coordinated, with activists using the technology to harass or overwhelm their opponents, for example through aggressive trolling, doxing, hashtag hijacking or DDoS attacks (a distributed denial of service attack, an attempt to make an online service unavailable by overwhelming it with traffic from multiple sources). There are many similar examples across the world of journalists, political activists, and even people simply participating in online political discussions, experiencing online harassment for expressing political opinions. In Thailand, pro-government Facebook vigilante groups 'perform public witch-hunts against people whom they accuse of being disrespectful of the monarchy'.[26] In Sri Lanka, Indonesia, Mexico, and India, the *New York Times* has reported, Facebook and its subsidiaries, have been used to inflame existing ethnic and political tensions, sometimes overflowing into real life violence and lynchings.[27] The UK is not exempt either. A review by the Committee on Standards in Public Life found that during the 2017 UK election a 'significant proportion of the candidates' experienced harassment, intimidation, and 'persistent, vile and shocking abuse' and concluded that the 'widespread use of social media platforms is the most significant factor driving the behaviour we are seeing'.

The third area where the use of personal data and digital campaigning threaten existing democratic protections is in our ability to maintain a fair and level playing field between candidates. Again, in the UK, democratic protection to ensure this fairness developed during the nineteenth century, culminating in the landmark 1883 Corrupt and Illegal Practices Act. This Act, on which successive subsequent UK election legislation has been based, sought to ensure that 'the length of a man's purse will not, as now, be such an important factor [in electoral contests]; and the way will be opened for many men of talent, with small means, to take part in the government of the country, who have been hitherto deterred from seeking a seat in the House of Commons by the great expense which a contest entails'. In contrast to other democracies, such as the US, the UK has managed to maintain this commitment to fair and equal access by constraining campaign spending, particularly at a local level.

Limits on local constituency spending are fundamental to this commitment. A candidate can, during the short campaign in the weeks leading up to a general election, spend a maximum of around £10–15,000 (depending on the size and density of the constituency). Spend more than this and he or she is liable to prosecution on criminal charges. Separately, and in addition, each political party can spend a much larger amount on a national campaign, up to £19.5 million in 2017, depending on how many seats the party is contesting. The distinction between the local and the national campaign has never been absolute but used to be relatively distinct when national campaigns were defined by newspaper and billboard advertisements and general party election literature. Yet, since central campaigns have shifted online, and since they have been able to direct messages at particular constituencies, and even particular constituents, via social media platforms, the distinction has blurred to obscurity. Parties can use national budgets to wage local campaigns in a small number of constituencies, making the constituency spending limit moot, and privileging the bigger and more well-resourced parties.

All the major UK political parties have used social media to direct advertising to specific voters via social media, though the Conservatives were the first to devote significant resources to it. For the 2015 election, the Tories identified twenty-three seats which they believed could, if won, give the party a parliamentary majority. They then used digital media, particularly Facebook, to direct ads at those voters in those constituencies who their research told them were most open to influence. In the words of the Conservative's 2015 joint digital director Craig Elder, the party worked

with Facebook using constituency targeting to focus just on the constituencies that were going to decide the election, and then based on what we already know about the demographics of the people who are going to decide this election, we could do demographic targeting, and interest targeting, to focus in on people and present different content to a young mum in Derby North to maybe a slightly older gentleman living in Rochester.[28]

According to the returns submitted to the Electoral Commission, the party ran up to forty-six different campaigns on Facebook. One, Campaign 24, invoice #9437 from May 2015, cost over £82,000. These invoices were allocated to national rather than to local expenditure, despite statements by those involved that the campaigns were focused on individual constituencies. The lack of any detailed, geographically itemised invoices, and the fact that none of the ads sent was open to public scrutiny, means it is impossible to know whether or not the campaign breached electoral rules. Yet, either way, their geographically targeted approach necessarily undermines the principle of a fair and level playing field at a local level.

The Conservatives may have stolen a march, but since 2015 all parties and campaign groups have used social media and targeted advertising extensively. During the 2017 general election campaign, the Conservatives sent highly targeted ads at certain constituents criticising the local Labour candidate. One such ad was sent to constituents in Ealing Central and Acton which read: 'Jeremy Corby and Rupa Huq want to tax over two-thirds of all homes in Ealing Central and Acton.'[29] Labour, Buzzfeed reported, ran a larger and more sophisticated social media campaign than they had in 2015, even using in-house software called Promote, 'to link individual voters to their Facebook profile'.[30] It then paid Facebook to encourage Labour supporters in specific constituencies to 'like' Labour's Facebook page, in order to nurture organic support. The party also went beyond Facebook to target individuals using Snapchat, YouTube and mobile phone games.

A fourth way in which the collection and use of personal data for political purposes challenges democratic rules and systems is concerned with the *value* that is put on data. This may seem slightly esoteric, but given how fundamental personal data has become to campaigns, it is fast becoming central. Without being able to put a value on the collection, analysis and use of personal data, for example, then many of the spending caps on elections and referendums will look increasingly anachronistic.

It has now been recognised, across many areas of commercial life, that data acts like an alternative currency. In May 2017, *The Economist* magazine illustrated its cover with a drawing of corporations like Google drilling for data as though it was oil, proclaiming that data was now 'the world's most valuable resource'. Big data and algorithms are, it is argued, rewriting the rules of business and competition. It is difficult to rationalise Facebook's $19 billion purchase of WhatsApp, for example, without taking into account the personal data and contact information that WhatsApp had (most notably its 600 million mobile phone numbers). In a book assessing the influence of big data on competition, two eminent legal academics, Ariel Ezrachi and Maurice Stucke, show how existing laws—particularly around monopolies and competition—fail properly to account for the use of data. Knowing people's online consumer habits, for example, can give certain online retailers much greater ability to discriminate on price. Knowing people's movements via their mobile phones gives companies like Google and Apple significant advantages should they want to design or run autonomous vehicles.

As in commercial life, so in public life and politics. Every self-respecting political campaign now has a database with as much information about voters as it can gather. Without such personal data, a modern campaign manager would feel naked. Which voters should we focus on? Where are they and what do they care about? Fortunately for them, even if they start without any data, there are many ways in which they can acquire it. They can go out and ask people for it. They can build apps which, in exchange for information or a game, require people to give their personal details. They can collect it more surreptitiously through online browser extensions or other tracking software. Or they can simply buy personal data from third parties, such as data brokers like Acxiom and Experian. Once they have it, they will need somewhere to store, clean, organise, analyse, access and use it. Equally, they will need people with the right skills to be able to assess it, manipulate it, and apply it. This means employing software engineers, database managers, statisticians and experts in mathematical modelling, as well as (or instead of) the sorts of people normally associated with political campaigns.

All this data has significant political value and can be a huge advantage to a modern campaign. Some of this value is straightforward to calculate in monetary terms. Buying data from a third party, for example, has a price tag. Campaign data managers, in most circumstances, have to be paid. However, a lot of the value of data is much harder to assess. Databases can be built and data collected by various different methods, and before an official campaign begins. Data can be stored and analysed outside the country in which it is being used—similar to money being offshored to tax havens like the Cayman Islands. Algorithms, statistical models, and election software, that have a high value in the commercial market, can be gifted or loaned to a campaign, or licensed at preferential rates. Similarly, spending on data expertise can be taken care of by third parties, and their support hidden or disguised. Existing democratic protections, as manifested in electoral law and regulation, struggle to capture the value of data in each of these cases. Monitoring the collection and analysis of personal data, and then tracking its use and delivery via digital platforms, is something that few electoral systems have the remit or the capability to do.

The official and unofficial Leave campaigns provide a good illustration of the challenges to existing law and regulation. Not because they are unique—these challenges are common to modern campaigns—but because they provide vivid examples on which there has already been some investigation and about which there is some documentation. In the case of Vote Leave, the campaign director, Dominic Cummings, made it apparent after the vote how valuable he thought data and data science had been to the campaign. 'One of our central ideas', Cummings wrote, 'was that the campaign had to do things in the field of data that have never been done before.'[31] He also emphasised the extent to which Vote Leave relied on intelligent data analysis, and on the work of physicists, data scientists, and 'people whose normal work was subjects like quantum information'. On top of which, at least 40 per cent of the campaign's total spending went on digital campaigning. Yet, beyond knowing the absolute amount spent, trying to work out how it was spent, what it was spent on, and what its value was to the campaign, is a black box. This is because all 40 per cent was spent with a single commercial company, Aggregate IQ, based off the west coast of Canada, on Vancouver Island. This opacity was made more troubling by the fact that three other campaign groups, all of whom supported leaving the EU, also spent substantial sums with Aggregate IQ. BeLeave, Veterans for Britain, and the Democratic Unionist Party together spent a further £808,000 on Aggregate IQ. None of them, when asked, explained what Aggregate IQ did for them. And yet, according to Vote Leave's director, this small and obscure foreign company was crucial. 'Without a doubt,' Cummings said, 'the Vote Leave campaign owes a great deal of its success to the work of Aggregate IQ. We couldn't have done it without them.'[32]

When it came to collecting personal data, neither the official nor the unofficial Leave campaign had the benefit of a pre-existing campaign database (the referendum having only been announced in 2015). Both, therefore, had to build their own. They did this using a combination of some of the methods described above. The official campaign, Vote Leave, took a particularly creative approach. As referred to earlier, it ran a football competition, with the offer of a £50 million prize if someone could guess the result of all the games in the upcoming European Cup. The campaign did not have £50 million to give away, but calculated that the chances of someone correctly guessing every game were so minute that it could risk it. So small was the chance of a win that they were able to insure themselves against significant loss. There is less clarity about how the unofficial Leave campaign, Leave.EU, gained its data. Arron Banks, who supported Leave.EU financially and worked closely with its figurehead, Nigel Farage, was certainly convinced of the tremendous value of personal data to the campaign, as he made apparent in his referendum memoir. He also committed, according to the campaign diary entry he wrote on 14 July 2015, to getting hold of all the data he could find and using call centre staff to help canvass. 'I'm going to exploit all the data I can find and use hundreds of call centre staff to convert as many as 10,000 people a day to the cause.' Yet it has been difficult to establish where this data came from, or its value. In evidence to the Culture, Media and Sport Select Committee almost two years after the referendum vote, Brittany Kaiser, an employee of Cambridge Analytica, claimed that Banks may have used data from his company's commercial insurance databases as part of Leave.EU's campaign, though Banks denied this.[33] Still, by the end of the campaign he was able to boast that Leave.EU had created 'an extremely useful database which enabled us to better understand the concerns of voters'.[34] The data that each campaign gathered, according to those running them, was central to their success, but the value of this data, in terms of its collection, its analysis, and its use, remained obscure.

Even the Information Commissioner's Office (ICO), which launched an investigation into the use of data analytics for political purposes, found it very hard to discover what Aggregate IQ, or other companies using data in the referendum campaign, actually did. In a slightly forlorn statement at the end of 2017, the ICO said their investigation was 'complex and far-reaching ... involving over thirty organisations including political parties and campaigns, data companies and social media platforms' some of whom complied, and some of whom did not.[35] Over and above the disturbing implications of this opacity for voter privacy and consent, it prevents any fair assessment of the value of this storage, analysis, or re-use of data.

There is also the difficulty of calculating the ongoing and future value of data to political campaigns. After the referendum vote, Arron Banks said he was considering setting up a new party. 'It'll be properly run with a national network and a solid structure' Banks wrote, 'Leave.EU has a million online followers and a huge database.' The database, Banks implied, was a powerful asset to the formation of a new party. Equally, it could be used to support an individual candidate for leadership in an existing party, or simply to mobilise people to particular political causes. This raises a further, and perhaps the most awkward, challenge of data. How to monitor and account for the actions of non-party individuals and organisations? This problem is accentuated in referendums and one-off votes, where new campaign groups emerge and then disappear. But it is already having an impact on elections and this impact is likely to increase as data storage, tools and methods become more affordable and accessible. Monitoring and regulating of major parties can be tricky, but it is far harder to keep track of private individuals, commercial organisations, and pop-up campaigns.

The fifth and final way in which digital campaigning appears to subvert existing democratic protections is with regard to sourcing and transparency of election literature. The same 1883 Act which limited election spending also stipulated that every piece of campaign literature have a clear indication of who it was sent on behalf of, and who published it. This was so that members of the public would know when they were receiving propaganda from a particular candidate, to provide some accountability for election literature, and to discourage campaigns from making misleading statements. The same stipulation does not apply to digital material. A voter can therefore receive a political advertisement in their Facebook or Twitter feed and have no way of telling who it has come from or who has paid for it.

These five areas each represent ways in which the radical transformation of our communications environment is challenging existing democratic protections. In Britain, some can be dealt with by changes to electoral legislation. The imprint law, for example, which requires the names of candidate and publisher, could be extended online. Others could be partially resolved by new legislation requiring greater transparency. Campaigns could, for example be forced to reveal what personal data they are collecting and for what purpose—though this in itself could compromise the privacy of voters. Political parties could be required to break down their spending by target group and by local area. Yet preventing campaigns from using big data to predict how people will vote, or stopping them from targeting susceptible voters with tailored messages, would be much harder—if either were even pursued.

These five areas are certainly not comprehensive. The profound changes in the way we communicate, the copious digital trails we now leave, and the spectre of ever-increasing automation, all raise questions not just about how campaigns are run, but about how we participate in politics, how we are represented, how we discover and verify our political news and information, and whether the digital environment supports or obstructs democratic deliberation. The revolution in communication forces us to rethink the way existing democracy works. Either that or watch its legitimacy progressively eroded.

Notes

1 B. Bimber, 'Digital media in the Obama Campaigns of 2008 and 2012: adaptation to the personalized political communication environment', *Journal of Information Technology & Politics*, vol. 11, no. 2, 2014, pp. 130–150.

2 Lexington's Notebook, 'Obama the great communicator', *The Economist*, 27 January 2010; https://www.economist.com/lexingtons-notebook/2010/01/27/obama-the-great-communicator (accessed 9 August 2018).

3 J. Allen and A. Parnes, *Shattered: Inside Hillary Clinton's Doomed Campaign*, New York, Broadway Books, 2017.

4 Statista, Number of Internet Users Worldwide, from 2005 to 2017; https://www.statista.com/statistics/273018/number-of-internet-users-worldwide/; Office for National Statistics, 'Internet users in the UK 2017'; https://www.ons.gov.uk/businessindustryandtrade/itandinternetindustry/bulletins/internetusers/2017; Ofcom, 'Adults' media use and attitudes report 2017'; https://www.ofcom.org.uk/__data/assets/pdf_file/0020/102755/adults-media-use-attitudes-2017.pdf; eMarketer, 'More than half of UK population will log on to Facebook this year', 25 February 2016 https://www.emarketer.com/Article/More-Than-Half-of-UK-Population-Will-Log-on-Facebook-This-Year/1013627 (all accessed 8 August 2018).

5 Reuters Institute & University of Oxford, 'Digital news report, 2017'; https://reutersinstitute.politics.ox.ac.uk/sites/default/files/Digital%20News%20Report%202017%20web_0.pdf (accessed 9 August 2018).

6 S. J. Miller, 'Digital ad spending tops estimates', Campaigns and Elections, 2017; https://www.campaignsandelections.com/campaign-insider/digital-ad-spending-tops-estimates (accessed 9 August 2018).

7 M. Moore, 'Facebook, the Conservatives and the risk to fair and open elections in the UK', *The Political Quarterly*, vol. 87, no. 3, 2016, pp. 424–430.

8 D. Cummings, 'On the referendum #20', 29 October 2016; https://dominiccummings.com/2016/10/29/on-the-referendum-20-the-campaign-physics-and-data-science-vote-leaves-voter-intention-collection-system-vics-now-available-for-all/ (accessed 9 August 2018).

9 D. Taylor, 'Tories knew they would win election three weeks before vote', *Times*, 13 May 2015; D. Bond, 'Facebook key to winning UK general election, political parties say', *Financial Times*, 14 May 2017; A. Banks, *Bad Boys of Brexit*, London, Biteback Publishing, 2016.

10 L. Beckett, 'Trump digital director says Facebook helped win the White House', *The Guardian*, 9 October 2017; https://www.theguardian.com/technology/2017/oct/08/trump-digital-director-brad-parscale-facebook-advertising; Recode, Interview with Jennifer Palmieri—full transcript, 11 April 2018; https://www.recode.net/2018/4/11/17226866/hillary-clinton-communications-director-jennifer-palmieri-recode-decode (both accessed 9 August 2018).

11 M. Di Stefano, 'Italy's new far-right star specifically thanked Facebook for the election result because of course he did', Buzzfeed, 7 March 2018; https://www.buzzfeed.com/markdistefano/italys-new-far-right-star-specifically-thanked-facebook?utm_term=.thmpymkPml#.yk3JpXQRXW (accessed 9 August 2018).

12 G. Kenningham, 'Why it's Facebook wot won it', Campaign Live, 8 June 2017; https://www.campaignlive.co.uk/article/why-its-facebook-wot-won/1435935#lh7k5oiMDUz1qzTM.99 (accessed 9 August 2018).

13 H. G. Wells, as quoted in E. Bernays, *Propaganda*, New York, IG Publishing [1928], 2004.

14 Reuters & Oxford, 'Digital news report, 2017'.

15 H. Allcott and M. Gentzkow, 'Social media and fake news in the 2016 election', *Journal of Economic Perspectives*, vol. 31, no. 2, 2017, pp. 211–236.

16 M. Kosinski, D. Stillwell and T. Graepel, 'Private traits and attributes are predictable from digital records of human behavior', *Proceedings of the National Academy of Sciences (PNAS)*, vol. 110, no. 15, 2013, pp. 5802–5805.

17 J. B. Kristensen, T. Albrechtsen, E. Dahl-Nielsen, M. Jensen, M. Skovrind, T. Bornakke, 'Parsimonious data: How a single Facebook like predicts voting behavior in multiparty systems', *Public Library of Science (PLoS) ONE*, vol. 12, no. 9, 2017, p.e0184562.

18 A. Glaser, 'Politicians are addicted to big data like it's campaign cash', Slate.com, 17 October 2017; http://www.slate.com/articles/technology/technology/2017/10/politicians_are_addicted_to_big_data_like_it_s_campaign_cash.html (accessed 9 August 2018).

19 M. Crook and T. Crook, 'The advent of the secret ballot in Britain and France, 1789–1914: from public assembly to private compartment', *History*, vol. 92, no. 308, 2007, pp. 449–471; J. Wasserman and E. Jaggard, 'Electoral violence in mid nineteenth-century England and Wales', *Historical Research*, vol. 80, no. 207, 2007, pp. 124–155; C. O'Leary, *The Elimination of Corrupt Practices in British Elections 1868–1911*, Oxford, Clarendon Press, 1962.

20 M. Fysh, Facebook, 5 May 2015; https://www.facebook.com/MarcusFyshForYeovil/photos/a.1437533486462035.1073741829.1405406096341441/1626144887600893/?type=3&theater (accessed 9 August 2018).

21 R. Savransky, 'Trump aide reveals "three major voter suppression operations"', The Hill, 27 October 2016; http://thehill.com/blogs/ballot-box/presidential-races/303034-trump-aide-we-have-three-major-voter-suppression (accessed 9 August 2018).

22 Cummings, 'On the referendum', 2016.

23 BBC News, 'Who spent what on Facebook during 2017 election campaign?', 31 March 2018; http://www.bbc.co.uk/news/uk-politics-43487301 (accessed 9 August 2018).

24 BBC Trending, 'Campaigns target voters with precision in final days', 7 June 2017; http://www.bbc.co.uk/news/blogs-trending-40177002 (accessed 9 August 2018).

25 Anti-Defamation League Report, 'Anti-Semitic targeting of journalists during the 2016 presidential campaign', 19 October 2016; https://www.adl.org/sites/default/files/documents/assets/pdf/press-center/CR_4862_Journalism-Task-Force_v2.pdf (accessed 9 August 2018).

26 W. Schaffar, 'New social media and politics in Thailand: the emergence of fascist vigilante groups on Facebook', *Austrian Journal of South-East Asian Studies (ASEAS)*, vol. 9, no. 2, 2016, pp. 215–234.

27 A. Taub and M. Fisher, 'Where countries are tinderboxes and Facebook is a match', *New York Times*, 21 April 2018; https://www.nytimes.com/2018/04/21/world/asia/facebook-sri-lanka-riots.html (accessed 9 August 2018).

28 T. Ross, *Why the Tories Won: The Inside Story of the 2015 Election*, London, Biteback Publishing, 2015.

29 BBC Trending, 'Campaigns target voters'.

30 J. Waterson, 'Here's how Labour ran an under-the-radar dark ads campaign during the general election', Buzzfeed, 6 July 2017; https://www.buzzfeed.com/jimwaterson/heres-how-labour-ran-an-under-the-radar-dark-ads-campaign (accessed 9 August 2018).

31 Cummings, 'On the referendum', 2016.

32 Electoral Commission, 'Details of major EU referendum campaign spending', 24 February 2017; https://www.electoralcommission.org.uk/i-am-a/journalist/electoral-commission-media-centre/news-releases-donations/details-of-major-campa

ign-spending-during-eu-referendum-published-by-electoral-commission (accessed 9 August 2018).

33 Select Committee for Digital, Culture, Media and Sport, written statement by B. Kaiser to the Fake News Inquiry, 17 April 2018; C. Cadwalladr, 'Price comparison site data may have been used by Leave.EU', *The Guardian*, 21 April 2018; https://www.theguardian.com/politics/2018/apr/21/price-comparison-data-may-have-bee n-used-leave-eu-brexit-cambridge-analytica (accessed 9 August 2018).

34 Banks, *Bad Boys of Brexit*.

35 Information Commissioner's Office, 'Update on ICO investigation into data ana-lytics for political purposes', 13 December 2017; https://ico.org.uk/action-weve-taken/investigation-into-data-analytics-for-political-purposes/ (accessed 9 August 2018).

9. Rethinking Democracy with Social Media

HELEN MARGETTS

SOCIAL MEDIA are blamed for almost everything that is wrong with democracy. They are held responsible for pollution of the democratic environment through fake news, junk science, computational propaganda and aggressive microtargeting and political advertising. They are accused of creating political filter bubbles, where citizens exist in ever narrower 'echo chambers' of personalised news and connections with like-minded people, which mean that they are exposed only to similar ideological viewpoints, feeding their own opinions back to themselves and creating a *'Daily Me'* news environment. In turn, these phenomena have been implicated in the rise of populism, political polarisation, waves of hate against women and minorities, far-right extremism and radicalisation, post-truth, political chaos, the end of democracy and ultimately, the death of democracy.[1] Discussion of social media's role in democracy sounds like a premature lament for a sick patient, without investigating the prognosis.

Yet, actually we know rather little about the relationship between social media and democracy. In their ten years of existence, social media have injected volatility and instability into political systems, bringing a continual cast of unpredictable events. They have challenged normative models of democracy—by which we might understand the macro-level shifts at work—seeming to make possible the highest hopes and worst fears of republicanism and pluralism. They have transformed the ecology of interest groups and mobilisations which challenge elites and ruling institutions, bringing regulatory decay and policy sclerosis. They create undercurrents of political life that burst to the surface in seemingly random ways, making fools of opinion polls. But although the platforms themselves generate new sources of real-time transactional data that might be used to understand this changed environment, most of this data is proprietary and inaccessible to researchers, meaning that the revolution in big data and data science has passed by democracy research. This chapter looks at the available evidence regarding the effect of social media on democracy, for which—as for Mark Twain—the report of death may be an exaggeration.[2]

What do we know? The value of small things

Social media—digital platforms which allow the creation, location and exchange of content—are entwined with every democratic institution and

Published by John Wiley & Sons Ltd, 9600 Garsington Road, Oxford OX4 2DQ, UK and 350 Main Street, Malden, MA 02148, USA

the daily lives of citizens, having reached incredible levels of penetration. Worldwide, Facebook has 2 billion users, YouTube has 1.5 billion, Whats-App 1.2 billion, Instagram 700 million, Twitter 328 million and the Chinese WeChat 889 million; nearly three quarters (73 per cent) of US adults use YouTube, while 68 per cent use Facebook.[3] In the UK, 66 per cent of the population are active social media users, with 57 per cent using social media on mobile (these groups overlap, with many using both).[4] Among younger age groups, usage of at least one social media platform is nearly ubiquitous, with 60 per cent of teenage smartphone users using Snapchat alone. When deciding whether to vote, to support, to campaign, to demonstrate, to complain, digital media are with us at every step. They shape our information environment through search engines and social information about what other people are doing, and extend our social networks by creating hundreds or thousands of 'weak ties', particularly for users of social media platforms such as Facebook or Instagram. So, these platforms have transformed the costs and benefits of every kind of political participation. But the key difference that social media have brought to the democratic landscape is a raft of new activities which are characterised by being really small, extending below the bottom rung of the ladder of participation. These activities stretch from small acts such as signing a petition, through voting, attending a political meeting and donating money to a political cause, right up to political violence or armed struggle. Following, liking, tweeting, retweeting, sharing text or images relating to a political issue, or signing up to a digital campaign, are tiny acts of political participation that have no equivalent in the pre-social media age (there is no precedent, for example, for reading President Trump's tweets). Even tweeting about a demonstration or political event that you have not attended is an act, because you have sent a tiny signal of viability to anyone looking at your tweet (or the +1 on a 'like'), and made it that bit more likely that they will act. These tiny acts are all around the democratic environment. They have enabled ordinary people across the world with no more resources than a mobile phone to challenge injustice, fight for policy or regime change, and shed light on corruption and inefficiency in public life. Until only twenty years ago, there was no way to participate in politics without joining a political party or organised interest group, attending meetings and knocking on doors. For many people, these costs in terms of time, effort or resources were too great, and politics has often been the province of an activist elite. Now, tiny acts are drawing new people into politics, particularly young people, whose absence political commentators have been bemoaning for years. For example, it is hard to imagine in a pre-social media era that US school children would demonstrate, under the hashtag #Enough, and walk out of school to campaign for gun control, as they did in 2018 in the wake of yet another school shooting.

Scaling up—or not

Taken individually, tiny acts of participation seem insignificant, and indeed for many years were dismissed as mere 'slacktivism' or 'clicktivism', denigrated as low-cost political acts that have minimal effect. The US political commentator, Malcolm Gladwell, published a widely cited *New Yorker* article[5] in 2010, arguing that small-scale actions and weak ties facilitated by social networking platforms could never give rise to political mobilisation on the scale of the civil rights movement, which provoked some controversy given the demonstrations, protests and even revolutions of the so-called Arab Spring which followed so soon afterwards. Tiny acts can and do scale up to large-scale mobilisations and campaigns for policy change that have brought major shocks and surprises to political regimes all over the world. Petitions to re-run the UK referendum regarding membership of the European Union (in 2016), or to block Donald Trump from a state visit to the UK (in 2017) immediately shot up to millions of signatures. There can be hardly a country in the world that has not experienced widespread demonstration, protest or campaigning for political change taking place on social media—demonstrations against the financial crisis and austerity in the US and UK in 2009 being examples of such. These mobilisations have challenged and even brought regime change in authoritarian states, as well as a whole host of policy changes in liberal democracies, from justice for victims of police brutality to the end of controversial health reforms. A few of these mobilisations have developed into new political parties across the ideological spectrum, from the Spanish Podemos to the Italian Five Star Movement to the German far-right Pegida, all highly disruptive forces in the political systems in which they have emerged. This scaling up of tiny acts appear also to play a part within conventional political events—such as election campaigns—by building up into waves of support for unconventional candidates such as Donald Trump (elected as US President in 2017), or Jeremy Corbyn (elected as leader of the UK Labour party in 2015 and again in 2016).

So, tiny acts of participation can scale up dramatically and rapidly. But they almost always don't. It may seem from the news media that it is relatively easy to get hundreds of thousands of people out in the streets or into a square, given the frequency with which such events appear to occur. But there is an obvious selection bias in favour of the successful mobilisations, which are reported on TV screens and circulate on social media, compared with all the failed mobilisations that we never see. So, for example, in the UK, over 99 per cent of petitions to the government fail to get the 10,000 signatures required for an official response and only 0.1 per cent attain the 100,000 required for a parliamentary debate (the same figure is 0.7 per cent in the US). This picture is replicated over and again across social media platforms from YouTube to Facebook, and across countries. There is no normal distribution of mobilisations; rather, a distribution that is more like that of earthquakes—a small number of extreme events and a huge number of insignificant ones. It is hard to predict (just as it is for earthquakes) which will succeed and which will fail. The shift towards new forms of mobilisation based on tiny acts of digital participation has brought an era of what we labelled in our book of the same name *Political Turbulence*,[6] where politics becomes harder and harder to predict.

Political turbulence means a challenge to two stabilising elements of democracy—political identity and institutions. Rather than identifying with issues, forming collective identity and then acting to support the interests of that identity (or voting for a political party that supports it), in a social media world, people act first, and think about it, or identify with others later, if at all. And even when a mobilisation does succeed in getting a million people on the street, or signing a petition, or even a revolution of sorts as in Egypt, the very fact that it is possible to get there without the normal organisational trappings (such as nascent parties or leaders) of a movement or revolutions means that it will usually be unsustainable. At the same time, turbulence threatens democratic institutions of all kinds, by showing that political figures from outside the mainstream—such as Jeremy Corbyn and Donald Trump—can win, or at least garner huge levels of support in surprising ways in a short space of time. Will the Labour party ever recover from Corbyn, the Republican party from Trump? Social media seem to inject instability into traditional democratic institutions.

Losing control of democracy

While traditional institutional actors are struggling in this new democratic landscape, new ones, of vital importance, have emerged. That is, when citizens are deciding to undertake one of these new tiny acts of political participation, they do so on digital platforms—and in particular, social media platforms. And these platforms shape crucially the information environment within which these decisions are made. They do so by exerting social influence, in the form of information about what other people are doing. In an earlier era, when we signed a petition on a street or expressed our support for some campaign, we knew little about how many other people supported the cause. On social media, on digital activism platforms, we know straight away how many people like, follow, share, view or discuss an issue or news item, and how close a campaign is to reaching its target. And decades of social science show that information like this is a crucial influence on how much we ourselves support something. For example, an experiment with music platforms has shown that if people are told that songs are popular, they are more likely to rate the songs highly themselves in comparison with being told they are unpopular, or being given no information at all, while we are more likely to contribute to public goods by recycling or voting or give to charitable causes if we know that other people are doing so.[7] This kind of influence has been shown to operate in the same way on digital platforms. For example, trending information, showing the most popular petitions, has been shown to concentrate petition signing in those petitions at the expense of the petitions not making it to the trending box.[8]

These chains of social influence, by which individuals undertake acts of participation and thereby send signals of viability to others, are the explanation for how small acts can lead to large-scale mobilisation or waves of support. This can start primarily on one platform, as with the so-called 'Twitter revolution' of Tunisia or 'Facebook revolution' in Egypt in 2011, or the largest demonstration in Romanian history in the autumn of 2017, with widespread protests against corruption in a newly elected government in Romania attempting to pardon themselves for past crimes, which appears to have been coordinated via the messaging app Slack. More recently, chains of influence operate across multiple platforms, particularly where young people are involved (with most teenagers in the US and UK being active on up to five social media platforms). In all these events, social media sent signals of viability through likes, shares, follows, views and so on, leading people to consider that mobilisations might succeed and be worth joining. That makes the digital media platforms themselves crucially important democratic actors, particularly the most popular giants of the social media world: Google (which also owns YouTube) and Facebook (which owns Instagram and WhatsApp). The design of their platforms shapes political participation in terms of what information people encounter, how people share information, and what they know about what other people are doing.

Furthermore, while a rise in political mobilisation and activism might be considered generally a positive development for democracy, the same mechanisms—tiny acts and chains of social influence—can also lead to anti-democratic phenomena. Just as social media platforms allow small acts of participation to become widely accessible and to (sometimes) scale up, they allow acts of misinformation, hate speech, abuse, threats, extremism, radicalisation and even terrorist influence to follow the same process. For this reason, social media platforms are implicated in a number of pathologies of contemporary democracy, including:

- *Echo chambers*, in which people are surrounded in online social networks by like-minded people and opinions that reinforce their own belief systems (in the same way that acoustic echo chambers use hollow enclosures to produce reverberated sounds);
- *Fake news*, where distorted or false versions of events are widely disseminated either for the purposes of disruption or for financial gain;
- Highly targeted *political advertising* to the extent that it is personalised, based on personal data;
- *Computational propaganda*, involving automated social media accounts (bots) which mimic real people through the dissemination of information or fake news across a range of platforms and networks, with the intention of manipulating opinion;

- *Hate speech*, where online abuse or threats are directed at individuals or groups on the basis of attributes such as race, religion, ethnic origin, sexual orientation, disability, or gender.

Critics of social media's role in democracy view these phenomena as operating in tandem. That is, automated bots are used to spread disruptive rumours in the form of fake news, which are spread around and reinforce the ideological position of echo chambers, whose inhabitants are vulnerable to these distorted versions of events and regard them as the truth. They are also used to disseminate hate speech to magnify its effect, surrounding victims with tirades of abuse and harassment from both human and automated 'trolls'. In this way, echo chambers lead to polarisation, dragging those in the middle ground towards more extreme opinions on either side of a duality, such as whether or not to remain in the European Union or whether to vote for Donald Trump. The view of these phenomena acting in concert rose to the surface of political commentary in March 2018 with the Cambridge Analytica affair (described in Martin Moore's chapter), where Facebook data generated by an application purportedly for academic research purposes was revealed to have been sold by the developer (thereby breaking Facebook's terms and conditions) to the political campaigning organisation Cambridge Analytica. The company then used this data for highly targeted advertising in the campaign to elect Donald Trump and (allegedly) in the UK referendum on EU membership. While none of the other protagonists in this affair—the Cambridge academic who developed the application, Cambridge Analytica, or the whistleblower Chris Wylie, who worked for the company—come out well, Facebook in some ways received the most opprobrium. For adherents to this view, the acoustics of social media, orchestrated by firms like Facebook, are implicated in the waves of political populism and even extremism that have swept across the United States and many European countries.[9] Although all of these phenomena—and in particular, the effect that they have—is contestable and under-researched, as discussed below, the perceptions that social media are somehow implicated in the downfall of democracy are real, and the journalist Carole Cadwalladr who exposed the Cambridge Analytica scandal believes strongly that social media platforms are leading us into a '9/11 of democracy'.[10]

Democratic grief

Political turbulence, the rising influence of social media platforms, and the loss of control for traditional institutions is traumatic for democrats. As noted in the introduction, many approach it as a death, with something akin to grief. It is possible to identify within the debate responses analogous to the famous five stages of grief: denial, bargaining, anger, depression and acceptance.[11]

Denial: politics as usual

The first response to the relationship between social media and politics has been denial. The way this view goes is that there is nothing new here, and that digital technologies in general are a neutral tool that (sometimes) make things work better (as Jane Austen might put it).[12] Although computer systems entered the machinery of government as early as the 1950s, when they first started to be used for large-scale administrative processing in the UK and US, they have been largely ignored in the media view of government outside the trade press. Before the 2000s, visual images of politics or political movies never contained technology—always venerable buildings, talking heads, pens, and desks. Any consideration of technological change still has no part in politics courses. Part of this resistance comes from the 'politics as pain' principle—particularly in British politics—that insists that politics that is automated or digitised in some way is not real politics. It should involve a long boring meeting or knocking on doors in bad weather or cut into the evenings, the view behind the dismissal of social media's role in politics as mere 'clicktivism' or 'slacktivism'.[13] It is interesting that this view manages to prevail, even while social media are being blamed for their massively pernicious influence.

Bargaining: the internet will make us free

Others take the second stage of grief—bargaining—to extreme. Here is the view that technology in the form of the internet is going to transform our political system and solve the traditional dilemmas of politics. We can live in a hyper-modernist world of direct democracy, where the bureaucratic state can disintegrate. But this can happen only if we preserve the internet as an icon of freedom, unconstrained by governance or regulation, following the original cyberactivist John Perry Barlow[14] in his Declaration of the Independence of Cyberspace, which proclaimed:

Governments of the Industrial World, you weary giants of flesh and steel, I come from Cyberspace, the new home of Mind. On behalf of the future, I ask you of the past to leave us alone. You are not welcome among us. You have no sovereignty where we gather. We have no elected government, nor are we likely to have one … I declare the global social space we are building to be naturally independent of the tyrannies you seek to impose on us. You have no moral right to rule us nor do you possess any methods of enforcement we have true reason to fear.

In this world, political life will be reinvented, a 'global social space we are building to be naturally independent of the tyrannies you seek to impose on us' as long as we are true to this cyber-libertarian dream. Even in a political world dominated by social media platforms run by huge internet corporations such as Google and Facebook (that might seem to have replaced the 'giants of steel'), adherents to this faith dream on, and for them any censorship or regulation of the internet or social media is opposed vehemently.

Even hate speech and microtargeted personalised advertising must all be allowed to continue unchecked.[15]

Anger: shoot the messenger!

This is currently the dominant view, where technology—particularly the internet, and over the last decade, social media—is to blame for everything bad in democracy, from the rise of radicalisation and the extreme right (or left), to the election of Donald Trump as US President in 2016. This is a special case of a more general tendency to blame the internet for every-thing, from plane crashes to teenage suicides. Here, social media is respon-sible for most pathologies of modern election campaigns, through the creation of echo chambers or filter bubbles of like-minded people, where citizens receive constant reinforcement of their own views, which somehow leads to political polarisation. These bubbles are reinforced in a number of ways, including the use of fake news, where third parties (non-media organisations) create completely untrue stories and tempt people to read them, thereby making money of advertisements alongside; political bots (robotic social media accounts that give the impression that a political campaign has more supporters than it actually has); or attempts generally to try to disrupt an opponent's campaign. The other accusation made against social media is that of hate speech (through the phenomenon of trolling against public figures, particularly women or people of the Muslim faith) and, more generally, a degeneration of civic discourse and a further polarisation of political discussion, as people on one side of a debate (such as whether to leave the European Union) react strongly to abusive lan-guage on the other.

Depression: post-truth

Depression is the next stage, where social media have led us to a post-truth world, where we cannot distinguish real news from fake news, and 'objec-tive facts are less influential in shaping public opinion than appeals to emo-tion and personal belief'.[16] Under this view, the internet corporations will continue steadily in their inexorable rise, taking over some roles from the state and turning citizens into ad-clicking data providers. Meanwhile, any genuinely 'social' media will be strangled, choking on their own hate, domi-nated by computational propaganda from massive political entities (such as the Russian regime) so that genuine political movements as characterised by the Arab Spring could never happen again. For some, this view is bound up in a more general rejection of technology's role in society, for example, in automating jobs, and a desire for a return to the past, which manifested itself so powerfully among Trump supporters in 2016, with their MAGA (Make America Great Again) hats, or in the Leave campaign in the UK refer-endum, with their (ironically, post-truth) red bus.

Acceptance: moving on from myths

Reaching the final stage of grief would be to accept that digital media platforms are part of our democratic system, the political weather, and that political systems must accommodate the change, through a process of institutional catch-up. Most social media platforms did not exist ten years ago, and they have been at the heart of our political systems for far less than that, so it is understandable that political institutions have failed to adjust, and the new institutions of democracy—social media corporations—have proceeded unchecked and unregulated, particularly given the power of the original cyber-utopian dream. In many ways, the myths of the other stages of grief—the denial of the importance of the internet, the denigration of social media activism as slacktivism and clicktivism (denial), the insistence that we can never regulate internet-related platforms (bargaining), the belief that social media are to blame for everything (anger) and the hopelessness of taking back any sort of control (depression), all work against the possibility of integrating and institutionalising social media platforms into democratic life.

The first stage in acceptance therefore would be to tackle some of these myths with research, to understand the scale and scope of the democratic pathologies outlined above. Such a task is not as straightforward as it might seem; ironically, because these platforms are based entirely on data, it is extremely difficult obtain the data needed to understand democratic processes, institutions and behaviour. While Twitter data is relatively open (hence the disproportionately high levels of scholarly attention it receives), WhatsApp is encrypted, Snapchat data is deleted as soon as it is read and so on. Most social media data from the more popular platforms such as Facebook and Instagram (which is owned by Facebook) is proprietary and closely guarded, especially in the wake of the Cambridge Analytica affair of 2018. Incidents like this, as with AOL's release of 1 million search records for research purposes in 2006, which were de-anonymised in a few minutes of release, have done much to stifle research into social media's actual (as opposed to gloomily hypothesised) impact upon democracy.

Examining the evidence for the death of democracy

One key research question is whether echo chambers and filter bubbles really exist to any greater extent than in non-digital settings (such as just reading the *Daily Mail* or only watching Fox News). After all, people have always sought out like-minded people and society has been structured around families. It is undoubtedly the case that social media firms can shape the kind of news environment and social networks that form on their platforms, for example through whether they provide trending information (Twitter always does this and Facebook did for a several years but stopped doing so in 2018), or by showing certain elements of the news feed. Facebook took the decision at the beginning of 2018 to prioritise interactions with friends and family, rather than passive consumption of news, arguing that this was more conducive to well-being. The most ardent believer in the echo chamber phenomenon, the US legal scholar Cass Sunstein, has moved from his pessimistic 2001 and 2007 predictions for the use of search engines for news consumption—made before use of social media became widespread—to a full blown characterisation of '#republic' as 'divided democracy', defined by polarisation, personalisation, social fragmentation of the public sphere through the echo chamber effect and 'cybercascades' of social and political influence.[17] Much of the scholarship directed at echo chambers is polemical (including Sunstein's argument). But where there is evidence based on available data, it suggests that algorithms play less of a role in exposure to attitude-challenging content than individuals' own choices and that 'on average more than 20 per cent of an individual's Facebook friends who report an ideological affiliation are from the opposing party'.[18] The evidence further shows that those who do not use social media on average come across news from significantly fewer different online sources than those who do use social media[19] and that social media are actually reducing polarisation.[20] These findings suggest that although the design of platforms clearly affects the extent to which echo chambers exist, they are nowhere near as determined or 'hermetically sealed' as some critics suggest.

Similarly, for fake news, there is a lack of rigorous empirical evidence and it is also difficult to identify what should and should not be labelled as fake news, particularly given President Trump's indiscriminate and overuse of the term. Where there is data, it has suggested that on Twitter, false political news tends to spread more quickly and further than verified news (perhaps because of the novelty of false news) and that humans rather than robots were responsible for this faster spread.[21] Research has also started to suggest that the volume and effect of fake news has been exaggerated. Research in France and Germany found a very limited reach of identified disinformation providers on the open web, with only a few of them generating high levels of engagement on Facebook.[22] Evidence from the US 2016 presidential election, combining survey responses with individual-level web traffic histories, estimated that approximately one in four Americans visited a fake news website between 7 October and 14 November 2016. Trump supporters visited the most fake news websites, which were overwhelmingly pro-Trump. In this way, there is a tendency for fake news to preach to the converted, reducing its overall effect; fake news consumption was heavily concentrated among a small group—almost six in ten visits to fake news websites came from the 10 per cent of people with the most conservative online information diets.[23] Likewise, another study examined online visitation data across mobile and desktop platforms in the months leading up to and following the 2016 presidential election and found that the fake news audience comprises a small, disloyal group of heavy internet users.[24]

For computational propaganda, there is little doubt of the scale, and it is being extensively gathered and analysed by the Computational Propaganda project at the University of Oxford.[25] An analysis of 9 million tweets from the 2016 presidential campaign found that one-third of pro-Trump Twitter traffic was driven by accounts that were bots or highly automated, compared with one-fifth of pro-Clinton traffic, and such an analysis has been performed for several elections since then. However, establishing the effect of such automated propaganda is far more difficult. This is especially the case with the now evidenced Russian activity in the 2016 election which, as a *Wired* article put it, was 'designed to look like it was coming from authentic American voices and interest groups', using automated accounts across platforms pushing out what was so-called native content—including video, visual, memetic, and text elements designed to push narrative themes, conspiracies and character attacks, rather than promoted or paid-for advertisements. This produced distorted social information, making it far more difficult for voters to assess where stories and narratives were coming from, whether they were real or propaganda, whether they represented the views of neighbours or not. Many were not actually aimed at changing opinion, but at reinforcing existing opinions and changing behaviour, making individuals feel strongly enough to do something. All were geared at disruption. As the *Wired* article noted, 'Persuasion and influence via social media cannot be estimated in linear terms; it requires looking at network effects. It is about the impact of a complex media environment with many layers, inputs, voices, amplifiers, and personalities. All of these elements change over time and interact with each other.'[26]

For hate speech, we know even less about the scale and scope of the phenomenon. Hate speech is clearly a problem that threatens to discourage a whole generation of women and ethnic minorities from public life, with misogyny towards campaigners for any issues connected with women's rights particularly prominent in the UK. And social media platforms have been very slow to react, as highlighted by the tirades of abuse and hate directed at Caroline Criado Perez, the UK activist whose successful campaign in 2013 to have women represented on bank notes led to sustained and vitriolic harassment on Twitter, highlighting the problem for the first time and causing Twitter to change their complaints procedure. In 2016, several platforms (including Microsoft, YouTube, Facebook and Twitter) agreed a code of conduct with the EU to remove offensive material within twenty-four hours of reporting. According to EU figures, they were managing this in 81 per cent of cases by the end of 2017.[27] While there are qualitative studies of online misogyny[28] and new centres of quantitative research[29] focusing on hate speech, particularly on Twitter where data is available, we have little idea of the scale of hate speech, or the extent to which it relates to isolated individuals or is orchestrated by far-right groups, or the extent to which verbal threats relate to instances of actual hate crime (through 'doxxing', for example, where personal details and physical locations are revealed). Without such research, it is impossible to understand the extent to which the hate peddled by trolls is something new, somehow caused by the ease of expressing it through the availability of tiny acts of hate which then scale up, or whether it merely reveals society's dark secrets that were hitherto concealed as thoughts and never translated into any sort of action. Certainly, the apparent rise in hate is not restricted to its online form, as the campaigner Gina Miller, who instigated the Article 50 legal case against the UK government (and has received unprecedented levels of threats and harassment) put it:

The idea that this abuse is the work of keyboard warriors is just not the case. These people take the time to make posters with vile images, put them in envelopes and post them. They go to the trouble of finding my email address or office number. This is really premeditated stuff.[30]

We need the data to understand the claims of the anger-ridden and grief-stricken mourners of democracy in order to understand the scale and scope of hate and the mechanisms which drive it, and that means developing research partnerships with the most popular social media platforms.[31] Facebook has now announced some positive moves, including the development of a data-sharing arrangement for reputable academic researchers, using a model developed by the Harvard political scientist Gary King and the Stanford lawyer Nate Persily.[32] They have also announced a new interface which will open up data on political advertising, the other threat to democracy posed by social media, in a move welcomed in May 2018 by the US *ProPublica* journalist Julia Angwin, who has done much to highlight the issue of highly targeted person-alised political advertising. It is possible to discern a note of hope for the future role of social media in democracy from the ensuing exchange, which also high-lights the importance of public service journalism in keeping up pressure, when on 11 May Facebook thanked Angwin (on Twitter) as follows:

Source: Twitter, 11 May 2018.

Taking back control? Building transparency and accountability back into democracy

Any institutional catch-up for democratic systems to account for the new actors will need to be carried out at multiple levels; there is no simple solution or quick fix. First, as highlighted above, there is a role for public service journalism and social activism in keeping up the pressure on social media platforms to make more transparent their processes and algorithms which shape the information and news that people consume and use to make political decisions (such as whether to join a campaign and for whom to vote). From around 2013 onwards, social media platforms have taken a series of actions to tackle the problems of hate speech, fake news and computational propaganda, and these moves have mostly been in response to public pressure. Facebook, for example, has employed thousands of fact checkers and moderators and in May 2018, published a transparency report[33] of the amount of content taken down on the site. The data highlights the scale of the challenge faced, with 3.5 million pieces of violent content and 2.5 million pieces of hate speech removed during the first quarter of the year, and the disabling of an astonishing 583 million fake accounts. The report illustrates the technical challenge and the importance of innovation in this area; while automated machine learning can deal with violent and even terrorist content relatively easily, hate speech is far more difficult to remove and only 38 per cent is dealt with automatically. And when it comes to the growing phenomenon of political bots directed by electoral campaigns or external forces wishing to disrupt elections, the answer may be a counter-spiral of automation by the internet corporations themselves. While an early example of this, the Microsoft 'Tay' chatbot driven by artificial intelligence, was a miserable failure (because it learnt quickly from the company it kept to spew out racist and abusive venom in all directions), more recent examples have been more successful.[34] Technologists and philosophers will have a role here, particularly in the building of ethical bots that do not go either native, or beyond their remit.

While there is a clear role for public pressure, regulation should not be removed from the policy table, and indeed when Mark Zuckerberg appeared before the European Parliament in May 2018, he made his first public acknowledgement that regulation was 'important and inevitable' and that Facebook was performing a public role. Although the German route of treating platforms legislatively like publishers (introduced in October 2017) is believed by many to be impossible to police,[35] the European Union's General Data Protection Regulation (GDPR) which came into force in May 2018 shows how regulation can effect meaningful behavioural change by commercial firms (as evidenced by the hundreds of emails and opportunities to discontinue relationships that everyone received in the preceding weeks). It also illustrated how the European state is leading in the way in the regulatory space.

There is a limit, however, to what regulation can achieve. In attempting to ban encrypted platforms such as WhatsApp in 2017, the then UK home

119

secretary Amber Rudd declared that 'enough is enough'—an even more meaningless statement than 'Brexit means Brexit'. Such a move would poison relations with, for example, Facebook while driving miscreants to far darker and harder-to-reach places, representing a massive act of environmental pollution. Another potential area for regulation is in challenging the monopolies of the huge platforms. The fact that Facebook was allowed to buy Instagram and WhatsApp, its key competitors, was a signal that the Federal Trade Commission (FTC) had totally underestimated the importance of this market. In the wake of the Cambridge Analytica affair, a new campaign, #freedomfromFacebook has emerged, for the purpose of lobbying the FTC to break up Facebook into these constituent parts. The political journalist Paul Mason has suggested that we should ferret around in the short history of social media to find those platforms, like Soundcloud, Medium and Twitter, that encourage co-operation and creativity and are 'worth saving', and establish new (co-operative) ownership models.[36]

We also need to stop denigrating tiny acts and extend our idea of what is democratic participation. For example, another way of tackling fake news may be to enlist the support of volunteers for fact checking and reporting false stories, in the same way that Wikipedia was formed. Confronting hate online at the individual level has been shown to be possible for some public figures, such as the TV academic Mary Beard, who confronted her trolls individually —and there may be creative ways of crowdsourcing such confrontations to avoid individual harm or risk. We also need to improve the education of children in terms of news consumption. It is by now clear that young people do not take news from conventional sources, as in national newspapers, TV or radio, where established brands are known as trusted sources, with flagged political standpoints and some kind of indicators of quality. News items on social media platforms, which is the only place where young people are likely to see them, could come from anywhere and are surrounded by advertising, and people navigate this environment with very little help.

Stabilising democracy in the social media age

Digital platforms now form the basis of our democratic environment and we must protect them rather than rushing to despairing of their influence as a terminal illness. While these platforms undoubtedly shape the information that we consume and the political decisions we make, the pathologies that they introduce are not terminal, but rather, chronic and under-researched, requiring careful study and long-term management. We need to work out ways to take over the reins that at present, technology companies seem to hold—although their control is very much less absolute than we tend to believe. Any rethinking of democracy in the social media age must be multifaceted, thoughtful, collaborative and evidence based. It will involve ethical and legal frameworks to guide as well as mandate good behaviour; working with tech companies rather than only making enemies of them; smarter policing of activities that are already illegal; and crowdsourcing safety in online spaces, so that people and social enterprises play a role.

This is not a sleek hyper-modernist vision of democracy, in spite of the high technology content. Indeed, by highlighting political turbulence and the messy chaotic nature of contemporary politics, I have tried to convey how an element of randomness has entered political life with social media. We have an understandable tendency to assume that because something important has happened, it was somehow inevitable. For example, the vote to leave the EU feels like the inevitable result of the clear pathologies of a divided country, where those with few resources had gained little from either Europeanisation or globalisation. Other seemingly landmark political events, such as the election of Donald Trump, have this same aura of inevitability, in spite of the surprise that greeted their arrival. Yet there is an alternative view. When we look in detail at the waves of support that led up to the vote for Leave, or Trump, or any of the other closely fought political contests with surprising results that have taken place over the past few years, perhaps it could have been different. The interconnectedness of our political life means that every tiny act of support for the Leave (and Remain) campaigns sent a tiny signal of viability out to other voters in a connected cluster of support—even if it was just a comment on a TV debate—which have scaled up to some kind of success, within some political microclimate (such as a locality, or institution, or profession), but could have fizzled out into failure. Learning how to manage this unpredictability in democratic life is crucial for a stabilising of democracy in the social media age. This is a democracy built on workarounds and fixes, a messy solution for a disorganised, chaotic politics.

Notes

1 S. Levitsky and D. Ziblatt, *How Democracies Die*, New York, Crown, 2018.
2 'The report of my death was an exaggeration', written by Mark Twain to Frank Marshal White, the English correspondent to the *New York Journal*, 31 May 1897, in response to rumours of his serious illness and death, and published in the journal on 2 June.
3 'Facebook now has 2 billion monthly users…and responsibility', Techcrunch.com, 27 June 2017; https://techcrunch.com/2017/06/27/facebook-2-billion-users/ (accessed 19 August 2018).
4 'Total number and the share of population of active social media and mobile social media users in the United Kingdom (UK) in January 2018', Statista.com; https://www.statista.com/statistics/507405/uk-active-social-media-and-mobile-social-media-users/ (accessed 11 August 2018).
5 M. Gladwell, 'Why the revolution will not be tweeted', *The New Yorker*, 4 October 2010.
6 H. Margetts, P. John, S. Hale and T. Yasseri, *Political Turbulence: How Social Media Shape Collective Action*, Princeton, Princeton University Press, 2015. See this book also for analysis and visualisation of the data cited above.

7 M. J. Salganik, P. S. Dodds and D. J. Watts, 'Experimental study of inequality and unpredictability in an artificial cultural market', *Science*, vol. 311, no. 5762, 2006, pp. 854–856.

8 S. A. Hale, P. John, H. Margetts and T. Yasseri, 'How digital design shapes political participation: a natural experiment with social information', *PloS one*, vol. 13, no. 4, 2018, p.e0196068.

9 For a discussion, see H. Margetts, 'Political behaviour and the acoustics of social media', *Nature Human Behaviour*, vol. 1, no. 4, 2017, s41562-017.

10 Carole Cadwalladr made this point at an event hosted by Damian Collins MP and the Latvian Embassy on 'Resisting the onset of post-truth in democracy' in Parliament, 15 May 2018.

11 E. Kübler-Ross, *On Death and Dying*, Abingdon, Routledge, 1969. Originally developed by Kübler-Ross to describe the emotions experienced by the dying, these five stages have been used widely to encapsulate the way in which people respond to bereavement and grief more generally.

12 'The Musgroves, like their houses, were in a state of alteration, perhaps of improvement', J. Austen, *Persuasion*, 1817, chap. 5.

13 For a discussion, see D. Karpf, 'Online political mobilization from the advocacy group's perspective: looking beyond clicktivism', *Policy & Internet*, vol. 2, no. 4, 2010, pp. 7–41.

14 J. Perry Barlow, 'A declaration of the independence of cyberspace', Electronic Frontier Foundation, 8 February 1996; https://www.eff.org/cyberspace-independence (accessed 11 August 2018).

15 This is the view of *Spiked*, the advocacy group and magazine promoting free speech; http://www.spiked-online.com/ (accessed 11 August 2018).

16 Definition of 'post-truth', designated word of the year in 2016, *Oxford English Dictionary*.

17 The most recent of which is C. R. Sunstein, *#Republic: Divided Democracy in the Age of Social Media*, Princeton, Princeton University Press, 2017.

18 E. Bakshy, S. Messing and L. A. Adamic, 'Exposure to ideologically diverse news and opinion on Facebook', *Science*, vol. 348, no. 6239, 2015, pp. 1130–1132.

19 R. Nielson, A. Cornia and A. Kalogeropoulos, 'Challenges and opportunities for news media and journalism in an increasingly digital, mobile, and social media environment', Council of Europe Report, 2016; http://reutersinstitute.politics. ox.ac.uk/sites/default/files/research/files/Challenges%2520and%2520opportun ities%2520for%2520news%2520media%2520and%2520journalism%2520in%2520an% 2520increasingly%2520digital%252C%2520mobile%2520and%2520social%2520me dia%2520environment.pdf (accessed 11 August 2018); N. Newman, R. Fletcher, D. A. L. Levy and R. K. Nielsen, Reuters Institute Digital News Report, SSRN Scholarly Paper No. ID 2796534, 2016. M. Duggan and A. Smith, 'Political content on social media', Pew Research Social Science Research Network, 25 October 2016, also supports this view; http://www.pewinternet.org/2016/10/25/political-content-on-social-media/ (accessed 11 August 2018).

20 P. Barberá, J. T. Jost, J. Nagler, J. A, Tucker and R. Bonneau, 'Tweeting from left to right: is online political communication more than an echo chamber?', *Psychological Science*, vol. 26, no. 10, 2015, pp. 1531–1542.

21 S. Vosoughi, D. Roy and S. Aral, 'The spread of true and false news online', *Science*, vol. 359, no. 6380, 2018, pp. 1146–1151.

22 R. Fletcher, A. Cornia, L. Graves and R. Nielsen, 'Measuring the reach of "fake news" and online disinformation in Europe', Reuters Institute factsheet, 2017; https://reutersinstitute.politics.ox.ac.uk/our-research/measuring-reach-fake-news-and-online-disinformation-europe (accessed 11 August 2018).

23 A. Guess, B. Nyhan and J. Reifler, 'Selective exposure to disinformation: evidence from the consumption of fake news during the 2016 US presidential campaign', 2018; https://www.dartmouth.edu/~nyhan/fake-news-2016.pdf (accessed 11 August 2018).

24 J. L. Nelson and H. Taneja, 'The small, disloyal fake news audience: the role of audience availability in fake news consumption', *New Media & Society,* February 2018, 1461444818758715.

25 The Computational Propaganda Research Project, University of Oxford; http://comprop.oii.ox.ac.uk/ (accessed 11 August 2018).

26 M. McKew, 'Did Russia affect the 2016 election? It is now undeniable', *Wired*, 16 February 2018; https://www.wired.com/story/did-russia-affect-the-2016-election-its-now-undeniable/ (accessed 11 August 2018).

27 Reuters, 'Social media companies accelerate removals of online hate speech', 19 January 2018; https://www.reuters.com/article/us-eu-hatespeech/social-media-companies-accelerate-removals-of-online-hate-speech-eu-idUSKBN1F806X (accessed 11 August 2018).

28 Qualitative studies include D. K. Citron, *Hate Crimes in Cyberspace*, Cambridge MA, Harvard University Press, 2014; K. Mantilla, *Gendertrolling: How Misogyny Went Viral*, Westport, Praeger, 2015. B. Poland, *Haters: Harassment, Abuse and Violence Online*, Lincoln NE, University of Nebraska Press, 2016.

29 Such as the ESRC-funded Social Data Science Laboratory, at the University of Cardiff.

30 L. O'Carroll, interview with Gina Miller, 'I've been told that "as a coloured woman", I'm not even human', *The Guardian*, 25 January 2017; https://www.theguardian.com/politics/2017/jan/25/parliament-alone-is-sovereign-gina-miller-speaks-out-after-article-50-victory (accessed 11 August 2018).

31 One example is Denmark, where the government has appointed a 'digital ambassador', in an effort to build closer ties with internet giants such as Apple and Google.

32 Facebook news, 'Facebook launches new initiative to help scholars assess social media's impact on elections', 9 April 2018; https://newsroom.fb.com/news/2018/04/new-elections-initiative/ (accessed 11 August 2018).

33 Facebook news, 'Facebook publishes enforcement numbers for the first time', 15 May 2018; https://newsroom.fb.com/news/2018/05/enforcement-numbers/ (accessed 11 August 2018).

34 V. Woollaston, 'Following the failure of Tay, Microsoft is back with new chatbot Zo', *Wired*, 6 December 2016; https://www.wired.co.uk/article/microsoft-zo-ai-chatbot-tay (accessed 11 August 2018).

35 Free Speech Debate, 'The UK can show the way on platform regulation. But not by treating Facebook and Google as publishers', 6 November 2017; http://freespeechdebate.com/discuss/the-uk-can-show-the-way-on-platform-regulation-but-not-by-treating-facebook-and-google-as-publishers/ (accessed 11 August 2018).

36 P. Mason, 'Why social media is like the railways—and must be saved', *The Guardian*, 9 January 2017; https://www.theguardian.com/commentisfree/2017/jan/09/social/media/fake-news-soundcloud-medium-facebook (accessed 11 August 2018).

10. Post-Democracy and Populism

COLIN CROUCH

BRITISH DEMOCRACY reached an ugly moment on 3 November 2016, when the *Daily Mail* and *Daily Telegraph*, the country's leading press representatives of conservative opinion, devoted their front pages to displaying photographs of three judges of the Supreme Court under the banner headlines, respectively, 'Enemies of the people' and 'The judges vs the people'. The judges' offence had been to rule that Parliament had a right to have certain votes on the process of the United Kingdom leaving the European Union (EU). In subsequent days some government ministers echoed the phrases, until the Home Secretary, under pressure from judges, issued a statement stressing the importance of the rule of law. However, the government itself continued in the same spirit when it attempted later to rule that, because a majority in the referendum on EU membership had voted to leave, none of the individual measures it would implement in order to revoke EU legislation—ranging across virtually all fields of policy—needed to come to Parliament. The people had spoken; government would interpret their will. Parliament, it seemed, like the Supreme Court, was a potential enemy of that will.

This was a confrontation between two concepts of democracy: does it (as in liberal democracy) denote a set of institutions that include expressions of popular will, but which surround them with others that ensure elaboration of that will, guarantee continued debate so that democracy can function again at a future date, and even limit the powers of those who claim the right to exercise the popular will? Or is it (as in populist democracy) the direct, unmediated voice of a people expressed on a particular day? This confrontation is by no means limited to the UK or to the Brexit debate, and it is a very old theme in democratic theory. In practice, the countries that are normally regarded as stable democracies have resolved the conflict in favour of the former concept. So well established did it seem that in 1992, the US political scientist Francis Fukuyama earned lasting renown for arguing that in western liberal democracy, humankind had reached the summit of its social evolution.[1] That questioning the viability of liberal democracy is now a live issue requires understanding. Equally intriguing is that fact that attacks on it from the political right, more or less silent since the fall of the Portuguese and Spanish fascist regimes in the 1970s, have returned to prominence across large parts of the world. The Marxist left has long been suspicious of liberal democracy, sometimes advocating the 'people's democracy' considered to have been achieved in the state socialist societies. Since their collapse, the left had retreated into utopian dreaming, but has more recently seen new opportunities in the waves of populism, even though these are mainly being led from the right.

Published by John Wiley & Sons Ltd, 9600 Garsington Road, Oxford OX4 2DQ, UK and 350 Main Street, Malden, MA 02148, USA

A basic premise of liberal democracy is that, outside small communities, the expression of popular will is highly problematic and has to be mediated through representative institutions. There then arises the problem of the relationship between the people and the representatives whom they elect. The latter are equipped with power, which they have many temptations to abuse, ranging from simple corruption to the suppression of their opponents. The day-to-day activities of parliament as a check on the executive, the rule of law (to which governments must be subordinate), independent statistical agencies and central banks, guarantees that open debate and the organisation of opposition will continue so that there can be future, seriously contested elections, and rules about transparency and the prevention of corruption all spring logically from the fact that there will always be potential conflicts of interest between governors and governed, and that the governed must retain the right to change their minds.

The populist challenge to liberal democracy is impatient with these intermediary institutions. The people express a will, and elect a leader to execute that will—no one sensibly maintains that a people comprising several million persons can act without any mediation at all. Anything that moderates or conditions the behaviour of that leader constitutes a frustration of the people's will. Populism thus requires total faith by the people in the leader. This is its overwhelming defect. Institutions that might have protected the people from betrayal, corruption, manipulation and ultimately repression by the leader have been swept away in impatience with their apparent interference in the popular will.

This lesson is now being unlearned in many different places. As the above example shows, in the UK it is at the heart of the conflict over how democracy deals with Brexit. In the United States Donald Trump has made use of very similar themes of discontent with the functioning of institutions, making allegations of corruption against the Establishment, while his own entourage is riddled with nepotism. There was nothing about corruption in the Brexit debate, but only three years previously, the *Daily Telegraph* had waged a well-researched campaign against the misuse of expense accounts by Members of Parliament. While this was thoroughly justified, it seemed odd, coming from such an Establishment newspaper. Looking back now after the Brexit debates, it seems to have been part of a wider pattern of undermining parliamentary and some other institutions by the political right.

Populist movements expressing disgust with parliamentary democracy can come from the right, the left or from nowhere easily recognisable. In the French presidential elections of 2016, all major established parties were cast aside while a populist of the centre, Emmanuel Macron, beat one from the extreme right. In Hungary and Poland, nationalist rulers have increased their popularity by denouncing the institutions of liberal democracy barely a quarter of a century after their populations had celebrated ecstatically their entry into that same political form. A new far-right anti-Islamic populist group (Alternative für Deutschland) has become the third largest party in the German Bundestag. Two anti-Establishment parties now dominate the Italian parliament, though one (La Lega) being from the far right and the other (Movimento Cinque Stelle, M5S) of very indeterminate political colour, they do not constitute a single movement.

In 2003, I described a process that I labelled post-democracy, whereby all the institutions of liberal democracy survived and functioned, but where the vital energy of the political system no longer rested within them, but had disappeared into small private circles of economic and political elites.[2] I did not say we had arrived at such a point in the settled democracies, but that we were on the road to it.[3] For democracy to be flourishing, I argued, movements emerging from the population at large, unprocessed by the elite's political managers, must from time to time to be able to give the system a shock, raising new questions that the elite would sooner not discuss. I mentioned three movements that had been still capable of doing this in recent years: feminism, environmentalism and xenophobic populism. What I did not anticipate was that the lead would be taken by the last of these to a massive extent. This raises two questions: why has xenophobic populism become so dominant? Should one welcome it as a democratic irruption against the complacency of liberal post-democracy, and if not, why not?

Why the popularity of xenophobic populism?

I identified two principal causes of post-democracy—neither anybody's fault and neither easily reversed. The first was the globalisation of the economy, which took the most important issues of economic regulation beyond the reach of national politics, the level at which democracy was usually best established. The second was the decline of the social identities of class and religion that had shaped the main party identities of twentieth-century democracy. The reasons why the first of these would lead to a rejection of contacts with 'foreigners' and a desire to hunker down into the nation state are fairly clear. The role of the second is less obvious, but ultimately more important.

Most people are not highly political and usually feel remote from what goes on in parliaments and local council chambers. They will have a strong political identity only if it relates clearly to a social identity that has meaning for them. Historically this has been most likely to occur if the social identity has been relevant to struggles over inclusion in and exclusion from citizenship rights.[4] For example, if one is a member of an established religion, one might want to support policies to limit the rights of those of other religions or none. If one is a member of a class excluded from political participation by property qualifications, one is likely to support parties advocating the rights of that class. Nearly all established liberal democracies have party systems based on struggles over these two key issues—class and religion—dating back to the nineteenth and early twentieth centuries. (There are exceptions, principally the United States and Ireland, where parties are based on out-comes of past civil wars, but these too were initially struggles over inclusion.)

Once the concept of universal adult citizenship was accepted, these identi-ties survived as the representation of different interests within a system of overall inclusion, usually as the basis of party organisation and identity. As such, they became the central links between citizens and democracy. With time, the original struggles became a memory of the struggles of past gener-ations rather than an experienced reality. Then the class structure itself chan-ged, with the decline of the occupations of the industrial society on which it had been largely based. Religion too has declined in social significance (the US is again an exception). Many, probably most, people in the contemporary established democracies no longer have strong social clues to indicate a political identity for them.

Two further social identities offer themselves as candidates for struggles over inclusion and exclusion: gender and nation. The former is central to much political conflict, but it is difficult for it to become the basis of party identity, because such identities need to be rooted in communities, and men and women do not form separate communities. Nation does not have this handicap and is far more potent, being a social identity that people have long been encouraged to feel strongly, and which has clear political implica-tions. For a long time after the defeat of fascism in the Second World War, mainstream politicians were careful not to exploit the dangerous possibilities of these. This has changed. While class and religion have declined as moti-vating forces for political participation, major movements of migrants and refugees, with the added frisson of occasional acts of Islamic terrorism, have raised the salience of appeals to apparently threatened national identities. If one adds to this the feelings of loss of national control facilitated by globali-sation, the rise of xenophobia as a major political force presents no mysteries of understanding.

Setting the growing importance of nation against the declining salience of class and religion may also enable us to explain some otherwise puzzling features of the present situation. The advanced northern European welfare states—the Nordic countries as well as the Netherlands, Austria—all have major xenophobic populist movements, despite their wealth, low levels of social insecurity and of inequality. (Germany is a different and more com-plex case, because of its particular history of racist politics and its recent uni-fication with a former communist state.) Portugal and Spain—relatively poor (especially Portugal), with less developed welfare states, high levels of inequality, recent victims of imposed austerity policies following the eurocri-sis—lack such movements. It is possible to explain the paradox if one recalls that these countries did not enter liberal democracy until the 1970s, three decades later than the rest of western Europe. The hypothesis that political identities based on struggles over inclusion around class and religion 'wear out' over time should lead us to predict that these identities should be holding up better on the Iberian Peninsula than elsewhere in western Europe. Those struggles had been particularly harsh under the fascist regimes.

How then does one explain the particular virulence of xenophobia in central and eastern Europe, where liberal democracy is even younger, barely a quarter of a century old? Here one must remember the inversion of class struggle that had occurred under state socialism. The working class was deemed to be the leading class, but in reality, there was no political citizenship for anyone outside a tiny elite of *nomenklatura*. Universal inclusion was universal exclusion. It was therefore difficult for people in that part of the world to relate to the political structures familiar in the West. For a few years after 1990, it seemed that something like Christian and social democratic parties might become the basis of party systems, but these movements fragmented. There was instead a plethora of small, transient parties, with an occasionally larger movement based on a rich individual and his client groups. Meanwhile, all the formal institutions of democracy were in place. Democracy seemed very rapidly to become post-democracy.

Viktor Orbán in Hungary was the first central European ruler to realise that nationalist sentiment could provide a base for an enduring connection between politicians and a mass public. As a linguistically distinct country with various long-standing cultural minorities within its borders, Hungary was a likely location for this discovery to be made. Orbán has now been imitated by similar movements in Poland, followed by the Czech and Slovak Republics. A *causus belli* was provided in these cases by the EU's attempt to get the central European countries to help share the burden of refugees landing on the coasts of Greece and Italy. Poland is the only one of these countries to have a potential religious basis for party division, and the prime minister, Jarosław Kaczyński, uses it, but by itself it is problematic. In western Europe, Catholic parties are strongly pro-European. Seeking a political position largely hostile to European integration could not therefore be built on religion alone, but required a strong nationalism. Like Orbán, Kaczyński has admired the Russian regime of Vladimir Putin, a major symbolic figure for this new movement. Putin is post-democratic in using the formal institutions of democracy, while ensuring that these institutions are void of content, but populist and very different from classic post-democrats in appealing to xenophobic and traditionally conservative sentiments. At Putin's rallies banners depict himself with Trump and Marine Le Pen, the leader of the French far-right populist Front National.

Nation was potentially available as an identity that could be used by any party to refresh declining mass political attachments, but it has mainly been carried by new movements. This does not mean that established parties have not embraced it. Trump was the official candidate of the Republican party. Brexit is now the policy of both the Conservative and Labour parties. In Austria the established conservative Österreichische Volkspartei (ÖVP) turned itself into a populist anti-Islamic party. However, even these exceptions demonstrate the resistance of established parties to the xenophobic wave. Trump emerged as an outsider within Republican ranks, not initially favoured by the establishment. Brexit is ostensibly about a legal and economic question of membership of an international organisation and only secondarily (though powerfully) about nationalist resentment of foreigners. The ÖVP undertook its anti-Islamic turn only after it had been beaten into third place in Austrian politics by the Österreichische Freiheitspartei, itself a long-standing but outsider, post-Nazi party.

Established conservative, liberal, Christian and social democratic parties had become accustomed to relating to voters through professional media campaigns, confident that they could shape elections through top-down communication. Further, they had nearly all been complicit in the neoliberal policies that had led to the combined menace of unregulated, irresponsible global finance and declining public services that burst open in the financial crisis of 2008. It was therefore left to new invaders to articulate discontent— a discontent that was then mainly targeted, not at deregulated finance and a deteriorating public realm, but at an incoherent combination of old political elites, immigrants of various kinds but especially Muslims, and international organisations.

Populism as a problem

If, as I argued in *Post-Democracy,* democracy expresses itself in disruptive challenges emerging from the citizenry and challenging the complacency of elites, I have to welcome the initial appearance of these various movements as refreshments for democracy. There is, however, a separate question whether the continued presence of a movement on the scene maintains that refreshment.

To consider this, we need to become more precise about what we mean by 'populist' movements. At its most general, the term refers to movements that are not contained within established political parties and which have themselves weakly structured, inchoate organisations. When they first appear, they do not behave in ways that follow the rules (formal and informal) of political conduct, but operate as the voice of their supporters, who are in general political outsiders, having neither experience of nor respect for such rules. Populist movements burst uninvited, loudly and rudely, into a room where groups of people are having polite conversations.

Beyond that point, we need to differentiate. The populist mode of politics contains three possibilities for future development, which can run into each other or can go in different directions. First, populism may simply be the form taken by a new movement when it bursts on to the scene. Newcomers who lack prior invitations cannot enter a room without disturbance, and how is change in political representation to take place without the occasional arrival of the uninvited? If an existing system of representation is wearing out, standing for social structures and issues of the past, renewal is bound to take forms disturbing to the parties of that system—the people already in the room, engaged in polite conversation. Naturally, these resent the intrusion and stigmatise the newcomers as populists, meaning movements that have no overall programme or roots in society, but just exploit any available discontents in order to advance their own position. If populist movements are something better than that and represent not rootlessness but interests that have been neglected, they will eventually become parties with structures and programmes; they will 'settle down' and take their place in the room, behaving like everyone else.

However, this is in itself ambiguous. It might mean that the movements stop behaving in ways that threaten the rules of behaviour that prevent abuse of power; but it might mean that they adopt practices that they had criticised during their earlier phase. For example, the German Green party, originally a disruptive outsider, eventually became part of governing coalitions. Some of its leaders later became lobbyists for motor industry and energy corporations. In Italy, M5S draws much of its energy from attacks on the corruption that is rife in Italian public life. It became a major force in local politics in 2016 when its candidates won mayoral elections in Rome and Turin. Within months, both mayors were involved in corruption scandals around public contracts.

A second possibility is that populist movements do not seek to become the 'new normal' in a renewed party system, but want to continue confronting established politics with a different way of doing public business, one less institutionalised and bearing the direct voice of the people. Strictly speaking, populist movements have no fixed substantive policy agenda, but follow what 'the people' demand. Oddly for movements that despise formal procedures, they represent a procedural form of politics; it is the way in which the voice of the people is heard that matters to them, not the content of that voice. M5S has until now been a fairly pure form of that approach. It has been clearly driven by discontent with how the Italian political elite behaves; its policies on actual issues are formed through crowd-sourcing.

The question of breaking with formal rules and, in particular, impatience with intermediary institutions that check the exercise of democratically elected power, brings us to the third question of the direction in which populism moves, and to the core issue of whether its continuity makes the same contribution to democracy as its initial irruption. On the one hand, the notion of direct people power is always a sleight of hand. There are always leaders whose job it is to interpret the people's will, and whom the advocates of populism have to view as the incorruptible, unmediated voice of the people. This was well analysed by Yves Mény and Yves Surel in their prescient 2001 study of populism, when the current resurgence was in its infancy.[5] Populist movements, they argued, always required a charismatic leader in whom total trust was placed, as populism is intolerant of intermediary institutions. This requires a naïve view of the perfection of the human nature of leaders. On the other hand, established elites and wealthy interests are usually in a good position to make those institutions work for them. They own the property that under a system of private ownership provides protection from the power of the state; can afford to take cases through law courts; can afford to own and control the means of mass communication.

Human history is replete with cases where central power is grasped by individuals and small groups speaking in the name of the people to challenge the institutionalised rule of wealthy families and organisations, often but not necessarily going on to become dictators oppressing the people who supported them in the first place. The original Greek *tyranoi* were leaders of people whose interests were excluded from consideration in polities dominated by aristocratic interests. Having no formal possibilities for representing these interests, they used extra-institutional means, like mercenary soldiers, to do so. Sometimes they then used those means to support their personal positions against everyone else in the society, giving birth to our modern understanding of the word tyrant as a ruler necessarily oppressive and vicious—a change in the meaning that was first engineered by Plato. The French and Russian revolutions echoed that ambiguity in more recent centuries. But the problems faced by *tyranoi* in trying to represent those without means of representation were real.

The most prominent modern example of a successful populist leader was Huey Long, governor of Louisiana during the 1930s. He burst on to the political scene, taking over the state Democratic party at the head of groups outside the party's normal power structures, introduced the most radically egalitarian public policies ever seen in the US, and was confronted by the might of the oil companies, who tried to use the law to stop him taxing their activities. To consolidate his power base, he used political clientelism in appointing people to jobs throughout the public administration and interfered in the appointment of judges. He was assassinated by the son-in-law of a judge whom he was trying to dismiss from his post. Whether he would have dispensed with elections, had he been head of a national rather than a US-state level government, we shall never know. As it was, Long remained within democratic frameworks and abused power no more than many more orthodox politicians. He was certainly a tyrant in the pre-Platonic sense; whether he deserves the later twist to its meaning is difficult to determine.

Similar ambiguities surround the recent cases of the 'pink wave' of Latin American leaders elected during the early years of this century: most prominently Hugo Chavez (Venezuela), but also Evo Morales (Bolivia), Daniel Ortega (Nicaragua) and Rafael Correa (Ecuador). Each pursued policies of egalitarian redistribution, encountered strong opposition from displaced wealthy elites, elites usually supported by the US, and each rode roughshod over checks and balances on the exercise of power, including the rule of law. On the other hand, and unlike the right-wing dictators whom the US had often maintained in power in Latin America, they never abolished elections.

These examples all concern essentially left-oriented forms of populism, targeting wealthy national (sometimes international) elites and championing redistributive policies. Some of the currently important populist movements belong to this camp: Syriza in Greece, Podemos Unidos in Spain, France Insoumise, possibly M5S. The only one so far in power, Syriza, has done nothing to threaten democratic institutions or the rule of law. But far more prominent today is right-wing populism. Since by definition the political right supports established elites, especially national ones, it has to define its enemies in terms other than wealth and power. One of the most readily available forms of this are ethnic minorities, other countries, external institutions, foreigners in general. Rightist populism is therefore likely to be xenophobic. Mény and Surel listed hostility to immigrants alongside the existence of charismatic leaders as a defining characteristic of populism, a term which they confined to the rightist form.

The recent greater salience of 'foreigner' than class issues therefore helps explain why the political right has been in a better position to make use of discontent over the 2008 financial crisis, even though this was ostensibly a class issue, and therefore why the majority of new populist movements are on the right. There are exceptions. The only important centrist populist movement, Macron's En Marche, far from using xenophobia, is explicitly cosmopolitan. On the left, Syriza, Podemos Unidos and the Bernie Sanders movement in the US have avoided all use of immigration in their campaigns, though M5S, France Insoumise and the Labour party of Jeremy Corbyn have been more ambiguous.

There is an asymmetry in the relationship to established politics of rightist (xenophobic) and leftist (class-based) populism. As seen from the above examples from the Americas, leftist populism runs into an immediate confrontation with powerful interests. Although rightist populism criticises established elites, it then deflects the criticism towards foreigners, internal and external, letting the local elite off the hook, as it were. Elites under serious threat are therefore likely to accept rightist populists as the best of a bad job. This was astoundingly the case when Paul von Hindenburg, as president of Germany, appointed Adolf Hitler to be Chancellor in 1933, following elections in which the Nazi party's support had declined. The Weimar Republic was extremely unstable, and had Hitler the rightist populist not been appointed, the leftist Communist party might have been the next to threaten a takeover. Similarly, in 1922 the King of Italy called Benito Mussolini to form a government following his not particularly impressive March on Rome, to avert the risk of a communist challenge.

Donald Trump is not a fascist, though formally similar processes were at work when the Establishment of the Republican party decided to support him as its presidential candidate and subsequently to sustain him in office, despite his decidedly anti-Establishment stance. He turned popular rage at stagnating living standards, which might have focused on the banks and US capitalism in general, against Muslims and Mexicans.

While right-wing, xenophobic populism raises less of a threat to established interests than its leftist variety, it does threaten those institutions that surround democracy and protect citizens from their elected rulers. This happens because of the fundamental drive behind most examples of populism of all kinds, which is a belief in the inherent rightness of their cause and the rejection of all opponents as illegitimate. This was well analysed by Mény and Surel, and more recently by Jan-Werner Müller.[6] The charismatic leader of a populist movement claims to speak for '*the* people'. There is always a definite article here, leaving no scope for minorities. Those who do not share the majority view are therefore hostile to the people and have no democratic rights. All intermediate institutions that might stand in the way of, or modify the expression of the people's will are likewise anti-democratic enemies. Given that the people's will is singular and straightforward, it needs only one representative, the charismatic leader. There is no need for parliamentary or other debate. The people's will is revealed in a singular vote or plebiscite, after which all interpretation of its nuances is left to the leader and those entrusted by him or her. There may be subsequent general elections (as in state socialist regimes) or referenda on specific issues (as practised by Francisco Franco in Spain), but only after all organised opposition has been declared illegal, liquidated or (as in contemporary Russia) considerably handicapped by bans and arrests.

The regimes of Hitler, Mussolini and Franco were pure examples of rightist xenophobic populism. Those of the Soviet Union and its allies were cases of leftist populism, though eventually Stalin added hostility to Jews and various other types of foreigner to the initially class-oriented line. Today's instances are moderate in comparison, and it is important not to over-stress similarities between them and today. Institutions are better grounded and better able to be defended. It is therefore important to make an estimate of the strength of the threat that neither under-estimates nor exaggerates.

For example, in Hungary Orbán has used a nationalistic, anti-European, anti-Muslim and anti-Jewish rhetoric to justify changing the constitution to subordinate the law courts to political control, dominating state broadcasting media and purging many public offices of persons supporting opposition parties. However, this was done through parliamentary means. Orbán's Fidesz party had achieved a two-thirds majority, which under the country's constitution (similarly to that of many other countries) permitted constitutional change. In Poland, a similar rhetoric has been used to justify subordinating law courts to political control. This is, however, being done without parliamentary authority to make constitutional change, which is why the European Union is sanctioning Poland but not Hungary for its actions. In western Europe, xenophobic parties that have in the past held government office (Austria, the Netherlands), or hold it today (Austria again, Finland, Norway) have been as junior members of coalitions or support a minority centre-right government without holding office (Denmark). They therefore lack any power to pursue institutional destruction.

In the US and UK, we certainly observe populist attacks on institutions, but with limited effect. Trump has vilified various bodies, ranging from law courts to the security services. He has also made political appointments to the Supreme Court, but that has long been a vulnerable point in the US Constitution, a right exercised by all presidents. The Court derives its independence, despite the political nature of its appointments, through the fact that judges serve for life and cannot be removed, weakening the impact that any one president can have. However, towards the end of President Obama's term of office a Republican-dominated Congress refused to permit him to fill a vacant place on the court, in the eventually successful hope that there would soon be a Republican president. This would not have happened in earlier decades, but no one sees any risk that Trump will try to prevent future elections or have any power to hobble the Democratic opposition.

Brexit bears many of the hallmarks of xenophobic populism. Its campaign was targeted against internal (immigrant) and external (EU) foreigners. It was a plebiscite with decidedly anti-parliamentary overtones. The defeated minority, although large (48 per cent) is expected to surrender the usual democratic right to continue debating, and with the conversion of the Labour party to support leaving the UK, the minority has no major political voice. The rhetorical attack on claims that Parliament should submit the process to scrutiny, and the stigmatisation of the Supreme Court as 'enemies of the people' for saying that Parliament should have this role, is pure populism. Equally, so is the doctrine that the people had their right to speak on the day of the referendum; any right to vote on the issue again would be hostile to the people's will, as that will is defined as an almost sacred event happening on one day alone.

However, the British case is odd in that the populism is limited to this one issue—though it is an issue with important implications for virtually every field of policy. There is to date no hint that the intolerance of debate and opposition will be used to delegitimise political disagreement in general and no threat to future elections. Several leading advocates of Brexit have said that, outside the EU, the UK can become the 'Singapore of the Atlantic', but by this they refer to that island's weak welfare state, high level of inequality and low level of labour rights rather than to the highly flawed nature of its democracy. A further oddity is that, since the demise of the populist party, UKIP, the leadership of British right-wing populism is in the hands of core Conservative politicians and the editors of the *Daily Mail* and *Daily Telegraph,* both bastions of the Conservative Establishment. Somewhat like the Trump phenomenon, though through different means, Brexit represents a kind of palace coup populism from within the Establishment.

Recent developments in social media demonstrate the potentiality of such or even false populism. An early development in the US was the Tea Party movement founded around 2009. It is a mass populist movement supporting most policies associated with US conservative Republicans. It styles itself a grassroots movement, and gives the impression of resources pouring into it from masses of little individuals, who shape its agenda, while in reality it is heavily funded by a small number of billionaires who control its policies.

This has led its critics to style it an 'Astroturf' movement. However, by 2016 the Tea Party seemed to be an exponent of outmoded technologies. Today, if one has the resources (which means if one is part of a very exclusive elite of the very rich) one can develop complex technologies that send out social media messages that have the appearance of coming spontaneously from masses of individuals, whereas in fact they come from one manipulative source. People are more likely to believe that an event has taken place, or that a view is sound, if it seems to come to their personal social media site from many different points than if it comes from just one. At the time of writing details are emerging of the role of a US billionaire, Robert Mercer, who through various channels funds Cambridge Analytica, a technology firm that specialises in this kind of centralised message crowding. Mercer is very close to Trump, and Cambridge Analytica was active in both the Trump and Brexit campaigns.

Ironically, this kind of manipulative artificiality was very much part of my vision of politics under post-democracy, but it is being practised by those claiming to be the populist challengers to Establishments. Rightist populism appears not as an antidote to post-democracy, but an extreme extension of it.

Conclusion

The initial irruption of populism within a society may well invigorate its democracy, bringing neglected issues to the table and putting established parties and elites on their mettle. However, unless it rapidly changes its character to accept restraining institutions, its continued presence can threaten democracy. Democracy requires the protection of the people from potential manipulation by their leaders. It endangers itself if it is deemed to justify political control over the law and other intermediary bodies. Also, there must always be another election, and opposition and government parties alike must have the right to go on debating and using political resources in preparation for that moment, and those that come after. Today's minority may become tomorrow's majority, which also means that majorities must beware how they treat minorities, as that may be their position in a few years' time. This expectation of a changing balance of power is the best safeguard we have that those currently with power will not abuse it. The tendency of populist movements to regard themselves as the perfect and final manifestation of democracy renders them as its enemies.

But the deficiencies in democratic institutions revealed by the rise of populism remain. It is essential that rallying calls to oppose populism do not lapse into defences of corruption, of the plutocratic capture of government, of party systems that do not represent society's most important divisions. Rude invaders must be welcome, provided they accept that they themselves must become subject to constraints that safeguard democracy's future. That itself will partly depend on whether new, or radically reshaped old, parties can locate themselves within rooted interests within the social structure, with which they are engaged in genuine two-way communication, not a post-democratic, manipulative, top-down use of social media that pretends to speak for a 'people' defined so vaguely that it can be held to want whatever the leaders decide it wants.

But are post-industrial, post-religious, post-modern societies capable of producing such rooted interests, or are we just a mass of loosely attached individuals blown around by confusing blasts? The political right has produced an answer to that question: rootedness in nation, though many moderate conservatives and liberals will be in despair at that outcome. Do the left and centre have anything of similar strength to offer, roots in deeply felt social identities? Cosmopolitan liberalism by itself risks failing to have the courage of its lack of convictions. Debate on the left and centre must now turn to this search.

I have space here to offer just one possibility. I have written elsewhere that, just as the original labour movement was essentially a male phenomenon that interpreted the problems of all working people through the eyes of 'breadwinner' men, in post-industrial society, many of the problems of such people may be best articulated by women.[7] They experience more keenly issues of work–life balance, of precariousness in the labour market, of deficiencies of care services, of the manipulation of consumers, though these are problems that men share too. They are found in large numbers working in the public and care services that embody the main challenges to both neoliberal and intolerant world views. This is unlikely to mean the formation of women's parties, and in any case the hope is that women will become the spokespeople of many men too. It does require a strong civil society surrounding formal politics with other forms of representation, including organisations that express women's continuing experience of various kinds of exclusion and the development of political agendas to counter them.

There is perhaps a further element. Much about rightist populism is very macho: from the male swaggering of leaders like Putin and Trump to the violent fringe that attaches to most xenophobic movements. Is it fanciful to see in the very recent widespread resurgence of feminism a reaction against that ugly face of masculine politics? We were all taken by surprise that, when a popular reaction against 2008 occurred, it took the form of xenophobia rather than a class critique. Perhaps the events of International Women's Day on 8 March 2018 were in turn an unexpected reaction against rightist populism.

Notes

1 F. Fukuyama, *The End of History and the Last Man*, New York, Free Press, 1992.
2 C. Crouch, *Postdemocrazia*, Bari/Rome, Laterza, 2003. Published in English in 2004 as *Post-Democracy*, Cambridge, Polity.

3 I was writing some years before the financial crisis of 2008 saw saving the banks from their earlier irresponsibility accorded the highest priority in public policy; before the eurocrisis saw elected governments displaced in order to pursue strategies of bank rescue. I tried to incorporate some of their implications in 'The march towards post-democracy, ten years on', *The Political Quarterly*, vol. 87, no. 1, 2016, pp. 71–75.

4 For a more detailed exposition, see C. Crouch, 'Globalization, nationalism and the changing axes of political identity', in W. Outhwaite, ed., *Brexit: Sociological Perspectives*, London, Anthem, 2017, pp. 101–110; and C. Crouch, 'Neoliberalism, nationalism and the decline of political traditions', *The Political Quarterly*, vol. 88, no. 2, 2017, pp. 221–229.

5 Y. Mény and Y. Surel, *Populismo e democrazia*, Bologna, Il Mulino, 2001.

6 J.-W. Müller, *Was ist Populismus*, Berlin, Suhrkamp, 2016; published in English as *What is Populism?*, Philadelphia, Pennsylvania University Press, 2018.

7 Op cit, fn 4, 'Neoliberalism, Nationalism and the Decline of Political Traditions'.

11. Relating and Responding to the Politics of Resentment

GERRY STOKER

Introduction

THE POLITICS that delivers democracy is an imperfect but very human process. Citizens engage as much or as little as they see fit and politicians use every tool available to win support. There are structural flaws in the process that have been widely identified. Our democracy since universal suffrage has been blighted by the negative impact of social and gender inequality, respectively, in terms of the extent of citizen participation and representation in national and local elected assemblies. Democracy may be under increasing threat from big data manipulation or developments in artificial intelligence. But in this chapter, I will focus on the strengths and weaknesses associated with the dominant political vehicles that have emerged to deliver democracy. My concern is less with individual institutions—such as parliament or parties—and more with the frameworks of politics in which they have operated. How politics is done matters hugely to the delivery of democratic ideals, and we have entered the most troubling period since near universal suffrage arrived on the scene a century ago, with the emergent dominance of a politics of resentment.

During the century since 1918, Britain has found its politics delivered through three political vehicles: class, competence, and most recently, resentment. Each vehicle contains a mix of interest, identity and values in its construction. Each has a defining question for citizens about their political leaders. To what do I owe my loyalty? Who can get the job done? Why are others getting what I deserve? Broadly, in Britain we have cycled through these frames and reside today with a democratic politics dominated to a large extent by resentment. A relationship driven by resentment is fuelled by a mixture of disappointment, anger, and fear. It is arguably the least healthy of the frameworks for doing democratic politics so far tried, yet we appear stuck in its grip.

We start by noting the inherently imperfect foundations to politics before exploring the political vehicles that have emerged to translate democracy into action. In the period since universal suffrage, different vehicles have dominated, yet each has had to give way to another practice in response to changes in context and political strategies. That analysis then provides the basis for the concluding discussion about how to break the grip of the politics of resentment. Democratic politics has found ways of reinventing its core practice over time and I explore the seeds for a future reinvention.

Published by John Wiley & Sons Ltd, 9600 Garsington Road, Oxford OX4 2DQ, UK and 350 Main Street, Malden, MA 02148, USA

The imperfect foundations of politics

Democracy is an ideal that relies on the human practice of politics to deliver it. The result is that there is a continuous tension between the hope embodied in the idea of democracy and the disappointment associated with its provision. Most citizens are regularly inattentive to politics, careless in their reasoning about it and casual in the use of evidence about issues. Social identity, emotion and hunches play a big part in the decisions that people make. Citizens muddle through to make sense of politics and its choices. Some optimistic observers argue that citizens can use heuristics—mental short cuts requiring little effort or information to be brought into play—to make judgements that are good enough. These heuristics provide a reliable guide to what they might choose if they had more information, a better framed task or put in more cognitive effort into making the judgement. Yet others argue that citizens' judgements in this fast thinking, intuitive mode can be partial and prone to bias.

For those more directly involved in political decision making—political leaders and activists in parties, thinks tanks and lobby groups—their engagement with politics can be more intense, detailed and reflective than that of most citizens. Indeed, politics can appear to be a laudable practice when, for example, a set of political leaders clinch peace plans or when politicians usher in life-altering or epoch-defining changes through legislation or spending. There is perhaps also quieter nobility in the politician who fixes a tricky problem for a constituent, who tries to help sort out a difficult issue through some gentle diplomacy, or who supports events, businesses, and organisations in their local community. But for long periods, there appears to be nothing noble about politics at all. Politics, after all, is a battle for influence and the exercise of power. That this activity involves politicians in hustle, intrigue, lies and deceit provides little surprise to most citizens, who have long understood that politics is prone to such a dynamic. Politics has the quality of being both the decent pursuit of the common good and a rather unedifying process that involves humans behaving badly.

The main weapons at hand in this messy world are interest, identity and ideology. Interest is the most straightforward in many ways, as few would dispute the idea that politics is a battle over interests and to an extent exists because people have different interests. Interest politics is largely about the distribution of resources. What someone understands as in their interest is not always a reflection of their objective social or economic position, but may well reflect the influence of the forces of identity or value choices on their outlook. Identity too is a familiar axis for politics. It is primarily about recognition. It can be defined by a practical, social and emotional commitment to a sense of belonging to a group and wanting that belonging to be rewarded. Values are the human face of ideology; decades of public opinion research tend to show that citizens do not generally form their views into clear cut ideological positions. Values—beliefs about how the world should be—are held by citizens but not necessarily in a coherent or consistent way. Political leaders can and do try to appeal to the values that people have.

Since the introduction of near universal suffrage, Britain has experienced politics through three political vehicles: class, competence, and most recently, resentment. Each vehicle contains a mix of interest, identity and values in its construction and each has its strengths and weaknesses. We explore each vehicle in the sections that follow, focusing most effort on resentment, as it is the vehicle that is currently dominant and proving to be particularly problematic.

Class, identity and politics

There is probably little dispute that the early practice of politics in the era of universal suffrage was framed to a large degree by class. The occupational background or more generally the economic position of an individual was a good predictor of their party choice and political loyalty. Other influences might come into play, reflecting ethnic, regional or religious factors, but particularly in Britain, these other influences were less powerful in their impact, leaving class as the dominant feature of politics. Yet by the 1960s, still roughly only two-thirds of the manual working class supported Labour, the party claiming to represent their interests, with the remaining third regularly voting Conservative. As Frank Parkin[1] notes, the explanation of this phenomenon encourages an understanding of politics that combines looking at economic factors with cultural concerns. Broadly, Parkin argues that Labour supporters were sustained in their outlook by networks within community and workplace and by other social factors that encouraged an identification with the Labour party. Conservative working class voters were often from communities that lacked those networks because of the nature of their industrial and economic circumstances.

Politics in this framework was a struggle both over redistribution (in that it concerned resources available to different interests) but was also given vibrancy and loyalty by way of a politics of identity built around class. Labour politicians, for example, could mobilise support based on promises to deliver resource benefits to their voters, but at the same time rely on a sense that voters were loyal and felt that the only choice that people like them had was to vote for the party that represented them. This framework of politics delivered sufficient stability and loyalty to Britain's democracy that American academics in the 1960s were moved to identify the presence of an effective civic culture that combined an appropriate mix of deference and activism and revealed through some of the earliest detailed survey work undertaken in this country a great pride in Britain's system of government and a modest sense that people could influence outcomes.[2] Its disadvantages as a way of articulating the democratic ideal are in hindsight also clear. It failed to address the concerns of those who found that class politics did not capture their concerns over resource redistribution or those seeking to secure recognition for non-class identities (of gender, race, sexual orientation, race, and so on). Moreover, it gave little space to activism or broader civic engagement: it offered what was perceived as a rather thin form of democratic politics with most of dynamism in the hands of political elites.

Changes in social and economic structures led the basis of class politics to unravel, reflected in partisan realignment, voter volatility and the emergence of a more complex class structure. Class-identity politics was a dominant force in electoral politics and provided a settlement suited to the industrial age, but it began to break down as the forces of deindustrialisation became more obvious. Other forces entered politics, building an identity and redistributive politics around, for example, nationalism in Scotland and Wales. Non-party campaign groups began to reset and expand the agenda of politics, focusing on gender issues, race inequality, gay rights, green and environmental concerns. Class, with its complex mix of redistributive and identity dynamics, remains a mobilising force in British politics but without the power that it once had.

Politics and competence

Political exchange has, during the period of universal suffrage, always been about competence of political leaders to a degree, that is, where citizens ask primarily and are offered evidence of the competence of the political leader to get the things done that they care about. As the membership of political parties declined and voters became less loyal in the 1970s and 80s, there emerged greater scope for a different politics that was based on the competing competence of leaders: a vacuum that the politics of competence stepped in to fill. Moreover, loss of empire and industrial decline had contributed to a loss of confidence in the capacity of government, as reflected in the debate over governing overload captured in one of several seminal works by the late Anthony King.[3] That analysis might have been flawed, but it captured the mood of the times and the prominence of two key ideas: that there should be less of a role for government and that what it did do, it needed to do better. Part of the response was the privatisation and rolling back of the state in areas of welfare, brought to the fore in the Thatcher years of the 1980s, but its partner was new public management and an audit culture targeted at making government more effective. 'What matters is what works' became a core mantra of the Blair Labour governments from the late 1990s onwards.

The political vehicle associated with these changes focused on competence. In political science the term valence politics[4] has been used to capture some of the features of this political practice, although in fairness the model stretches beyond the narrower focus on competence, while it does have that at its heart. The argument is that voters are primarily focused on the ability of governments to perform in those policy areas that people care about most,

141

especially the economy. Central to this argument is the idea that perceptions of party leaders crystallise people's thoughts about the likely performance of political parties in office. Can they be expected to deliver? Citizens, it is argued, can engage in quite complex judgements. Green and Jennings[5] show how political parties come to gain or lose 'ownership' of issues, how they are judged on their performance in government across policy issues, and how they develop a reputation for competence (or incompetence) over a period in office. Their analysis tracks the major events causing people to re-evaluate party reputations, and the costs of governing which cause electorates to punish parties in power.

At first glance, only positive outcomes could come from this form of political exchange from the perspective of the delivery of democratic ideals. Citizens are engaging with politicians based on whether they deliver what they promise, and the incentives for political leaders are clear: provide the economic and social welfare that citizens seek and success will be yours, and if you fail to do so you will lose. Moreover, as issues of concern move up and down the agenda of public concern, so can the policy priorities of governments be adjusted, creating a dynamic of responsiveness in the system that approximates a crude model of operationalised democracy. It is probably the model of the way our political system works and is implicit in much of the media coverage of politics.

So why have doubts about this framework? First, as noted earlier, generally voters seem to be not very attentive to politics, and when it comes to retrospective judgement about the performance of government, they may lack the capacity effectively to allocate credit or blame to political leaders. Insofar as they do judge, those judgements are often quite myopic, based on the last few months before an important election.[6] Second, political leaders try to manipulate the way that citizens judge their performance. Messages are honed, voters targeted and campaigns planned with the competence, character and personal qualities of the leader, rather than the party as a whole, as the focus of attention. They send out messages about achievements, they produce lists of achievable promises (sometimes even put them on a block of stone), they produce reports and statistics to support their arguments. Valence politics has in practice become marketised and then offered through the 'mediatisation' of politics. It is presented and communicated through the 24-hour media frenzy—with its emphasis on news management, spin, and presentation of sound bites—so there is little wonder that many citizens struggle to connect to it with any depth of interest. Together with colleagues,[7] I have shown that if, in contemporary democracies, politics is conducted only through a series of fast-thinking exchanges, it is likely that citizens will become trapped in a cycle of negativity about politics. This negativity about the way politics is conducted in turn supports a level of cynicism and disengagement leading to questions about its sustainability. Far from promoting trust, paradoxically, the politics of competence may have contributed to the emergence of anti-politics that in turn has resulted in the politics of resentment.

The politics of resentment

The politics of resentment combines elements driven by interconnected differences of interest, identity and values. Voters are divided in their interests by the strength of their connection to the knowledge economy. Those who are educated to a higher level and located in a vibrant economy are in a stronger position to access better jobs. Citizens are divided by clashing identities, with one group seeing they are being left behind and others focusing on the struggle to get ahead. They are also divided by value differences on the virtues of multiculturalism, globalisation, immigration and other issues. While class as a political vehicle had spatial or place-based character, the politics of competence did not. If anything, the competence fixation reinforced a drive to centralism, with national agenda-setting, targets and performance frameworks. The politics of resentment has, in contrast, a strong place-based focus. The spatial separation of the experience of different communities provides a foothold for a politics of resentment, because groups who lack direct knowledge of one another can come or be persuaded to see 'the other' as a focus for blame and antipathy.

The politics of resentment finds its most obvious expression in Britain in the 2016 Brexit vote, which revealed a stark difference not only between people, but also between places. Similar patterns could also be observed in the 2017 general election.[8] The major cities of the UK voted heavily to remain in the EU, while less urbanised areas tended to vote to leave. This divided politics reflects not only a difference of identity and cultural outlook (described by some as a 'cultural backlash'), but also long-term forces of social and economic change that have created grievances and put different places on different tracks, leaving people living worlds apart in terms of their attitudes and everyday experiences. This dynamic is having political consequences— dubbed the 'revenge of the places that don't matter'.[9] Economic, political and social factors have created the conditions for this politics of resentment.

The emergence of a politics of resentment reflects long-term changes in the economy which has seen some locations connect to the emerging global and knowledge economic growth dynamic, with others left behind. However, the idea that uneven development is characteristic of liberal capitalism is hardly novel. In this new era, some towns and cities—primarily in the south of England—have found a niche in the new global order: they are highly connected, decidedly innovative, well-networked, attracting skilled populations and often supported by inward migration. They display the qualities of 'cosmopolitan urbanism'. In other locations, the focus is on 'shrinking' cities and regions, which are experiencing an outflow of capital and human resources. Add to that the impact of the austerity policies imposed on public spending—especially from 2010 onwards—and, in some areas a decline in both economic activity and the delivery of public services, the conditions for a politics of resentment have been created. When people feel insecure and fearful about resources, the politics of resentment can find opportunity for expression.

Another factor that has helped to create the arena for a politics of resentment is that anti-politics attitudes have become more widespread and embedded within British society,[10] creating an environment where populist and also more mainstream politicians can label opponents not only incompetent but rather corrupt, unworthy and a despised 'other'. This rise of anti-politics—defined as negative attitudes towards politicians and institutions—has three noteworthy features. First, more and more citizens judge politicians to be out for themselves and part of a separate out-of-touch elite. Negativity towards politics and politicians is now close to universal. Second, as historical analysis shows, negativity toward politicians was present from the early days of the universal franchise but over the last century, it has expanded its range of complaints. Politicians in the 1930s or 40s might have been viewed as 'gas bags' and in it for themselves, but in the twenty-first century, citizens regularly judge politicians as not only self-serving and not straight-talking, but also to be out of touch, all of a type, a joke, and part of a broken and unfair system. A third feature of anti-politics is the mood of anger, despair and bitterness. In our study using mass observation (MO) data we found that in 1945, respondents wrote about politicians in relatively measured terms. This cannot be dismissed as simply a reflection a culture of deference at the time since, in the same responses, they wrote about clergy as 'intellectually dishonest' and 'spoil-sports'; doctors as 'uncaring' and 'protective of their own interests'; lawyers as 'tricksters' and 'money-grabbers'; and advertising agents as 'frauds' and 'social parasites'. By 2014, the negative terms for these other professionals had not really strengthened in the writing of MO panellists, but those used to capture their views of politicians had certainly strengthened. Citizens now described their 'hatred' for politicians who made them 'angry', 'incensed', 'outraged', 'disgusted', and 'sickened'. The words used to describe politicians were: arrogant, boorish, cheating, contemptible, corrupt, creepy, deceitful, devious, disgraceful, fake, feeble, loathsome, lying, money-grabbing, parasitical, patronising, pompous, privileged, shameful, sleazy, slimy, slippery, smarmy, smooth, smug, spineless, timid, traitorous, weak, and wet.

Further polarisation of political opinion can lead to opponents not being viewed as legitimate but instead, as lesser participants in the democratic process, to be defeated at all costs. Evidence that is not in keeping with one side can be dismissed as the product of fake news, and opponents within the movement can be accused of backsliding or of being traitors, and those outside the movement can be dismissed as heretics, enemies. The tone of politics, perhaps always intemperate, goes up a few degrees in negativity and mutual non-listening in the context of the dynamics of resentment. Developments in social media feed into and enhance these changes as like-minded contacts and focused news-feeds reinforce a sense a dialogue within camps but not between camps.

Key changes to the social structure have led to major shifts in the demographic order of Britain. Increased numbers of graduates and immigration are drivers and have been accompanied by wider changes in class related to occupation. An understanding of the complexities of what is involved is provided by Mike Savage, Fiona Devine and colleagues who map out a more fragmented social class structure for Britain that mixes economic, social and cultural dimensions in drawing its distinctions.[11] The mix differs by place and, in particular, between cosmopolitan areas—big cities and university towns—and suburban communities, post-industrial towns, rural and coastal areas. The latter have more of 'traditional' social groups such the established middle class and the traditional working class. Others groups, such as the new elite, technically skilled middle classes, emergent service workers, and the precariat, with marginal incomes, provide diversity and inequality within cosmopolitan areas. These changes have seen the idea of a simple split between working class and others—the basis of politics at the start of the era of universal suffrage—disappear. Once dominant players in politics, such as the manual working class, have seen their role diminished.

So, economic disconnect, political alienation and dramatic shifts in social structure have created the conditions for the emergence of a politics of resentment as the dominant political vehicle. Katherine Cramer summarises:

In this politics of resentment, when we tell ourselves and others about the reasons behind how events have unfolded, the stories hinge on blaming our fellow citizens. What I am calling the politics of resentment is a political culture in which political divides are rooted in our most basic understanding of ourselves, infuse our everyday relationships and are used for electoral advantage by our politics leaders.[12]

Cramer's empirical study is of rural America, but its dynamic can be applied to Britain today. Different places have developed diverse cultures in response to social interaction facilitated by proximity in location. These outlooks can be reinforced or sharpened further through framing from local or national political elites. Feelings of being 'left behind', for example, are socially constructed rather than simply a product of individual experiences. Low income and casual employment, and poor housing conditions, are factors in cosmopolitan areas, and high home ownership is a feature of non-cosmopolitan areas, alongside clear experiences of economic stress. There is not a simple story of poor versus rich areas to explain the politics of resentment. Rather, it is story of perceptions, of places where citizens increasingly see themselves and their communities heading in different directions.

Social scientists, in response, are taking renewed interest in 'place'.[13] Place provides the opportunity for regular engagement with others nearby and a process of social exchange encourages a search for shared ground and a common understanding. Cultural stereotypes come to define the understanding of the place where people live, who they are and what they represent.

Other places and their populations become defined as different, alien and not to be trusted. Politicians can play on and reinforce these feelings of difference to bolster their support and as a consequence, place-based identity becomes politically weaponised and a symbol to drive a more polarised politics. The broad argument is that context matters, because it shapes the way that people see their political choices and options. The use of short cuts or heuristics is integral to the way people think about politics and many other issues where information complexity and time shortages rule out more 'heroic' or extended reasoning. Place provides a convenient shorthand for developing a set of understandings and, in turn, can be exploited by political leaders. Comparisons between places are constructed and comparisons within places are made over time. How do citizens see the past and future of their place and how does that shape their political outlook? The dynamic of change in people's experience of their place opens up a shifting set of reference group comparisons which in turn feed into political outlooks and cleavages.

The politics of resentment could be seen as having positive impact for the delivery of democratic ideals. Politicians who speak up for groups who feel left behind could be celebrated within those communities: at last, they might argue, we have someone who understands our world and speaks to its concerns. For too long, politics has been in the hands of a university educated political elite—the Westminster and Whitehall bubble—which has little or no connection with people in communities whose primary experience has been one of decline and decay.

The problems of the politics of resentment as a vehicle for delivering democracy are, in part, tied to a populist framing that is associated with its practice. Leaders seeking to exploit resentment tend to express arguments in terms of an 'us' versus a 'them' and exploit divisions which encourage a view that dialogue or negotiation with the other is worthless. Doing so weakens democracy's reconciliation function. Populist expression within democracies could be seen as helping to identify sections of the community who perceive themselves as neglected, but it has the disadvantage that through its means of expressing concern, it threatens the usual dynamics and norms of democratic politics, leaving society generally less able to speak across divides. Leaders exploiting resentment talk of a rigged political system, a mechanism designed for a powerful few, not the deserving many.

Resentment itself has a negative dynamic in the contrasts it makes. It steps beyond the relative deprivation comparisons characteristic of British society in the 1960s—in the age of class politics. According to Runciman,[14] individuals felt their inequality at that time by making comparisons with their chosen reference groups, groups which generally were located quite close to them. Deprivation was felt when these groups appeared to be more successful in achieving what the individual experiencing relative deprivation could reasonably have expected to achieve. Relative deprivation was about a felt sense of lack of opportunity which politics could address through redistribution and through creating conditions for meritocracy and equal opportunity. Resentment allows for no similar political response. Resentment draws on a comparison that is more communal in focus and based on a sense that others are getting something they do not deserve. As Katherine Cramer argues, resentment is easier to express than envy—in that it has a moral dimension—but it is more stubborn and problematic. Resentment draws on emotion as well as reason, so that even if your group does not gain, but the resented better-off groups get to suffer, the response is to feel pleasure at their decline. They are undeserving, so simply they are getting their just desserts. Leave voters we are told,[15] would be willing to see significant damage to the economy, as well as the undermining of the Northern Ireland peace process or Scotland being pushed towards independence, in order to achieve Brexit. All this, despite the presence of evidence pointing to the longest and most significant damage being done by Brexit to the areas where Leave voters were strongly located.

On the other side of the fence are resentful social liberals in cosmopolitan areas. They are working hard, making their way in a global and knowledge-based economy and, in a post-Brexit world, find their future, their lifestyle and opportunities threatened by the mobilisation of a perceived resentful 'left behind' group. The two groups have only a limited understanding of one another and the networks that reinforce ties within each group, so the actions and reactions of each can come as a surprise, as in the case of the Brexit vote. The conditions for a politics of resentment exist on both sides of the divide that characterises much of British politics. Its consequences are unlikely to be healthy for the future of democracy. The way that politics is done matters and democratic ideals will fall further still from fruition if the politics of resentment is not addressed.

Finding a new political vehicle: a radical devolution?

The divisions that fuel the politics of resentment are as much about economic as they are cultural differences; or to put it another way, economic conditions are filtered by citizens through developing and changing social identities. Therefore, policies to create the conditions for an effective economic and social dynamic in so-called left behind towns and other locations will be needed, as well as policies to address the challenges of sustaining growth in cosmopolitan areas. These policies will need a degree of national framing, in order to ensure redistribution of resources to areas that need it and to prevent unhealthy competition for the same economic niche. But above all, what is required in politics is a substantial shift of power from the national to subnational levels. The case here is not driven by classic and rather uninspiring arguments for greater localism, but rather is seen as a direct response to the politics of resentment.

National politics has been the focal point for much of the era of universal suffrage, but there are reasons to argue that the next phase of politics will have to be developed outside the Westminster/Whitehall 'bubble'. The politics of resentment has a much more distinctively and developed territorial dimension to it than the previous iterations of ways of doing politics, and the circumstances that have led to that place-based focus are unlikely to disappear. Second, the bubble itself is substantially implicated in many citizens' understanding of the problems confronting our democratic practice. A London-centric and centralised politics—even if reframed—is not going to provide a way forward on its own.

The solution is much more likely to be found in the promotion of a radical devolved politics built around local government, city regions and national assemblies in Wales, Scotland and Northern Ireland. There can be little doubt that the scale of the reconstruction necessary is substantial, since—especially in England—the way that local government has faced startling spending cuts in the last ten years means that it has been denuded of power. A reconstruction would require the transfer of substantial powers over a range of domestic issues to devolved institutions (substantially most of those already granted in Scotland) and tax-raising and spending powers that go beyond those already provided for Scotland. Moreover, the efforts already started, but far from completed, in the devolved assemblies of Scotland and Wales to develop a more consensual, better gender-balanced and more open practice of representative politics would have to be extended to devolved institutions in England as well.

A core argument for a radical devolution to kick-start a new politics is that only such an arrangement can tackle the blight of the politics of resentment. An empowered devolved government system could lead to policies being designed to meet the different circumstances of areas that have experienced growth and connection to the global knowledge economy and for those that have not. In addition, the pressures of an aging population on the National Health Service and social care—with fewer people to staff them—is likely to be a major pinch point that will require imaginative local solutions in cosmopolitan and non-cosmopolitan areas alike. The Brexit vote was a visible expression of the diverse experiences and economic trajectories of people and places around Britain. It was not just a protest by 'left behind' areas, but rather a wake-up call to a policy system that has developed a policy process that is too national and centrally generated.

For cosmopolitan areas of growth, the challenges are most likely to be associated with congestion, housing shortages and sustaining a wider social and welfare fabric as the pace of work accelerates and costs of living in those areas become unsustainable for many. For those 'left behind' areas that are joining the new economy as latecomers, a clear specification of the niche and focus of their ambition as well as targeted financial incentives, infrastructure and training would be required. We may also have to accept that some areas will be forever left behind, as permanent stragglers in the global economy, and that there is a need to develop a planning system capable of managing decline and identifying ways to achieve lifestyle gains for citizens in those areas. In all areas, sustaining the NHS and creating better social care will require better local knowledge, interagency working and sharing of resources; none of which can be organised nationally.

A core new argument for devolution is that resentment grows in a centralised system where responsibilities and powers are misaligned. Central government, with its control over finance, can task local decision makers to solve problems but keep from them the financial means and powers to get the job done. Equally, local leaders can always blame London when something is not done or when schemes fail; or complain loudly about investment going elsewhere but not to their own area. This system of dual irresponsibility has contributed to and exacerbated the conditions for a politics of resentment. The advantage of a radical devolution is that if it combined substantial power and financial sharing, a clear link could be seen between decision making and responsibility. It would create the conditions for a more effective politics of competence, where local leaders are judged on whether they have used the extensive powers available to them to deliver the best solutions for their areas.

Conclusions

This chapter—as do most—needs some caveats. The political vehicles of class, competence and resentment capture some, but not all, of the dynamics that have delivered representative democracy since the arrival of near universal suffrage. Some might argue that ideology has also played its part. Ideology is a central and justifiable force in politics and the high points of its use have tended to occur in limited spurts: the Thatcher regime of the 1980s, the euroscepticism in both the Conservative party and UKIP from the 1990s onwards and the period from 2015 of the Corbyn leadership of the Labour party. But, as I argued at the beginning of this chapter, most citizens do not think in strongly framed ideological terms. Second, although I have suggested a sequence of moving domination from class, through competence to resentment in political vehicles, it can be conceded that a better understanding might be driven by seeing these different vehicles as layering on each other than simply replacing old with new. Finally, my argument for a radical devolution directly to attack the politics of resentment needs both further development and qualification: I am arguing for a shift in power but not for the abandonment of all national responsibilities. Moreover, there are challenges over persuading citizens that local and regional action can be made to work and make a difference, given the impact of a focus on centralised solutions and the denuding of local powers for much of the era of universal suffrage.

I am convinced that understanding the politics of resentment is central to the sustaining of democratic practice in the future. I have tried to break from a framing that seeks to view the phenomenon through either an economic or cultural lens and tried to show how a complex intertwining of those forces, plus a climate of anti-politics and populism, sets the scene for its emergence as a dominant force. My argument for a radical devolution is premised on the idea that it could be one factor in addressing the underlying causes of the politics of resentment. Political leadership that in words and actions seeks to reach across divides could be another. Division and despair are not new to the politics of the era of universal suffrage. Think, for example, of the portrait of England provided by George Orwell in his 1937 book *The Road to Wigan Pier* that depicted the desperate working conditions in Lancashire and Yorkshire and combined it with a brutal take-down of the political pretensions of left and right. Orwell concluded nevertheless that 'England is a family' before adding 'with the wrong members in control.'[16] That sentiment sums up my feeling about politics today.

Acknowledgements

This chapter is based on a lot of shared work with Will Jennings and Nick Clarke who both provided helpful comments on an earlier draft. A conversation with Pippa Norris also helped to sharpen my thinking. I thank them all but they have no responsibility for the arguments made here.

Notes

1 F. Parkin, 'Working-class conservatives: a theory of political deviance', *The British Journal of Sociology*, vol. 18, 1967, pp. 278–290.

2 G. A. Almond and S. Verba, *The Civic Culture: Political Attitudes and Democracy in Five Nations*, Boston, Little, Brown & Co., 1963 [reprint 1965].

3 A. King 'Overload: problems of governing in the 1970s', *Political Studies*, vol. 23, no. 2–3, 1975, pp. 284–96. A great commentary on the argument is provided by M. Moran, 'Whatever happened to overloaded government?', *The Political Quarterly*, vol. 89, no. 1, 2018, pp. 29–37.

4 H. D. Clarke, D. Sanders, M. C. Stewart and P. Whiteley, *Political Choice in Britain*, Oxford, Oxford University Press, 2004.

5 J. Green and W. Jennings, *The Politics of Competence. Parties, Public Opinion and Voters*, Cambridge, Cambridge University Press, 2017.

6 C. Achen and L. Bartels, *Democracy for Realists*, Princeton, Princeton University Press, reprint edn. 2017.

7 G. Stoker, C. Hay and M. Barr, 'Fast thinking: implications for democratic politics', *European Journal of Political Research*, vol. 55, no. 1, 2016, pp. 3–21.

8 W. Jennings and G. Stoker, 'The bifurcation of politics: two Englands', *The Political Quarterly*, vol. 87, no. 3, 2016, pp. 372–382; and W. Jennings and G. Stoker, 'Tilting towards the cosmopolitan axis? Political change in England and the 2017 general election', *The Political Quarterly*, vol. 88, no. 3, 2017, pp. 359–369.

9 A. Rodríguez-Pose, 'The revenge of the places that don't matter (and what to do about it)', *Cambridge Journal of Regions, Economy and Society*, vol. 11, no. 1, 2018, pp. 189–209.

10 N. Clarke, W. Jennings, J. Moss and G. Stoker, *The Good Politician. Folk Theories, Political Interaction, and the Rise of Anti-Politics*, Cambridge, Cambridge University Press, 2018.

11 M. Savage, F. Devine, N. Cunningham, M. Taylor, Y. Li, J. Hjellbrekke, B. Le Roux, S. Friedman and A. Miles, 'A new model of social class? Findings from the BBC's great British class survey experiment', *Sociology*, vol. 47, no. 2, 2013, pp. 219–250.

12 K. Cramer, *The Politics of Resentment*, Chicago, Chicago University Press, 2016, p. 21.

13 In addition to Cramer above see also R. D. Enos, *The Space between Us: Social Geography and Politics*, Cambridge, Cambridge University Press, 2017.

14 W. G. Runciman, *Relative Deprivation and Social Justice: A Study of Attitudes to Social Inequality in Twentieth Century England*, London, Routledge & Kegan Paul, 1966.

15 See YouGov research; https://yougov.co.uk/news/2017/08/01/britain-nation-brexit-extremists/; and A. Menon, ed., *Brexit: local and devolved government*, ESRC/King's College London, The UK in a Changing Europe, 2018; http://ukandeu.ac.uk/research-papers/brexit-local-and-devolved-government/ (both accessed 21 August 2018).

16 G. Orwell, *The Road to Wigan Pier*, London, Left Book Club, 1937 [Penguin edn., p. viii].

12. A Hundred Years of British Democracy

ANDREW GAMBLE

IN 1918 THE UK made a decisive step towards universal suffrage. All male citizens over the age of twenty-one and all female citizens over the age of thirty were given the vote. Full universal suffrage had to wait another ten years. Britain was a representative democracy at last. In the previous hundred years, Britain had slowly extended the franchise, in small steps—1832, 1867, 1884—but the forces marshalled against full democracy were strong, and Britain's progress was slower than in several other countries. The prestige of British political institutions was not because they were democratic, but because they embodied a mixed constitution credited with preventing the kind of autocracy so familiar elsewhere. Royal absolutism had been destroyed by the two revolutions in 1649 and 1688 and never recovered. The supremacy of Parliament and the independence of the courts were permanent legacies from the upheavals of the seventeenth century. Foreign observers admired the liberty that had resulted from the balance between the different institutions of the state, the energy this released in civil society, and the skill of the British political class in allowing incremental reform and forestalling revolution as it presided over the momentous change from agrarian Britain to industrial Britain, and from aristocratic to democratic Britain.

When democracy finally arrived in Britain, it was an add-on to the existing liberal constitutional order and its representative institutions, not a new kind of state. In 1918 the British state had enjoyed uninterrupted continuity of its institutions since 1688. It had avoided revolution at home and external invasion. It controlled the world's largest empire, and had enjoyed for much of the nineteenth-century financial, industrial and commercial supremacy. Its key institutions—Crown, Parliament, the judiciary, the civil service, the armed services, the Church, the universities, the media—had all been formed in pre-democratic times. There had been some broadening of the base of political power from the upper ten thousand families, but not much. The political culture of this Britain retained strong aristocratic and exclusive features and served a society which was highly inegalitarian, measured both by the distribution of income and wealth and by gender roles. There were very strong class and status divisions. There had always been a radical dissenting tradition in Britain, and it had had some successes but it had never managed to reshape the state. The old order persisted, in part because pragmatists among the political class generally prevailed over reactionaries, ensuring that timely concessions were made to incorporate new interests and contain popular pressures.

Published by John Wiley & Sons Ltd, 9600 Garsington Road, Oxford OX4 2DQ, UK and 350 Main Street, Malden, MA 02148, USA

Where stands that old order today? How successful has British democracy been in realising the hopes of those who struggled for so long to extend the vote to all its citizens and make Parliament truly representative of the people rather than just the oligarchies of land, industry and finance? Many critics of democracy have always maintained that democracy should be regarded simply as a procedural device for choosing which set of politicians should govern. It sets up a competition between rival parties and allows the electorate to choose which one formally becomes the government. As a procedural device, democracy is tolerable so long as it operates within basic legal and political constraints making impossible any challenge to the basic organisation of society, and specifically the rights of those who own property. The problem with democracy is that it introduces an element of uncertainty and in certain circumstances, politicians may be elected who do challenge property rights. This is why many supporters of capitalist market economies believe with Hayek that democracy is expendable in certain circumstances and an authoritarian government which guarantees the basic principles of a liberal market order is preferable.

There has always been another view of democracy, which sees it as not just about procedures, rules, and conventions, important though these are, but also about substantive outcomes. A liberal democracy is one that guarantees the rule of law and the rights of citizens and, crucially, the rights of minorities. Illiberal democracies do not. A social democracy is one that ensures security and opportunity for all its citizens, which it achieves through universal programmes on health and education and by actively intervening to counter disadvantage and to support citizens at all stages of the life cycle.

How well has Britain performed since 1918 as either a liberal or a social democracy? The Democracy Index of the Economist Intelligence Unit uses sixty indicators to assess how far a country conforms to the norms of a liberal democracy.[1] Its categories are full democracy, flawed democracy, hybrid regime and authoritarian regime. The UK in 2017 was rated a full liberal democracy, only one of nineteen of the 167 states surveyed which fell into this category. France, Italy and Japan were all rated as flawed democracies, as was the United States which had just been demoted, partly as the result of the election of Donald Trump. Britain came fourteenth on the list, behind Germany, Australia, New Zealand and the Nordic countries.

Stein Ringen in his book *What Democracy is For,* published in 2007, offered a comparative analysis of democracies as social democracies, measuring them not just by their political institutions but by the quality of the services they deliver to their citizens.[2] Ringen focuses on indicators that measure strength, capacity, security and trust as reflected in spending on health, child poverty, educational standards and social mobility. His index has the Nordic countries at the top—Sweden and Norway both score a maximum eight points—while Britain languishes down the table with three points and the United States even lower with just two. This was before the financial crash and austerity.

From these two snapshots it is evident in comparative terms that Britain since 1918 can claim to have had some success in building a strong liberal democracy, but its progress in constructing a social democracy has been less impressive. But even the construction of liberal democracy is far from complete. Democratic deficits continue to plague British democracy. These deficits seem smallest on the procedural side of democracy, but they are still real. On the positive side, there has been significant, incremental change since 1918, including extending the vote to all women at twenty-one in 1928, lowering the voting age to eighteen, removing anomalies like the university seats and extra votes for business in local elections. It is likely that the voting age will be further lowered at some stage to sixteen. This has already happened in Scotland, and there is a strong lobby for it in the other parts of the UK. There are flaws in the way voters are registered, but the conduct of elections has always been fair, with no suggestion of serious illegalities or corruption.

The biggest democratic deficit in Britain's procedural democracy is the voting system itself. For the Westminster Parliament this remains first past the post. Parliament came close to changing it during the minority Labour government of 1929–31, following agreement between Labour and the Liberals, but the government fell before the legislation could pass. So long as there is a two-party system in which the two main parties have a serious prospect of forming governments on a fairly regular basis, there is no incentive for them to back change to the electoral system. It is not that there has been no change. In recent years, different electoral systems have been agreed for many other elections, including the Scottish Parliament, the Welsh Assembly, the Northern Irish Assembly, and the European Parliament. But elections to Westminster itself and to local councils are still conducted under first past the post rules. The coalition agreement between the Conservatives and the Liberal Democrats in 2010 made provision for a referendum on the alternative vote system to replace the first past the post system. The referendum was duly held in 2011, but the reform proposal was heavily defeated.

Britain remains one of very few democracies anywhere in the world to persist with first past the post. It treats a general election as the sum of contests in individual constituencies. That system developed when electorates were small and national parties did not exist. Once there was a mass electorate, MPs stood for election as part of a national ticket, and the difference any individual candidate made to the vote became small, although it always did matter in a few cases. The consequence of elections being contested between mass parties with national leaders and national programmes on a first past the post basis has been many anomalies and huge variations between the numbers of votes cast for a party and the number of MPs elected. In 2015 UKIP polled four million votes and only elected one MP. That does not sound much like a representative democracy. Supporters of first past the post have always argued that it may be disproportional but it generally delivers a government with a majority to govern effectively for a full parliamentary term. It does this by transforming a small percentage lead in votes into a large majority in seats. The winning party has almost always been a minority party in terms of votes cast, still more so when non-voters are counted. Priority is given to forming a government able to get its programme through without opposition, rather than electing a parliament representative of the actual votes cast.

Parliamentary landslides under first past the post always exaggerate the support of the winning party. What first past the post generally avoids are hung parliaments and the need for coalition governments. That has generally been true of British politics in the last hundred years: in 70 per cent of the twenty-seven British general elections since 1918, one party had an overall Commons majority of more than twenty seats. There have been hung parliaments on five occasions 1924, 1929, 1974 (February), 2010 and 2017, and governments elected with majorities of less than ten on another three—1950, 1964 and 1974 (October). There have been three periods when the working of the party system has not delivered stable parliamentary majorities—the 1920s, the 1970s and the 2010s. In between there have long periods when one party has dominated, mostly the Conservatives—1931–1940, 1951–1963, 1979–1997. Labour's one spell of dominance (defined as a parliamentary majority sustained for at least two full parliamentary terms) was between 1997 and 2010. First past the post has generally delivered secure majorities whenever the two main parties have between them captured more than 80 per cent of the vote. The periods of hung parliaments and low majorities have been periods when the two main parties have dipped below that level.

When the two main parties cannot command more than 80 per cent of the vote, the legitimacy of first past the post comes into question. If such a period lasted long enough, then a change in the electoral system might conceivably be carried. But while the 2010 and 2015 results looked as though the grip of the two main parties had loosened again, the 2017 general election showed the two parties regain their dominance, with over 80 per cent of the vote between them. They even showed some revival in Scotland. But the election did not produce the landslide for the Conservatives which they had expected in calling the election early. Instead, it resulted in a hung parliament. What is not clear as yet is whether this election is an oddity, heavily influenced by the divisions over Brexit and the new alignments which the referendum vote displayed, or whether it is the beginning of a new period, in which the two main parties reassert their dominance. Given the fluidity of voting this seems unlikely.

The obstinate attachment to first past the post is a symptom of a deeper problem. Many other countries became democracies through a revolution or a decisive event which marked a new beginning, such as the end of the Fascist dictatorship in Spain in 1975 with the death of Franco. Such moments allow a fundamental review of the constitutional order, and the creation of appropriate rules and institutions for a democratic polity, often a new constitution. Britain has never had such a moment, which means that it has only had piecemeal and often incoherent reform of its constitutional rules and its institutions in the last hundred years. Most of its institutions and the way they functioned were inherited from the pre-democratic era.

Unlike most democracies, the British polity was never based on popular sovereignty. Instead, sovereignty is still located in the Crown—not the absolute Crown but the Crown-in-Parliament. Even after the ascendancy of Parliament was confirmed after 1688, royal powers and prerogatives were carefully preserved. But they were exercised increasingly by Prime Ministers rather than sovereigns, whose power became increasingly attenuated. Crown-in-Parliament has always meant that the initiative lies with the executive in the British system not the legislature, and the executive has always sought ways to control the legislature, whether through patronage or after the rise of party, the whipping system. The rise of organised parties and national programmes increased the dominance of the executive still more after 1918, leading to much talk about the decline of Parliament as an institution. But Parliament has proved more resilient than many critics expected. A number of developments, including the number of MPs prepared to rebel against their party whips and the strengthening of the select committee system, has made Parliament more effective in holding the government to account, and providing some counter balance to the executive. This is particularly true in hung parliaments. But the central weakness of Parliament in the British system remains. It is not independent of the executive as Congress is independent of the executive in the United States, and its power to control the executive in the name of the people or anything else is limited.

The House of Lords is another idiosyncratic aspect of British democracy which belongs to the pre-democratic era. No other democracy has a second chamber like the House of Lords. In 1918 it had already lost its absolute veto power in the 1911 Parliament Act, but its composition was still predominantly the hereditary landed aristocracy. It is remarkable that one hundred years later this relic of the pre-democratic era still survives. Its powers of delay were further curtailed by the Attlee government, and its composition began to change with the Life Peerages Act of 1958. The hereditary element has gradually been reduced and the Blair reforms cut it to ninety-two hereditary peers. But the government could not get MPs to agree on how to reform the House of Lords or whether to have a second chamber at all. That remains the position today. Defenders of the status quo sometimes point out that the current Lords is the repository of a great deal of expertise, and this allows it to offer effective and often expert scrutiny of government legislation. But its legitimacy is a problem. By what right do unelected peers, many of them only present because of executive patronage, have a role in framing legislation in a democratic polity? This used to be an argument often rehearsed on the left, when the Conservatives enjoyed a permanent majority in the House of Lords because of the hereditary peers. More recently, it has become a refrain for populist nationalists and Brexiters. When the House of Lords recently passed amendments to the government's Brexit legislation, forcing another vote in the Commons, their behaviour was denounced as treason, and there were calls for the Lords to be stripped of its powers or even abolished outright.

Similar considerations apply to the Crown. The current form of the monarchy was fixed in the Victorian period, when it became an integral part of the idea of Britain's global empire. There is nothing democratic about a hereditary head of state, and although the monarchy has modernised slowly in response to the pressures of democracy and the media (a notable recent change has been the end to priority of males over females in the succession), it retains many of the trappings of the imperial monarchy and helps sustain an archaic honours and status system, which is hostile to a democratic political culture. The British are not citizens but subjects in this world, and the loyalty of public servants, and importantly the armed services, is to the monarch not to Parliament or people. The British monarchy derives its legitimacy not from any democratic decision but from its place in the old order, and that makes it an obstacle to a democratic culture and to popular sovereignty.

British monarchs remain a potent symbol of the old order. In the meantime, their powers are deployed by increasingly assertive Prime Ministers. Much has been made of the presidentialisation of British politics. But the scope for Prime Ministers armed with the prerogative powers of the Crown to act presidentially is not a new phenomenon. It existed from the start of the democratic era. Lloyd George and Churchill were early examples. Presidentialisation is in any case the wrong term. The office of Prime Minister can never evolve into a presidency because Prime Ministers are not directly elected by the citizens, and even the most powerful remains dependent on maintaining the support of his or her party. But that has not stopped Prime Ministers accruing great powers. The problem in the British polity is that there are no formal checks to the centralisation of powers in the British executive. The main obstacle to it has been divisions between departments and ministers. Even the most powerful Prime Ministers have to maintain the backing of their Cabinet colleagues. They cannot afford to lose the support of too many of them, as Margaret Thatcher found. Presidents have a much freer hand.

A key democratic deficit in Britain is that the old doctrine of Crown-in-Parliament has allowed Prime Ministers in the democratic era to accrue too much power without proper scrutiny or constitutional limit. Curbing the power of Prime Ministers and increasing the powers of Parliament would strengthen British democracy, but without a codified constitution there is no easy way to do that. One of the key reforms long demanded is to make the exercise of the prerogative powers dependent on parliamentary consent. These prerogative powers include the right to declare war, the right to sign treaties, the right to call elections, and the extensive powers of appointment and patronage. Moves to curb these have begun. Precedents have now been established that the UK government should get the approval of Parliament before committing British forces to significant military action. That occurred for the first time with the vote on the Iraq war in 2003, and it has been repeated on several occasions since. It still lacks proper formalisation. Parliamentary approval for key treaties has also gradually been established, often painfully as the ratification of the Maastricht Treaty under the Major government showed. The right to call elections was given up with the passage of the Fixed Term Parliament Act, one of the key demands of the Liberal Democrats when they joined the coalition with the Conservatives in 2010. It worked in the 2010–2015 Parliament, but in the next Parliament Theresa May called an election in 2017 after only two years. It showed that it was still relatively easy for the Prime Minister to do so whenever she chose, because the opposition parties were not prepared to oppose it for fear of seeming frightened of facing the voters. Patronage powers have gradually been transferred to independent commissions, but the influence of the government and of individual Prime Ministers remains strong.

The old order emphasised parliamentary sovereignty, never popular sovereignty, which was always alien to it both in theory and practice. 'The people' is not sovereign, Parliament is, and even then, not Parliament itself but the executive acting through Parliament. The direct expression of the popular will has always been mediated through its elected representatives. This has allowed considerable divergence between the people and its elected representatives over a number of issues. Capital punishment is one example. At the time it was abolished in 1965, opinion polls indicated there was a large popular majority to retain it. But popular sovereignty has a very limited role in the British polity. The working of British parliamentary democracy diffused the pressures of direct democracy, and insulated the executive from direct popular pressure. Referendums were never part of British democracy and were strongly opposed by Labour and Conservative politicians alike. Partly, this is because plebiscites got a bad name when they were used by Fascist governments in the 1930s to legitimate the dictatorships they established, but it was also that Britain's pre-democratic liberal order harboured huge distrust of the uneducated and ignorant masses, who were shallow, uninformed and easily manipulated by demagogues. Allowing a professional class of representatives to deliberate and decide on behalf of the people was always seen as a safer option than consulting the people directly.

Conservative writers on the constitution, like Leo Amery, were adamant that the tradition of a strong executive, Crown-in-Parliament, was the best way to ensure good and effective government, which meant that democracy had to be tightly controlled.[3] The Tory tradition had earlier defended monarchical sovereignty against parliamentary sovereignty but in the modern era, it defended parliamentary sovereignty against popular sovereignty. The Labour tradition was at first hostile to the established state and its institutions, because it was outside it and excluded from it. Labour built its own democracy through the Labour movement, and when the party entered Parliament and, after 1918, became the second party in the state, there was always a tension between the mass movement outside Parliament and the elected MPs inside Parliament. Consulting the people in the Labour tradition meant consulting the mass movement through its internal democracy.

Yet despite this opposition in both leading parties to consulting the people directly through referendums, they have crept into British democracy in the last fifty years. There have been three national referendums, two on Europe and one on the electoral system, and referendums in Scotland, Wales and Northern Ireland on the establishment of parliaments and assemblies, as well as one in Scotland on whether Scotland should become independent and leave the UK. The principle that major constitutional changes should not be decided by Parliament alone but should be put to a direct vote of the people has become firmly established. This was not the intention, at least for UK-wide votes. The referendums on Europe were a way of managing the deep divisions within the ruling party—Labour in 1975 and the Conservatives in 2016. Tony Benn campaigned strongly for a referendum on Britain's membership of the EU because he thought it right that the people should have the final say. He came to believe in popular sovereignty as a matter of principle.[4] He also favoured a radical constitutional overhaul to make that possible, which included abolishing the House of Lords, but he remained a strong proponent of first past the post, and a Parliament which was controlled by the people rather than the executive. But Harold Wilson did not agree to hold the referendum in 1975 because he believed in popular sovereignty, but because he knew that the Labour party was deeply divided over British membership of the European Community and that a majority was against it. The referendum was a way of settling the internal party debate.

In a recent report from the Constitution Unit, a Commission containing leading Brexiters as well as Remainers has reflected on the *ad hoc* and casual arrangements for holding referendums in the UK and suggested ways they could be improved.[5] If referendums are to be made compatible with representative parliamentary democracy, then it would be desirable that only those changes which command a majority in Parliament are then put to a referendum of the people. That means that if there is a vote for 'yes' there is no problem in implementing the decision. If it is 'no', the proposal is simply discarded. The problem of the 2016 referendum, where there was no majority in Parliament to implement a Leave decision, would be avoided. Radical advocates of popular sovereignty and direct democracy want to go further, because they seek not the strengthening but the dilution of parliamentary democracy, and a much more direct relationship between the executive and the people. But there are dangers of that route leading to illiberal democracy. The advantage of representative democracy is that it can be a bulwark in protecting the rights of minorities and the rule of law. New devices like referendums for consulting the people directly can help strengthen representative democracy, but only if the conditions are clearly specified.

The problem, as so often with British democracy, is that the lack of a codified constitution means that a decision on whether or not to hold a referendum and the way that referendum is organised is decided often arbitrarily because there is no agreed set of rules to which to refer. But the much deeper problem which this reflects is the doctrine of the unlimited sovereignty of Crown-in-Parliament. Many constitutional writers note that this doctrine can be traced back to Henry VIII and Thomas Cromwell. The break with Rome and the proclamation that England was an 'empire', meaning a sovereignty sufficient to itself with no external obligations, has shaped British politics ever since, as its territorial and commercial empires expanded. So many of the current problems of the British state, from the devolution settlements to Brexit, stem from the reluctance of the British political class to share sovereignty. Devolution was conceived as a way to stem the growth of nationalism, but it has instead fuelled it in Scotland, and hostility to the privileges granted to the devolved administrations threatens to unleash it in England. An explicit federal union at some stage if the UK union is to be saved seems inevitable, but the English political class is unwilling to embrace it. England is too big a unit in relation to the other nations of the UK to make it possible, but breaking up England into regions is strongly resisted.

A broader democratic deficit arises from Britain's postimperial need to pool sovereignty in multilateral global and regional institutions such as NATO, the WTO, the UN and the EU. The remoteness of these institutions from citizens and the complexity and obscurity of their decision making means that their legitimacy is not directly conferred by democratic votes by citizens, but only indirectly through the agreement of national representatives who take the decisions. These multilateral institutions are vital to the ability of nation-states to find solutions to many of the problems which afflict them. But it is proving extremely hard to gain public support and understanding for these institutions, particularly in the period of recession and stagnation since the financial crash of 2008. The deeply flawed referendum in 2016 on the UK's EU membership has raised huge questions about Britain's identity, its place in the world, and whether its political culture is predominantly cosmopolitan or nativist. These have led to the sharpest divides in British political history since the divides in the pre-democratic era on Irish Home Rule. The Leave vote owed much to a desire to limit immigration, but also to the slogan 'take back control', returning Britain to being an independent sovereign country again with no foreign entanglements, an empire sufficient to itself. But in the circumstances of the modern world where pooling sovereignty, co-operation, burden-sharing have become a necessity for dealing with the very complicated challenges which governments face, the decision to leave the EU reflects the pre-democratic old order of the British state with its suspicion of power-sharing and mutual obligations.

This has emerged as a key political divide which affects the future of democracies everywhere. The backlash against multilateralism, international cooperation, tolerance and inclusiveness is spreading through all the western democracies. Populist nationalists are linking up across borders in their drive to restore a world of exclusive sovereignties. To its supporters, this is an assertion of raw popular democracy, taking back control from out-of-touch elites and reversing globalisation. Once uncorked, however, this populist nationalism is hard to contain. It is manipulated by those who seek to make democracy less liberal, less open and less pluralist by curtailing the rights of minorities.

In Britain, populist nationalism scored its first major success with the vote to leave the European Union. The Leave coalition was divided however between the rival Leave.EU campaign and VoteLeave campaign. Leave.EU wanted the referendum to be the first step in a new popular sovereignty, overthrowing the political class and using plebiscites to ensure the people stayed in control. The key issue in the campaign for them was control of immigration. VoteLeave, on the contrary, emphasised restoring the sovereignty of Crown-in-Parliament, freeing Britain from EU jurisdiction, in order to allow a British government to pursue a path of a deregulated and low tax economy, with a further major assault upon the welfare state.

Populist nationalism claims the mantle of democracy, but its effect everywhere it gains power is not to further democracy but to undermine some of the key civil, political and social rights democracy has secured. The dilemma for those who would resist it is that international institutions and global co-operation have indeed created an international political class which transacts within itself and is often remote from citizens. The latest phase of globalisation since the end of the Cold War has had winners and losers. The biggest gainers have been the super-rich, whose income and wealth have soared away, and the middle-income groups in rising powers like China and India. But many of the biggest losers, as Branko Milanovic has shown, are the middle-income groups in high-income countries.[6] These are the groups to whom the direct messages of the populist nationalists particularly appeal.

British democracy is at a crossroads. The Brexit vote has unleashed political forces which seek to weaken aspects of both the liberal and the social democracy which have been achieved in the last hundred years. Democracy in Britain was premised on the winning of civil and political rights and their gradual extension. The granting of those rights made possible the progressive extension of social rights, the transformation of the state into a welfare state for its citizens. Authoritarian governments have also, at times, promoted welfare, but the most significant pressure has come from the competitive party politics of mass democracies. Parties of the right as well as of the left came to support a comprehensive and universal welfare state out of electoral necessity. Democracies have tended to push their societies in a broadly egalitarian direction. Governments are put under pressure to combat discrimination, to extend rights, to reduce inequality and to provide opportunities for all their citizens. The story of British democracy in the last hundred years is in part, therefore, the creation of a welfare state funded out of progressive taxation. The transformative changes in services like education and health introduced in the 1940s have over time had an enormous impact. Despite the erosion of many services in the 1980s and again in the 2010s, there has been no return to conditions before the welfare state was established.

There remain, however, many democratic deficits. The basic conundrum of British democracy and of all other modern democracies remains what it was in 1918. Democracy was added on to a liberal constitutional order and a political economy in which there were huge inequalities of power, wealth, gender and race. The established institutions and much of the media were hostile to democracy, and many of them remain so. There has never been a level playing field. The struggle to achieve gender equality in work and in households has made advances, but painfully slowly. There has still not been a single Parliament or Cabinet in which women have been in the majority, and the discrimination against women in so many different aspects of life persists. The same is true for black citizens, LGBT citizens and many other minorities. The struggle to secure basic equality of treatment for all citizens is far from complete, although there has been much to celebrate. Britain in 2018 is a vastly different place than it was even in 1958. There has been progress towards greater equality for women and for minorities, and less tolerance of hate speech and discrimination.

In tackling the deficits that prevent the achievement of a full social democracy in Britain there has been less progress. The inequalities of power and wealth were reduced through the rise of the Labour party. Its incorporation into the state as the second governing party shifted the political dial and put class issues at the centre of political competition, leading to a substantial shift in the balance between capital and labour and the creation of a universal and comprehensive welfare state and a substantial reduction in inequality. But while the Scandinavian countries, with which Britain was level in 1950, moved on to the next level, Britain did not. Instead, in the political turmoil of the 1970s and 1980s, there was a successful retrenchment against the advances which had been secured and a new dispensation which led once again to rapidly rising inequality and weakening of universal provision in many areas, as well as withdrawal of services for many minorities. Some of this was reversed during the Blair government, which saw important reforms like the minimum wage and higher rates of increased spending on core services—such as health and education—than in the history of the welfare state. But many of these gains have been undone since 2008.

What does the future hold for British democracy? The popular anger against the political class which the Brexit vote expressed is both positive and negative for the prospects for democracy. It is positive because so many citizens engaged in the process, many of whom had stopped voting in other elections. It is negative, however, because the political forces which led the Brexit campaign and are now fighting over what kind of Brexit should be delivered, seek to use the Brexit vote as a pretext for altering key features of Britain's liberal democracy and its social democracy, either by celebrating nativism or reviving features of Britain's pre-democratic constitutional order. They are being held at bay for the moment by a Conservative government seeking to balance its internal factions and cope with its lack of a parliamentary majority, by seeking to deliver the softest Brexit possible. But it is under siege and may be swept away. The threat to British democracy as to many other western democracies at this time is that if Brexit is mishandled and if the international economic situation further deteriorates, populist nationalist parties may soon win power in the UK, as they have in Italy.

Avoiding this fate will need some bold and imaginative political leadership which takes British democracy on to a new stage by addressing some of the key democratic deficits that the Brexit vote has highlighted. This cannot be done by retreating from participation in multilateral institutions and international cooperation, since any hope of policies which can address global challenges like climate change and nuclear proliferation depend on not just maintaining, but deepening this cooperation. But it does require a rethinking of how citizens relate to their governments, and how citizens can feel once more that they are in control. This means that many policy areas which have been depoliticised need repoliticising, and the power of corporations which has been unchecked for so long in so many areas has to be countered again.

One of the key reforms is empowering local governments to take responsibility for local economies, ensuring that they are properly representative of their local communities and have real powers to make a difference. British governments have always talked about devolving power to local government, but have never delivered. The UK, even after devolution, remains a highly centralised polity. Transforming local democracy and developing a national programme to tackle inequalities of wealth and power, which have become so marked in so many fields, would be the first step in ensuring that Britain will enjoy not just a second century of democracy, but a democracy which moves forward and extends the gains of the last hundred years.

Notes

1 Economist Intelligence Unit, *Democracy Index 2017;* https://www.eiu.com/topic/democracy-index (accessed 22 August 2018).

2 S. Ringen, *What Democracy is For: On Freedom and Moral Government,* Princeton, Princeton University Press, 2007.

3 L. Amery, *Thoughts on the Constitution,* Oxford, Oxford University Press, 1947.

4 A. Benn, *Arguments for Democracy,* London, Cape, 1981.

5 M. Russell, 'Take more care with referendums; democracy depends upon it', *Financial Times,* 10 July 2018; https://www.ft.com/content/f8f985cc-8375-11e8-9199-c2a4754b5a0e (accessed 22 August 2018).

6 B. Milanović, *Global Inequality: A New Approach for the Age of Globalization,* Cambridge MA, Harvard University Press, 2016.

Index

Note: page numbers in italics refer to tables and diagrams; alphabetical arrangement is word-by-word.